‘I was born on a storm-swept rock
and hate the soft growth of sunbaked lands
where there is no frost in men’s bones.
Swift thought and the flight of ravenous birds,
and the squeal of hunted animals
are to me reality.’

Liam O’Flaherty

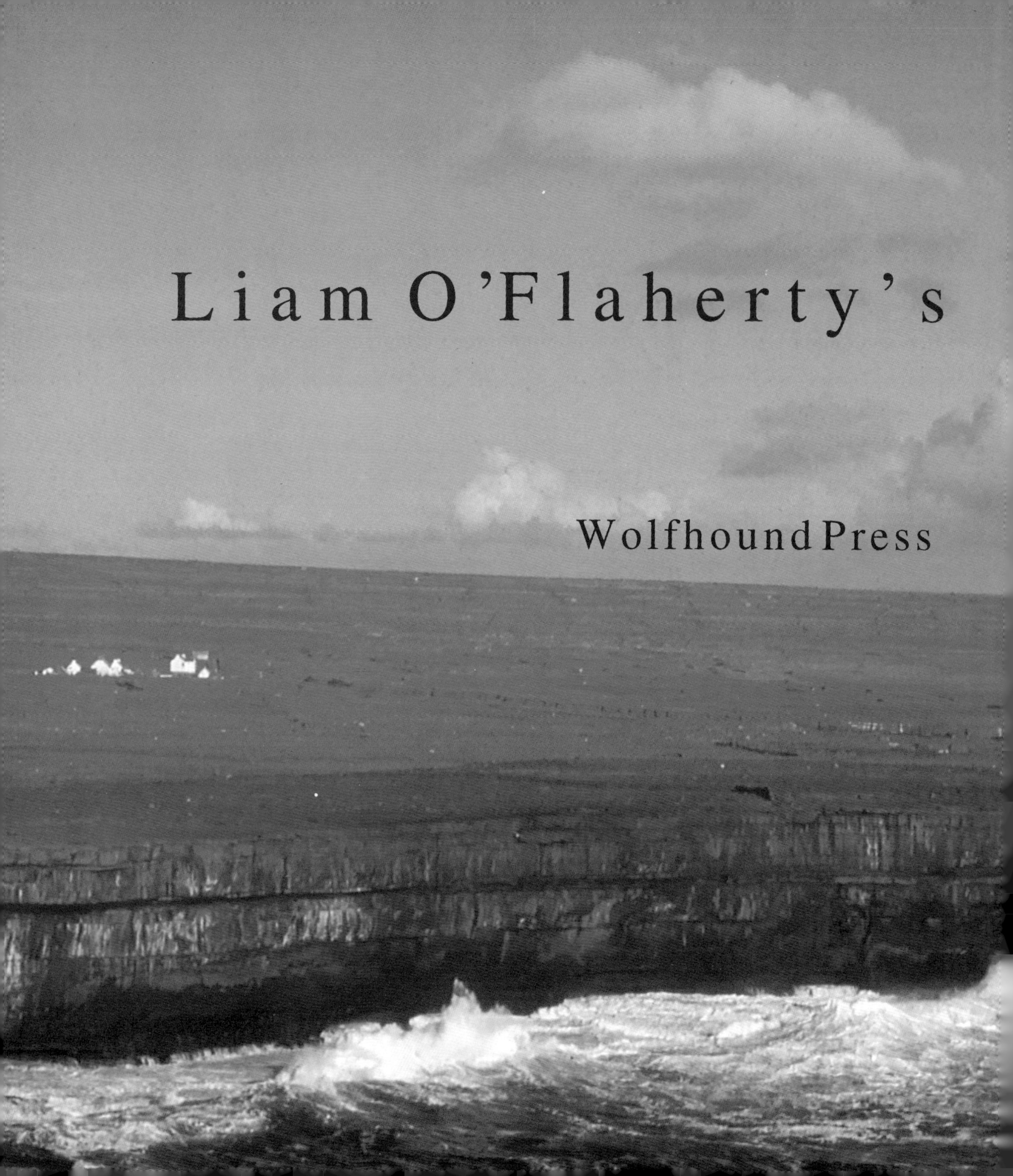

Liam O'Flaherty's

Wolfhound Press

IRELAND

Peter Costello

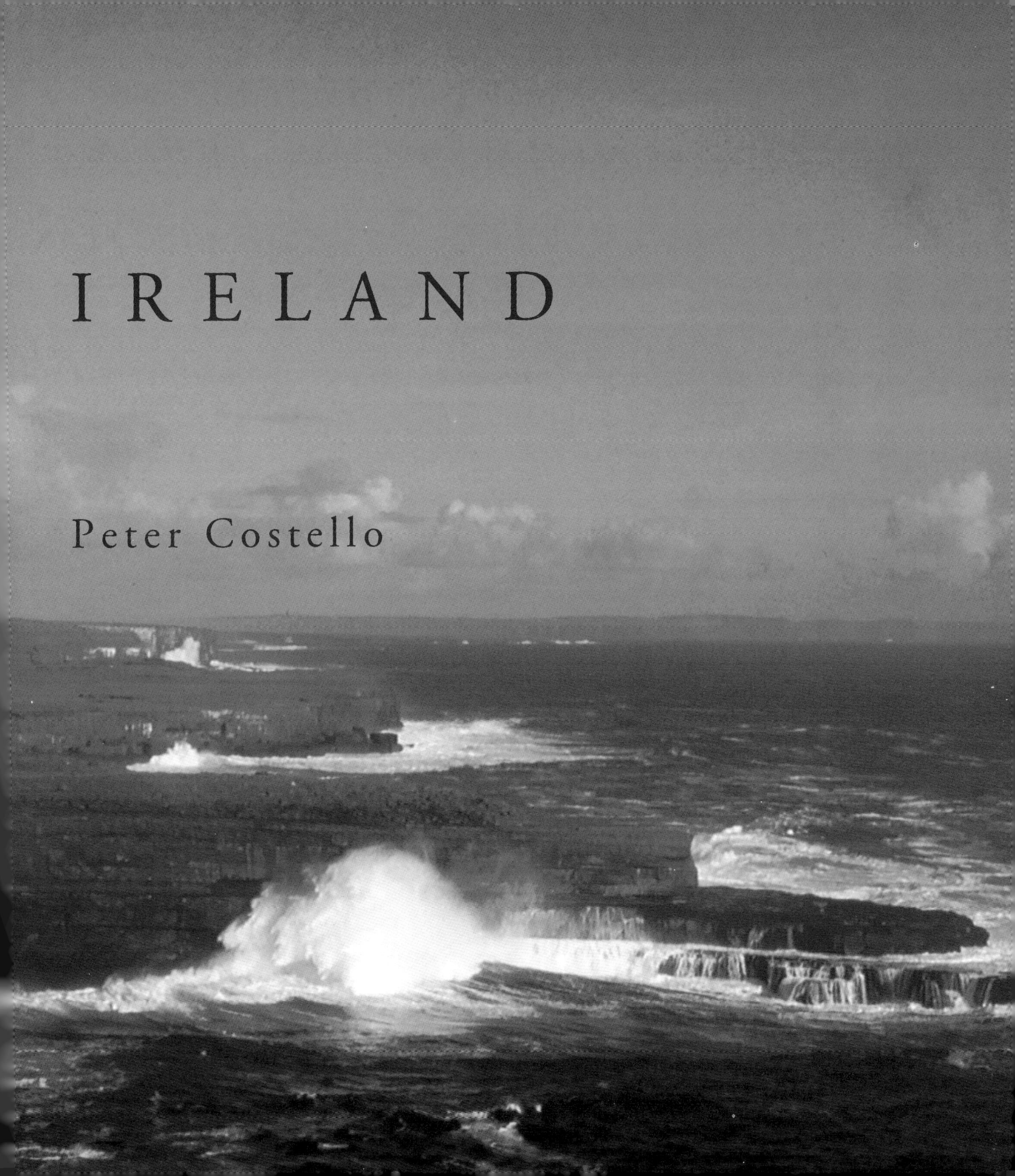

Dedication

To the memory of my friend Gus Martin,who did so much to change the climate in which Liam O'Flaherty is now read.

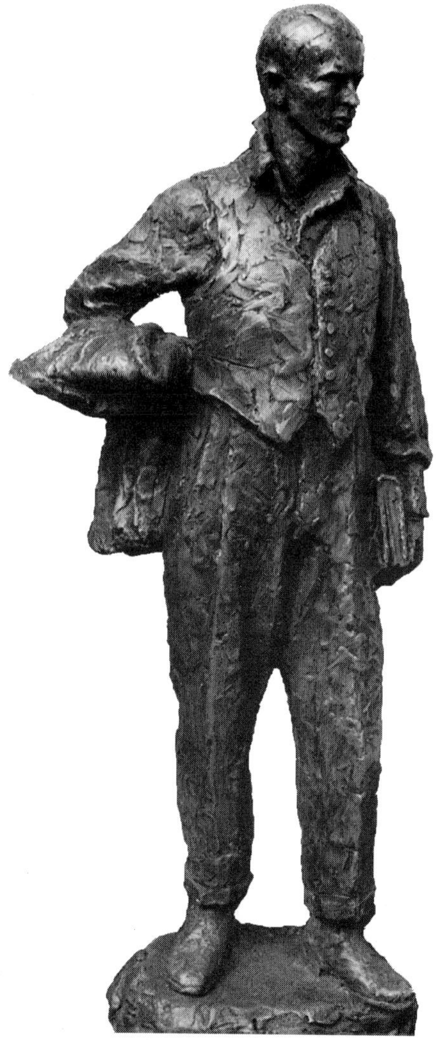

ABOVE: *Maquette for proposed life-sized figure in bronze of the young Liam O'Flaherty by sculptor Anthony Stones. Commissioned by The Liam O'Flaherty Trust, 68 Mountjoy Square, Dublin, which hopes to raise funds to enable completion of the work in 1997.*
PREVIOUS PAGES: *Aerial view over Aran from the west, showing the sea-battered cliffs with the houses of Liam O'Flaherty's birthplace, Gort na gCapall, to the left.*

First published 1996
Wolfhound Press
68 Mountjoy Square
Dublin 1
Ireland

Wolfhound Press receives financial assistance from the Arts Council/
An Chomhairle Ealaíon, Dublin.

British Library Cataloguing in Publication Data
A catalogue record for this book is available from the British Library

ISBN 0-86327-550-8

Cover Design: Slick Fish
Cover photographs: Portrait of Liam O'Flaherty by Hoppé; Aran seascape by Eoghan Kavanagh
Typesetting and Design: Wolfhound Press Ltd
Printed in Great Britain at the University Press, Cambridge

Contents

The courage and hardiness of the women of the west of Ireland was celebrated by Liam O'Flaherty in his stories and novels.

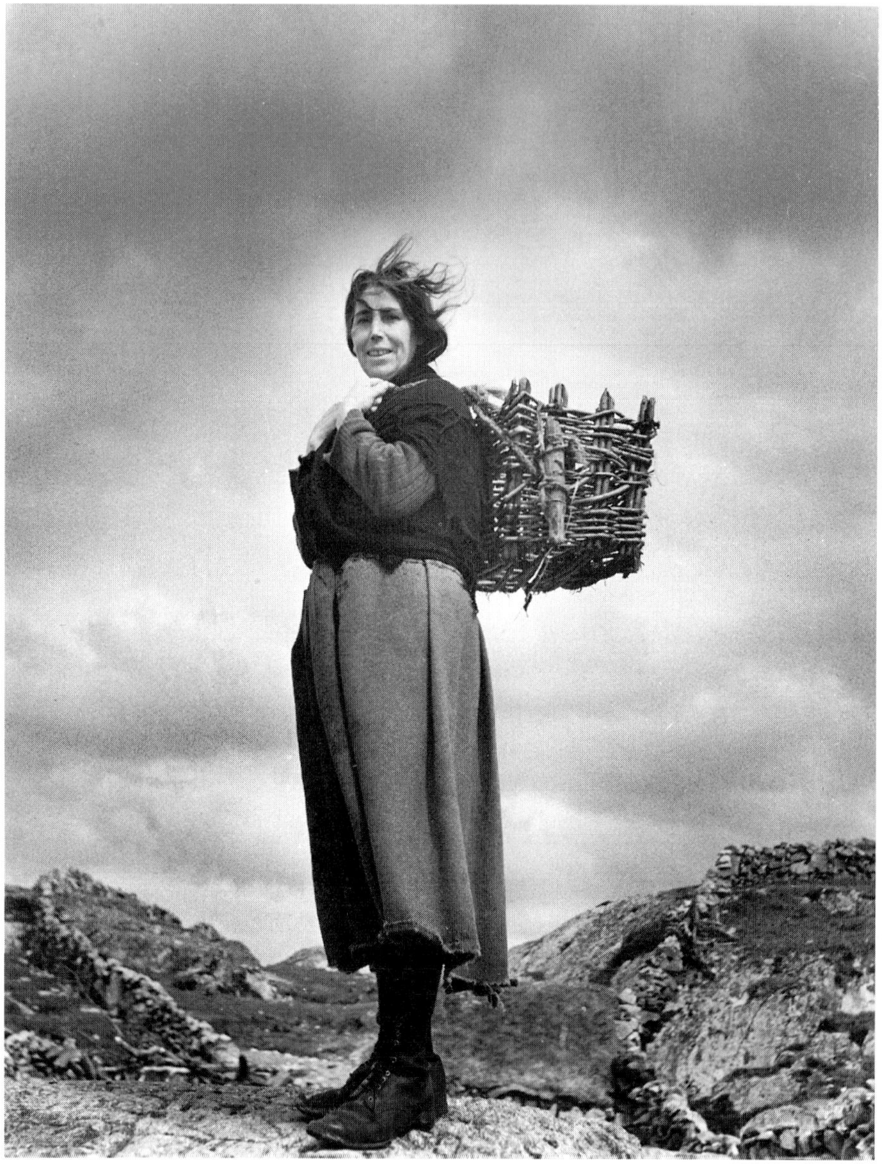

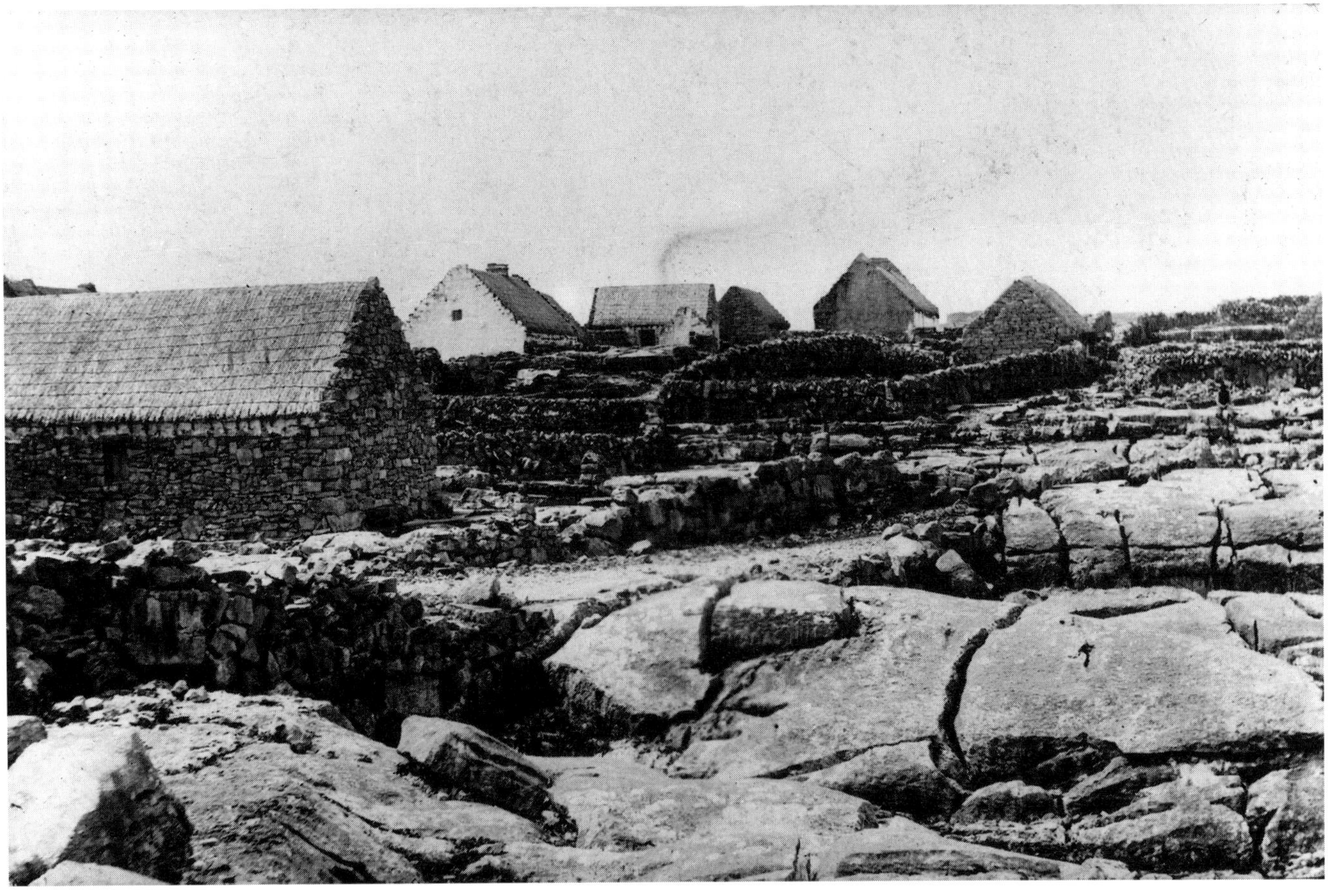

Gort na gCapall in 1900: the O'Flaherty house is the one with the small gable-end window.

As a child Liam O'Flaherty witnessed the back-breaking daily toil of life, in Aran and the west on which the very lives of the people depended. Here women (photographed in the late 1930s) carry up supplies landed by boat on the beach on Inishmaan. The Atlantic waves isolated the islands (see p10) and the people who lived there.

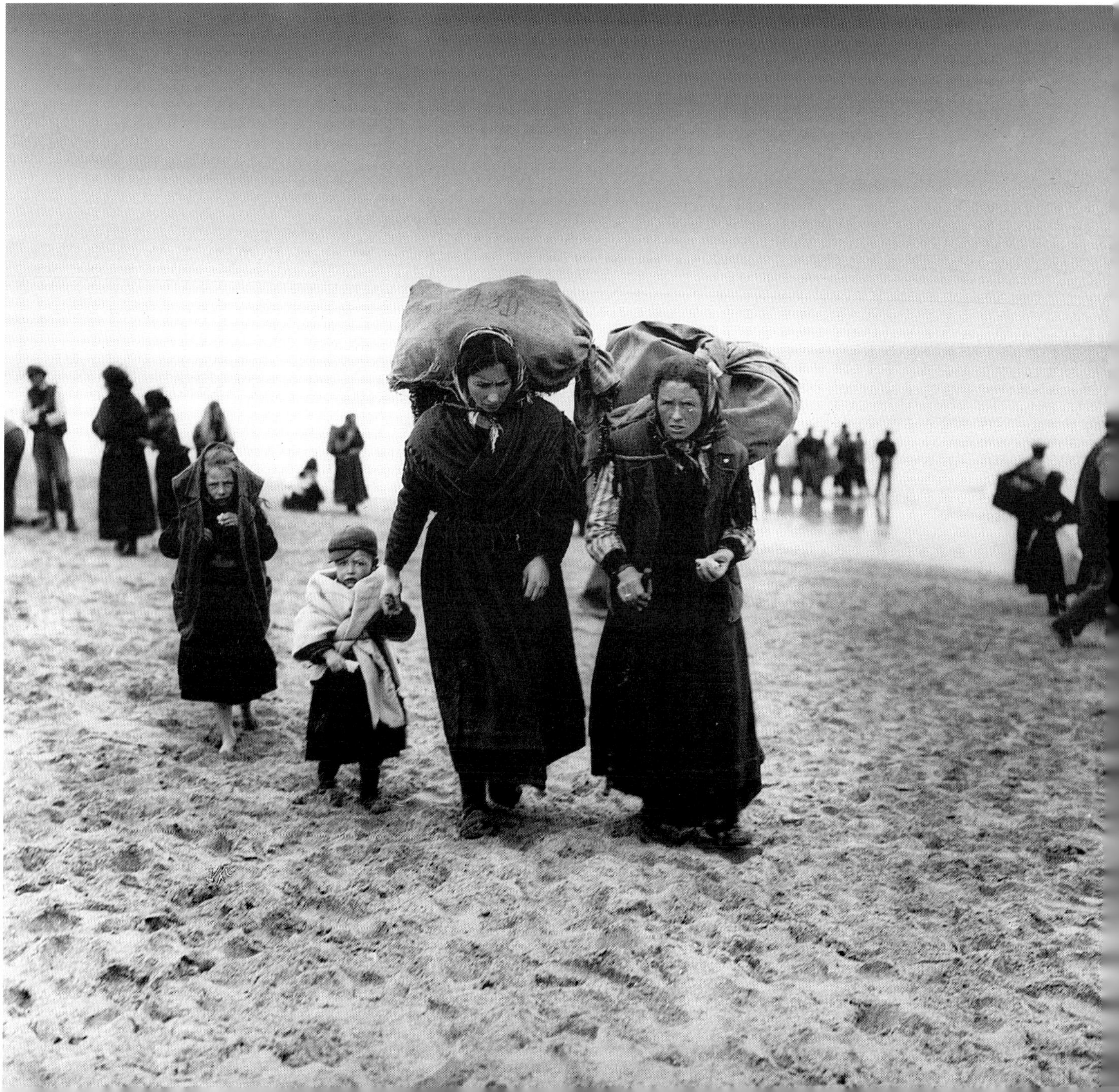

LIAM O' FLAHERTY was a child of the nineteenth century, and a man of the twentieth. Born in rural poverty, he died in urban comfort. Passionate in his love of nature, he abhorred everything brutish in man. An exquisite writer of short stories about man and beast on Ireland's western seaboard, ironically he is best known for *The Informer,* his novel of squalid communist intrigue in the back streets of Dublin (thanks largely to the famous film version by his cousin John Ford). Yet *Famine*, calmly dispassionate on the horrors of the Great Hunger, is regarded by all his readers as his greatest work. He was a man with a divided nature; even the Gaelic language of his childhood village was not the language his father wanted in the home. Solitary, he tried for many years to gain a foothold in crowded Hollywood. An individualist to the core, spontaneous and restless, by inclination a wanderer, he espoused the fervent communism so typical of those early twentieth-century writers who were filled with generosity and purity of heart; he was still reading Sartre and *Le Drapeau Rouge* in the last years of his life. Yet it was a cause that failed him, as it did so many other admirers of Lenin and Trotsky. In touch to his nerve-ends with the tides and eddies of creation, he loathed with great bitterness all organised religion, yet spent years studying for the priesthood. In the end he died with the blessing of a priest, reconciled with God if not with the institution he had so long rejected.

O'Flaherty was a strange, often contradictory man, unique among his contemporaries in Irish literature. In his writings we can see the beginnings of much that is now being done in both Gaelic and Irish literature. Though often neglected in the sweep of modern Anglo-American criticism, he was widely appreciated on the continent; and his own love of France and admiration for Russian literature suggest that he was more truly a European writer. From the dying remnants of an ancient culture, from the shattered fragments of a modern life, he composed the unities of his art.

This book is published to mark the centenary of Liam O'Flaherty's birth. It is intended to provide, through biographical commentary and extracts from his stories and novels, together with appropriate illustrations, a recreation of his varied experiences and his divided imaginative world. More than a decade after his death, it may also introduce him to new and to younger readers.

The dedication marks a debt which the sudden inappropriateness of death left largely unpaid.

Peter Costello
Dublin

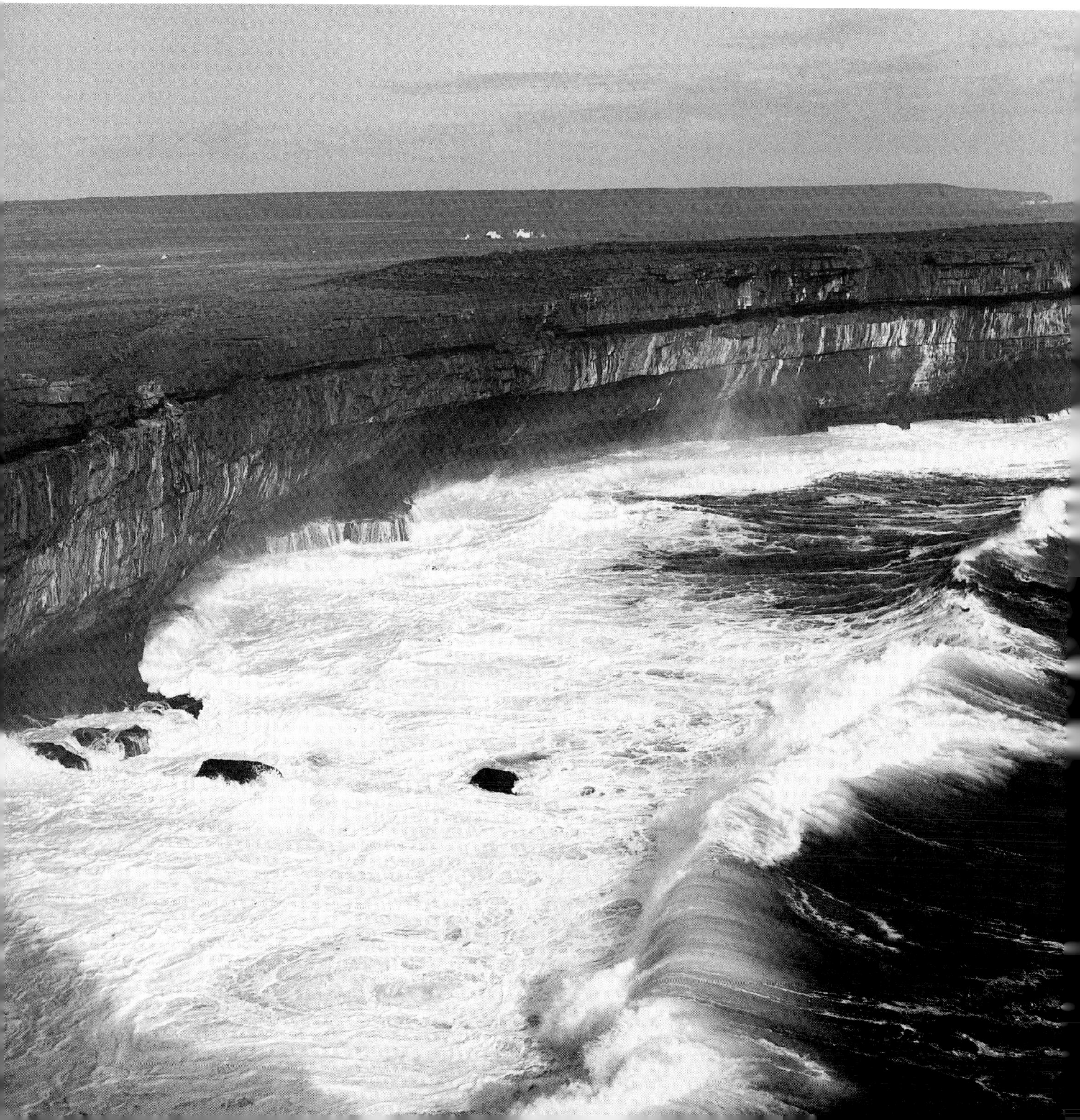

'The Wave' *by Liam O'Flaherty*

The waves hardly made any noise as they struck the cliff, and they drivelled backwards slowly. The trough of the sea between the reefs was convulsing like water in a shaken glass. The cliff's face was black, drenched with brine, that streamed from its base, each tiny rivulet noisy in the sudden silence.

Then the silence broke. The sea rushed back. With the speed and motion of a bladder bursting it sprang backwards. Then it rose upwards in a concave wall, from reef to reef, across the cove, along whose bottom the slimy weeds of the ocean depths were visible through the thin sheet of water left to cover the sea's nakedness by the fury of the rising wave.

For a moment the wave stood motionless, beautifully wild and immense. Its base in front was ragged, uneven and scratched with white foam, like the debris strewn around a just-constructed pyramid. Then a belt of dark blue ran from end to end across its face, sinking inwards in a perfect curve. Then came a wider belt, a green belt peppered with white spots. Then the wave's head curved outwards, arched like the neck of an angry swan. That curved head was a fathom deep, of a transparent green, with a rim of milky white. And to the rear, great lumps of water buttressed it, thousands of tons of water in each lump.

The wave advanced, slowly at first, with a rumbling sound. That awful mass of water advanced simultaneously from end to end of its length without breaking a ripple on its ice-smooth breast. But from its summit a shower of driven foam arose, from east to west, and fell backwards on to the shoulders of the sea, that came behind the wave in mountains pushing it to the cliff. The giant cliff looked small in front of that moving wall of blue and green and white water.

Then there was a roar. The wave sprang upwards to its full height. Its crest broke and points of water stuck out, curving downwards like fangs. It seemed to bend its head as it hurtled forward to ram the cliff. In a moment the wave and the cliff had disappeared in a tumbling mass of white water that yawned and hissed and roared. The whole semi-circle of the cliff vanished in the white water and the foam mist that rose above it blotting out the sky. Just for one moment it was thus. In another moment the broken wave had fallen, flying to the sea in a thousand rushing fragments. The cliff appeared again.

But a great black mouth had opened in its face, at the centre, above the cavern. The cliff's face stood ajar, as if it yawned, tired of battle. The mouth was vertical in the cliff, like a ten-foot wedge stuck upwards from the edge of the cavern. Then the cliff tried to close the mouth. It pressed it on it from either side. But it did not close. The sides fell inwards and the mouth grew wider. The whole centre of the cliff broke loose at the top and swayed forward like a tree being felled. There was a noise like rising thunder. Black dust rose from the tottering cliff through the falling foam of the wave. Then with a soft splash the whole centre of the cliff collapsed into the cavern. The sides caved in with another splash. A wall of grey dust arose shutting out everything. The rumbling of moving rocks came through the cloud of dust. Then the cloud rose and went inland.

The cliff had disappeared. The land sloped down to the edge of the cove. Huge rocks stood awkwardly on the very brink of the flat rock, with the rim of the sea playing between them. Smoke was rising from the fallen cliff. And the wave had disappeared. Already another one was gathering in the cove.

A Brief Chronology

1896	Liam O'Flaherty born 28 August at Gort na gCapall, Inishmore, Aran Islands
1908-1913	Attends Rockwell College, outside Cashel, Co. Tipperary; and Blackrock College, Dublin
1914	One term at Holy Cross College, Clonliffe; leaves in December
1914-1915	One year at University College Dublin, studying Classics
1915-1917	Serves in the Irish Guards (2nd Battalion) during Great War, in France and Belgium; wounded September 1917; discharged with disability pension; returns to England
1918	Treated at George V Military Hospital, Dublin; granted BA (War Service) by National University of Ireland
1918-1920	Travels as ordinary seaman to South America, Greece, Turkey and Canada; hobo, lumberjack and other jobs, in Canada and USA. Involved with Industrial Workers of the World ('the Wobblies'); joins Communist Party
1921	November: founder (with others) of Communist Party of Ireland
1922	January: seizes Rotunda with party of unemployed; fights in Civil War; flees Ireland
1923	First novel, *Thy Neighbour's Wife*, published in London; begins career as professional writer
1924	*The Black Soul*, a novel, and *Spring Sowing*, first collection of short stories, published; involved in publication of *To-Morrow*
1925	*The Informer* published
1926	Marries Margaret Barrington; birth of Pegeen
1927	*The Life of Tim Healy* published. Assassination of Kevin O'Higgins
1928	*The Assassin* published
1929	First film version of *The Informer*
1930	Visits Russia, returns through Poland, Germany and France. Birth of second daughter, Joyce
1932	Election of de Valera to government; publication of *Skerrett*; separation from wife
1933	Nervous breakdown
1934	*Shame the Devil* published. Lives in California for a year, where he meets Kitty Harding Tailer (d. 1990) who from now would be his life-long companion.
1935	John Ford's version of *The Informer*. *Hollywood Cemetery* published
1937	*Famine* and *The Short Stories of Liam O'Flaherty* published; French film version of *The Puritan*
1938	French film version of *Mr Gilhooley*
1940	Moves to United States; travels widely in the Americas with Kitty Tailer
1946	Returns to Europe; visits Ireland. *Land* published
1948	*Two Lovely Beasts* published. Ireland declared a Republic
1950	Last novel, *Insurrection*, published
1952	Settles in Dublin, with frequent visits to Paris
1953	Publication of *Dúil,* a collection of stories in Gaelic
1976	Publication of *The Pedlar's Revenge & Other Stories*, followed by reissue of many of his works by Wolfhound Press during the following years
1982	Death of Margaret Barrington
1984	7 September: dies in Dublin

Below: *The small house in Gort na gCapall where Liam O'Flaherty was born in August 1896.*

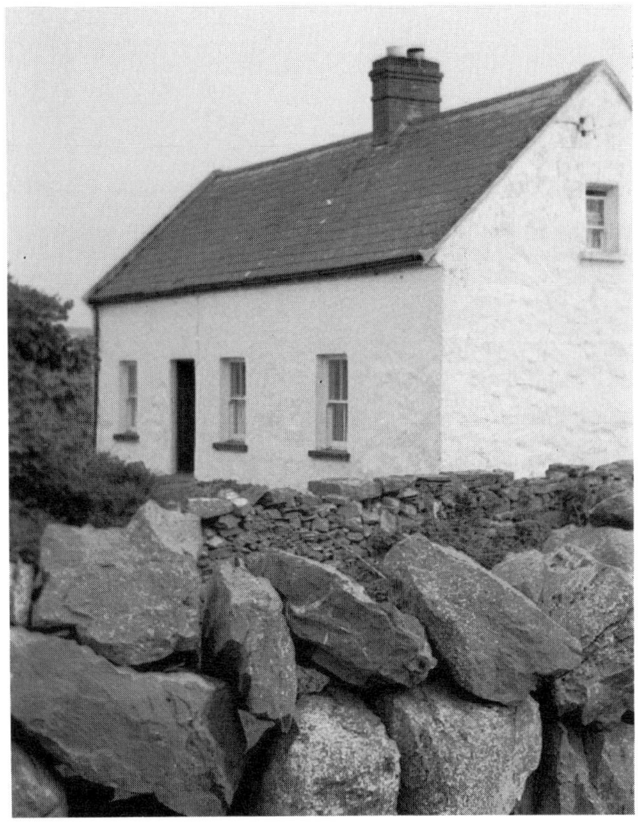

ARAN Liam O'Flaherty was born at Gort na gCapall on Inishmore, the largest of the Aran Islands which lie off the raw western coast of Ireland, on 28 August 1896.

On public records, such as the Census, which were kept in English, the family name sometimes appears as Flaherty, and the child's name as William. His father insisted, Liam later recalled, that English should be the language used in the family home. So, though Gaelic was the common daily language of their neighbours, it was not quite the child's second language, yet neither was it the writer's first language. His relationship with Gaelic, like his relationship with the Aran Islands, would be a significant but troubled one.

His father and mother had a romantic history. In February 1872 Michael O'Flaherty, then twenty-six, ran away with the beautiful Margaret Ganly, who was only sixteen, and married her. But the romance of their elopement faded quickly in the hard conditions of Aran life. Margaret O'Flaherty bore fourteen children alive, of whom only eleven survived into childhood. By the time Liam, who was the second surviving son and the eighth child, was born, his eldest sister had already emigrated to Boston, where she was joined later by another sister. They were part of a small colony of Aran Islanders in the New World.

The cottage where Liam was born had three rooms, a thatched roof and an outhouse for storing potatoes, and was typical of the island. Though the average size of a holding on Aran was one and a half acres, Michael O'Flaherty – whom Liam once described on an official form as a gentleman – had fifteen. These were on the rocky southern edge of the island, looking west towards the open expanse of the ocean, from which the winter storms came, out of the vast void of the Atlantic.

Of his family, his brother Tom and his younger sister Agnes were the most significant for Liam. He was a handsome little boy, spoilt by all the women of the village. He got his passionate nature from the O'Flahertys, proverbial in the west of Ireland for their wildness, and his love of nature and his storytelling powers from his Ganly mother. Her family were incomers, Plymouth Brethren from Ulster, who had come to Aran a generation before to build the lighthouse. She would sit with the child on the cliffs below their house and point out to him the wonders of the natural life that surrounded them. Liam's parents were famous in the islands for their dancing and singing skills. As a writer Liam would draw on his family background for many of his short stories and for his novels *Thy Neighbour's Wife*, *The Black Soul*, *Famine*, and in particular *Skerrett.*

Three weeks before Liam O'Flaherty was born in the summer of 1896, Inishmore was visited by the poet W.B. Yeats and his friends, the novelist George Moore and the English critic Arthur Symons. Later they would go on to stay with Lady Gregory at Coole; their friendships and experiences of this summer mark the beginning of the Irish Literary Revival, with the founding of the dramatic movement from which the Abbey Theatre and its achievements came.

A generation later Liam would make his own distinctive contribution to the reversal of that revival, re-channelling Irish literature in a new, realistic direction by rejecting with passionate contempt all that Yeats and his friends stood for. Yeats inspired J.M. Synge to visit Aran in the summer of 1897, so leading to *The Aran Islands* and *The Playboy of the Western World.* However controversial the nature of Synge's contribution to Irish writing was, it would be Liam O'Flaherty who eventually provided the wider world with the deepest insight into the life of the west.

Yeats and his friends saw the life of Aran in a romantic, idealistic, primitivist light, the light of summer. But Aran, when the visitors and teachers are gone, has its winter season too. By winter light life looks very different. Storm-swept and isolated, Aran was, like the whole nation, riven by personal, political and social divisions. These would become highly divisive during Liam's early years, and provide him with the material for some of his finest writing.

In 1897 Fr Murtagh Farragher, who had been a curate on Inishmore under the famous Fr O'Donoghue during 1887-91, returned as parish priest. His arrival led to the breakup and division of the Digby estate by the Land Commission, and the founding of the Aran Islands Fisheries Co-Operative. Fr Farragher also urged the islanders to settle the outstanding fine imposed on them for troubles during the Land League days, back in the 1880s. Liam's father and relatives had been leading figures in the struggles, driving the landlord's cattle over the southern cliff to their death in the sea. But the division of the land, though it was hoped it would hasten an improvement in the local way of life, was to have unhappy consequences.

These economic changes were part of a general change at the time, signified for some by the setting up on Aran of a branch of the Gaelic League by the Republican Patrick Pearse in the summer of 1898. A leading figure of the Gaelic League was the Oatquarter schoolmaster, David O'Callaghan. Like Yeats and his friends, Patrick Pearse and the members of the Gaelic League tended to view the island in a romantic light.

Both the priest and the teacher were trying to confront the poverty and deprivation, as they saw it, of the islanders. Typical of that hard life was the O'Flaherty household. Into the three rooms of the small house at Gortnagcapall (this was O'Flaherty's own preferred spelling) were crowded two adults and eight children at the time of the Census in 1901. Michael O'Flaherty supported them by growing potatoes and a few oats on his small holding, by farming some pigs, both to eat and for market, and by fishing in season. The population of the islands as a whole had been in decline since the Famine, and would go on declining during the coming decades. American Wakes for those going into exile in America, as Liam's sisters and other members of his family did, celebrated the loss of loved ones to a newer, and hopefully better, life.

As a child Liam played around the village and followed his father and uncles about their work. He wore the petticoats commonly put on small boys up to the age of thirteen – allegedly to confuse the fairies, but really for reasons of hygiene. His sharp eyes observed all the events of the cottages, and the lives of men and animals in the rocky acres and cliffs and beaches around him, storing the images which were to come so readily to his adult pen.

In the autumn of 1902, when he was six, he started at the Oatquarter school (which had been built in 1889). His first try at storytelling – a lurid romance of how a neighbour murdered his wife and buried her in the potato patch – dated from about this time. The story horrified his mother, who thought it might be true. Liam learnt early the value of shock, and also the sometimes bitter consequences of experiments in literature. In another version of this tale Liam says that the story was written when he was a little older, aged about nine, in 1906; and that his teacher beat him soundly for his temerity.

At the school he came under the influence of David O'Callaghan. O'Callaghan, then in his late forties and early fifties, was nevertheless to be the major influence on both Liam and his elder brother Tom. O'Callaghan was the first Sinn Féiner on the island, though not perhaps a Republican. From him Liam imbibed the nationalist sentiments which were coming to dominate public life and private debate all across Ireland.

O'Callaghan was from County Limerick, but his wife was from Galway. There may have been an element of the brash outsider putting things to rights about both him and the priest. It was about this time that Sir Roger Casement – then in the first flush of his interest in the Gaelic League – visited Aran, was impressed by the abilities of Tom O'Flaherty when he heard him reading in school, and offered to send him to Summerhill College in Sligo. But fate intervened in some unexplained way – perhaps through Casement's departure for South America – and nothing came of this.

It was with his brother Tom (then about sixteen) that Liam attempted his first novel. But they fell out over the plot, and it made no further progress. This would have been about 1907, the year that saw the publication of J.M. Synge's *Aran Islands* – which O'Flaherty, no admirer of the playwright, disliked when he came to read it. Even in that book, with its account of an island eviction, political troubles were not avoided.

In the summer of 1908 the difficulties over the Digby Estate came to a head. The land had been divided, but a cousin of Liam's father, Roger Dirrane, felt aggrieved and betrayed by the parish priest. While the priest was away (though his sister was in residence) Dirrane bombed the parochial house at Kilronan. For this act of anarchism he got three years in gaol; his supposed accomplice got three months. This sensational event led Fr Farragher to organise a boycott of the Dirrane family and their relatives – a large section of the island community – among whom were the Gort na gCapall O'Flahertys. This outlawed group were called Lucht na Tincans – the Tin Can Party – after the metal drums in which Roger had mixed his explosives. The priest's ban was supported by the reactionary United Ireland League. Questions were asked in the House of Commons, as often as not by the Craigs, whose names were to come to the forefront of Ulster Unionist politics a little later. Liam O'Flaherty, as a Tincan, adopted the anti-clericalism of his relatives – an attitude which lasted a lifetime.

Below: *The ferry boat, the vital link for islanders with the outside world in O'Flaherty's childhood,* c. *1910.*

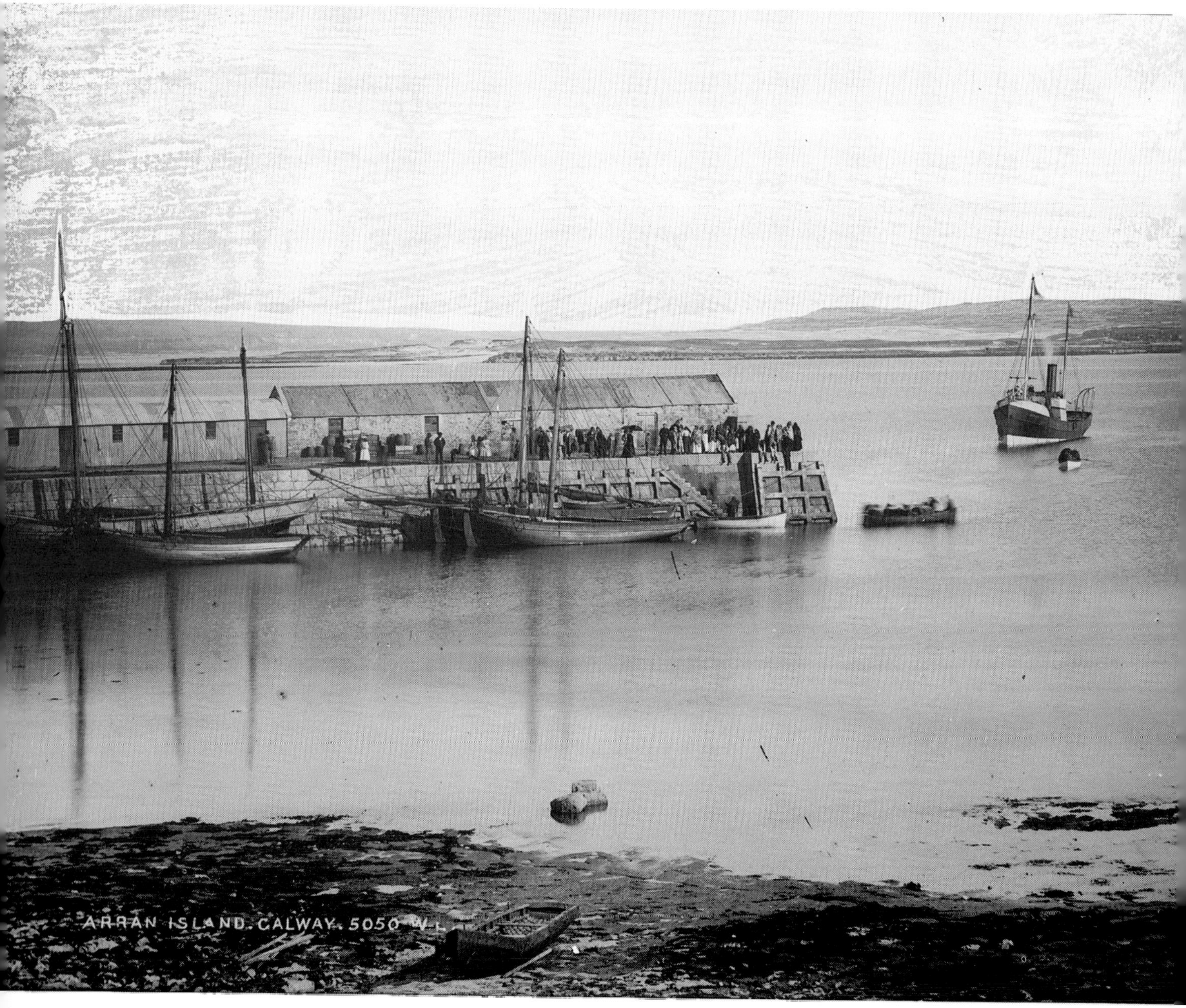

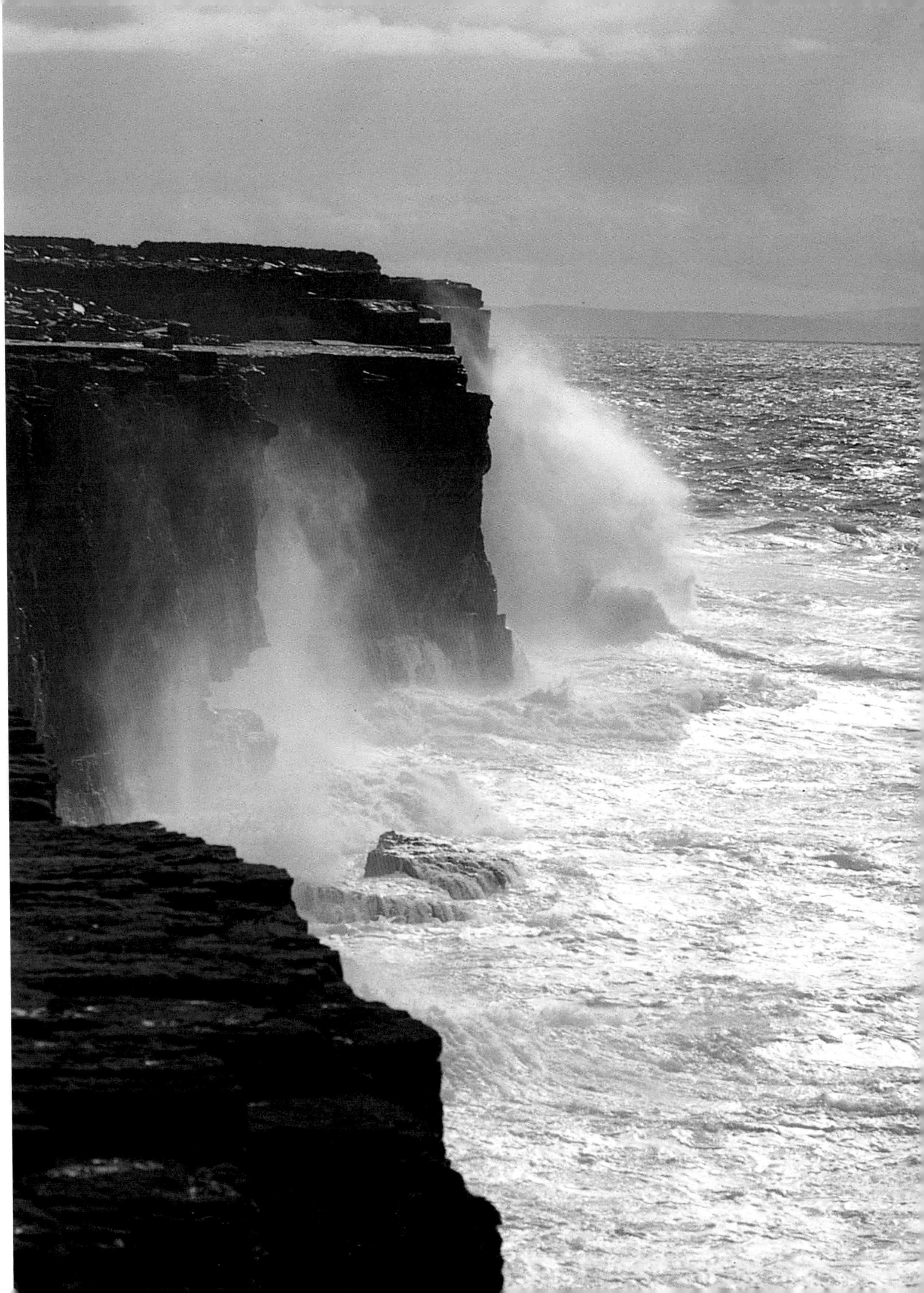

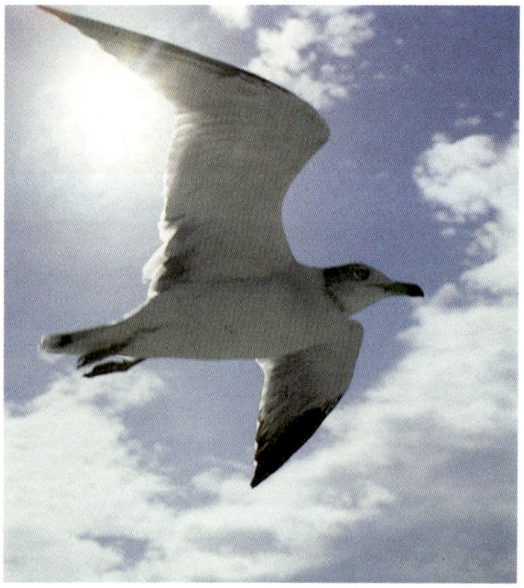

Previous page: *Liam O'Flaherty was born within the sound of the sea smashing on the cliffs of Inishmore, and all his life retained a love for the power and passion of nature that he had experienced as a child.*

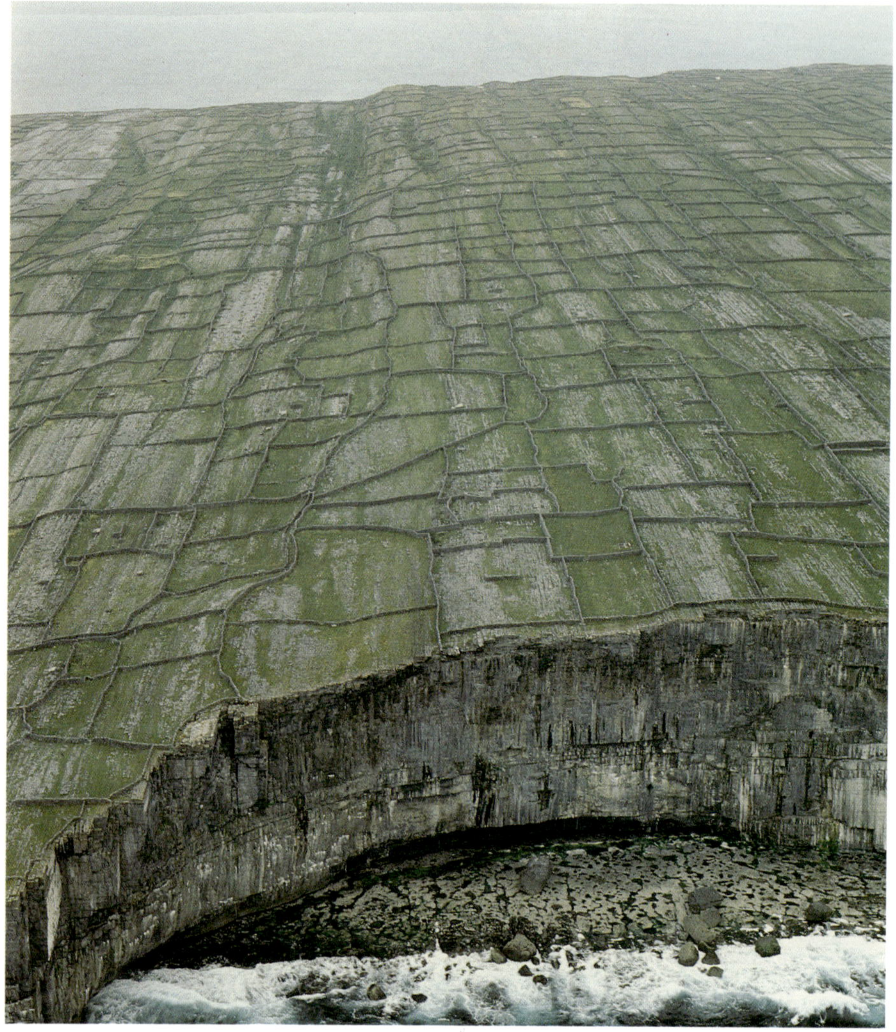

Above, left and below: *His stories recall the wild cries of the seabirds hanging over the small fields, divided by stone walls, built with back-breaking labour – the work of past generations of islanders. Wayside memorials kept alive the names of these dead. On Aran a child was always conscious of nature and history.*

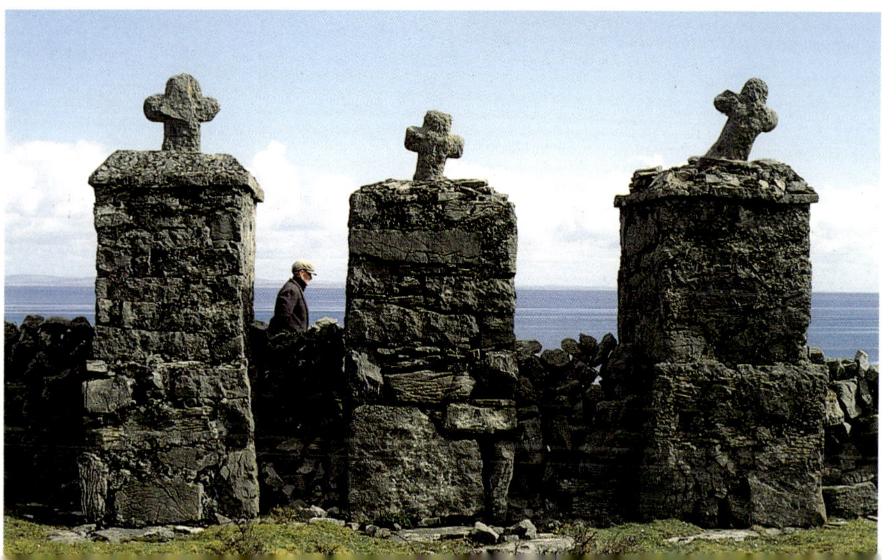

Right: *Existence in the west, where O'Flaherty was reared, was hard. Indeed, life itself, if only in the shape of a wildflower, had to force its way up out of the barren rock – a force of nature which could not be conquered.*

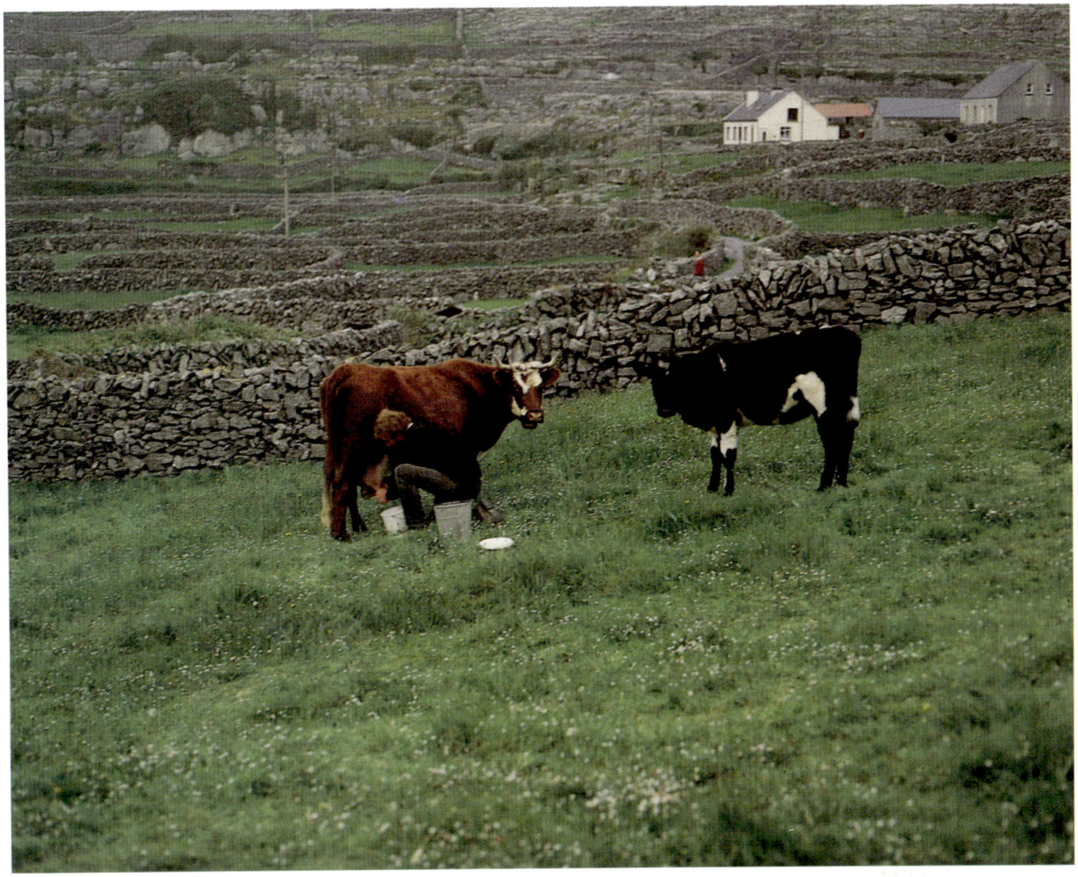

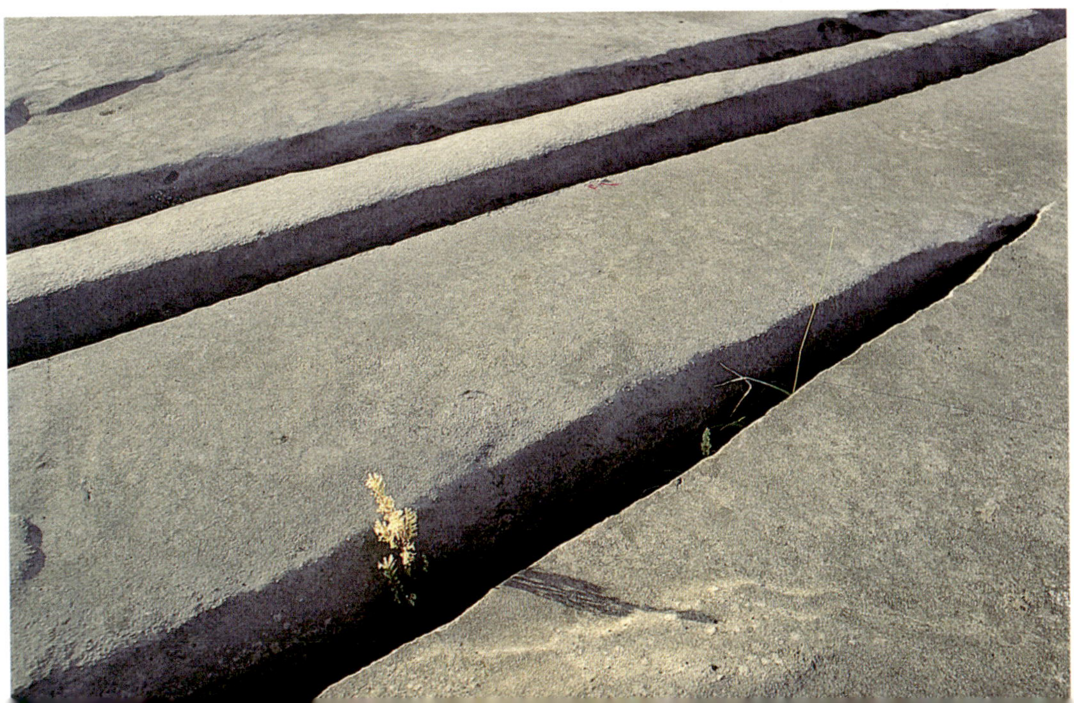

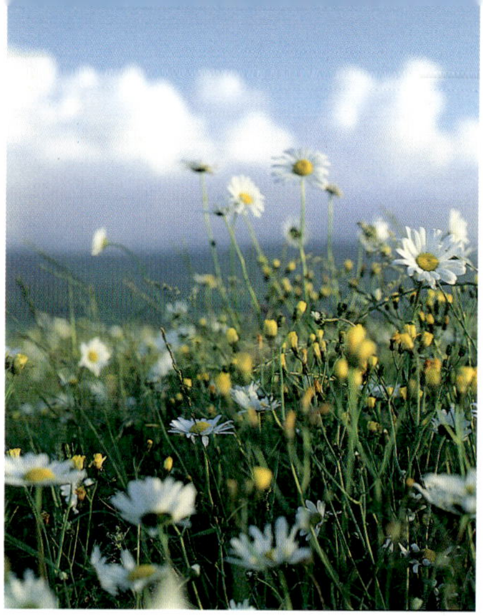

It was then that he noticed the wind, the lifting clouds, and the far-away sky. He smelt the wind as he breathed in great gasps . . . Then suddenly, he longed for the mountains and the wide undulating plains and the rocky passes and the swift-flowing rivers, away to the south in his own country. Freedom and solitude and quiet, with only the wind coming through the bog heather! Away, away, where nobody could catch him! To the mountains! To the mountains!

from *The Informer*

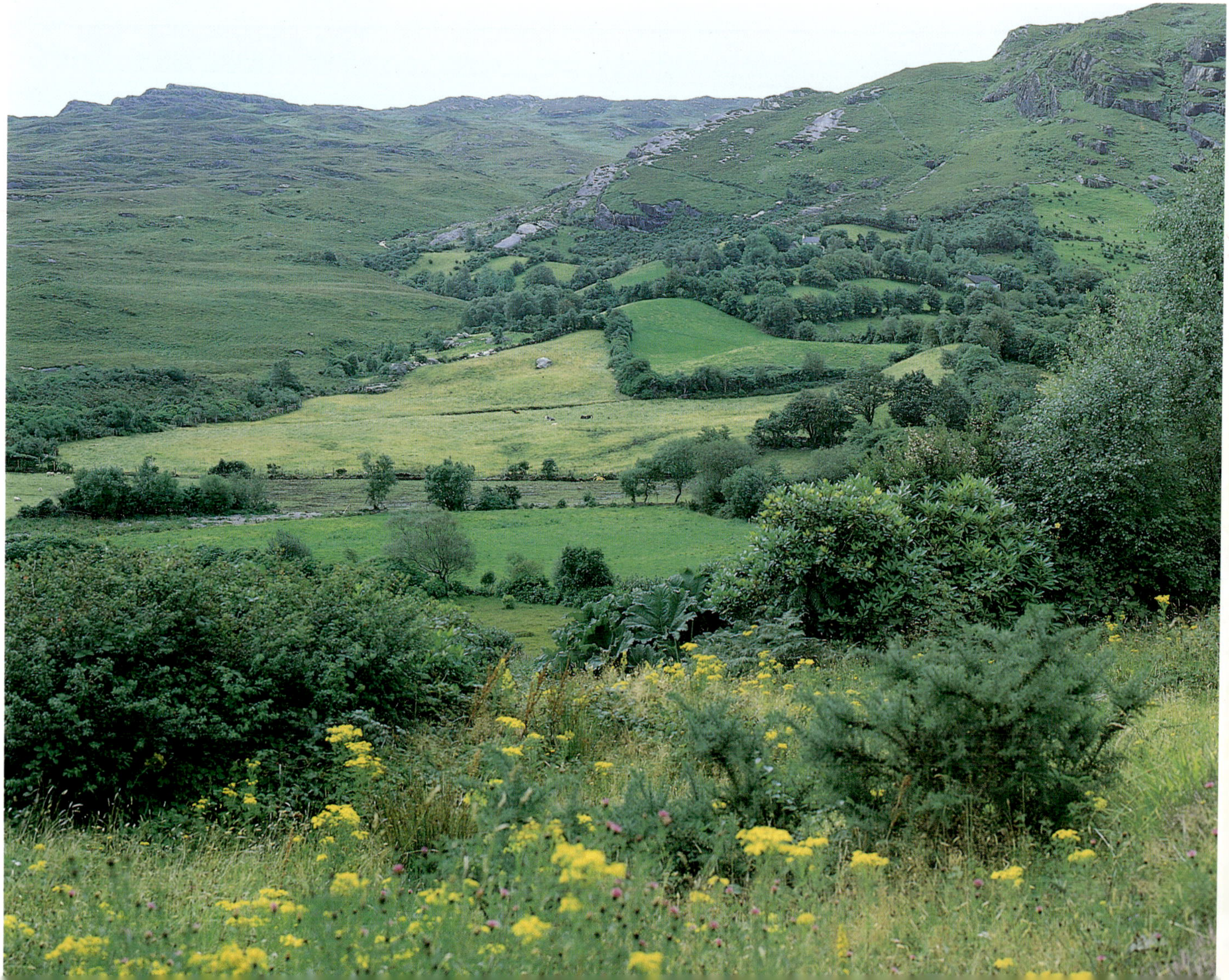

Left: *The images of nature, the wildflowers, the fields, the distant mountains, haunted O'Flaherty, as they do Gypo Nolan, his chief character in* The Informer, *longing to escape from the sordid city to the true freedom of his childhood home in Tipperary.*

Below: *O'Flaherty lived over many years in several places in the Wicklow Mountains (the scene below is near Sallygap), finding there among the trees and his herd of goats, his own special peace, his own true freedom.*

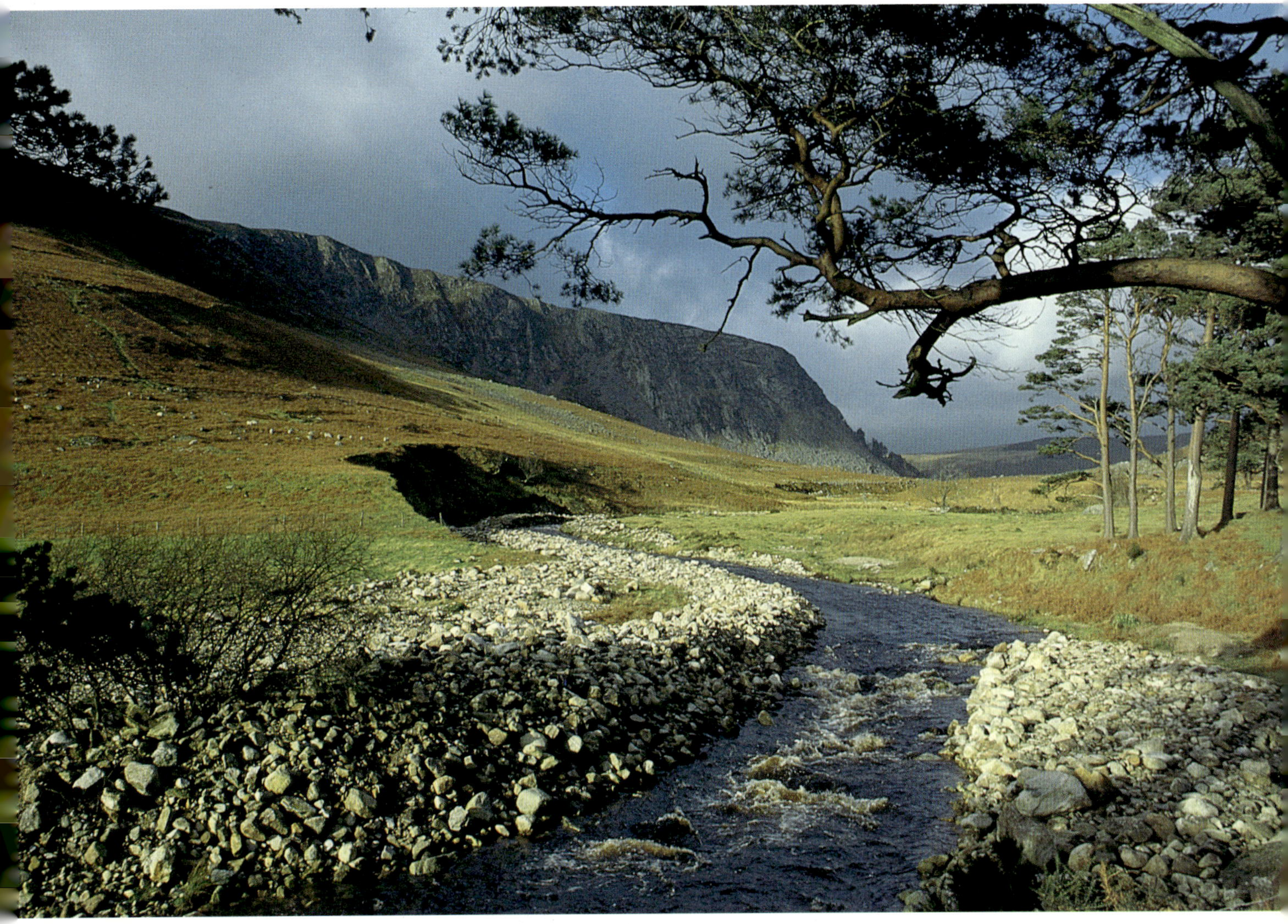

In his relationship with the land and with nature there was a mystical depth for O'Flaherty – for him, as for the old Gaelic poets, the wilderness was his salvation.

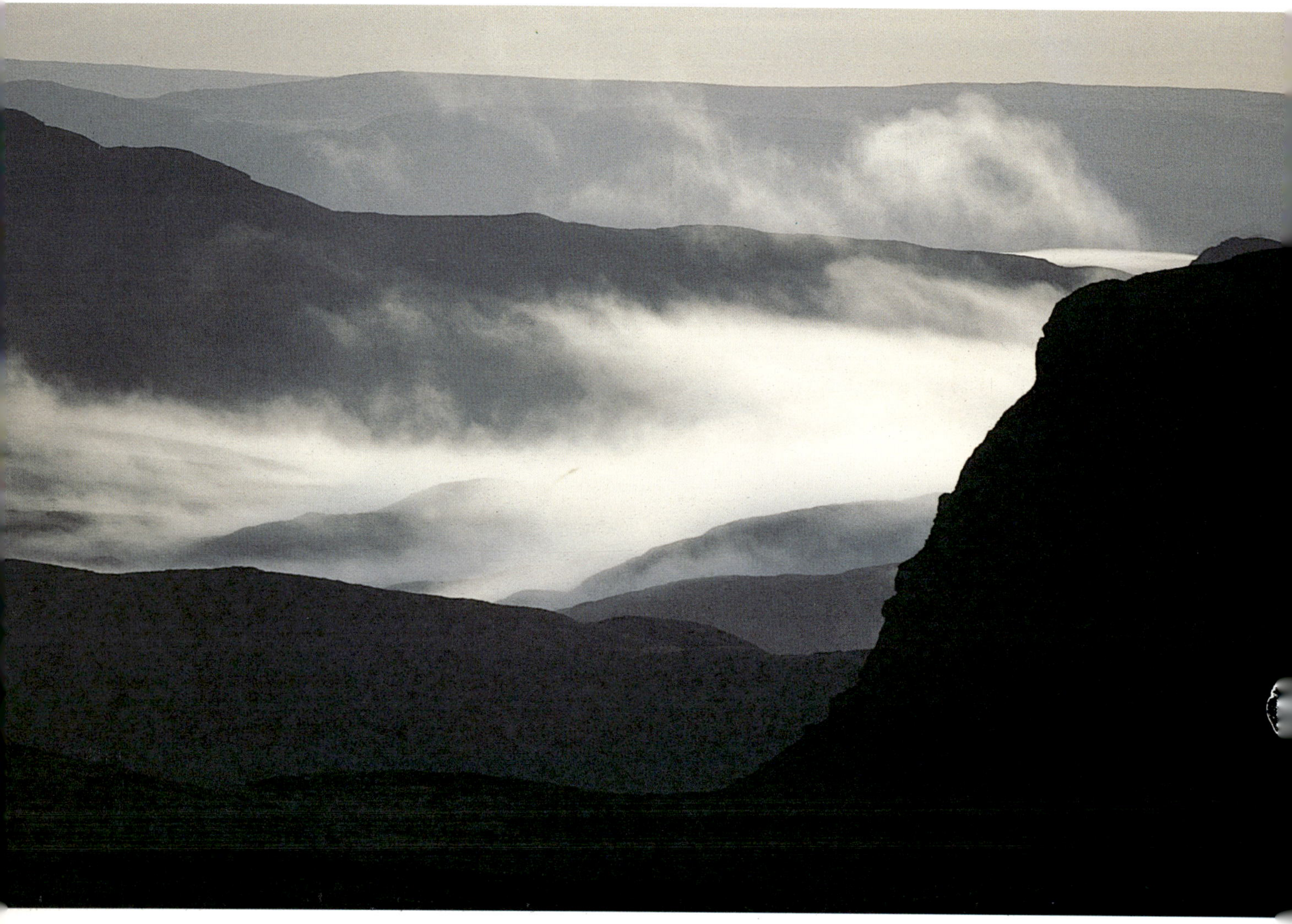

The moods of the land, often dark and sombre, were a reflection of his own volatile temperament – the sudden mists, the brilliant moments of vision.

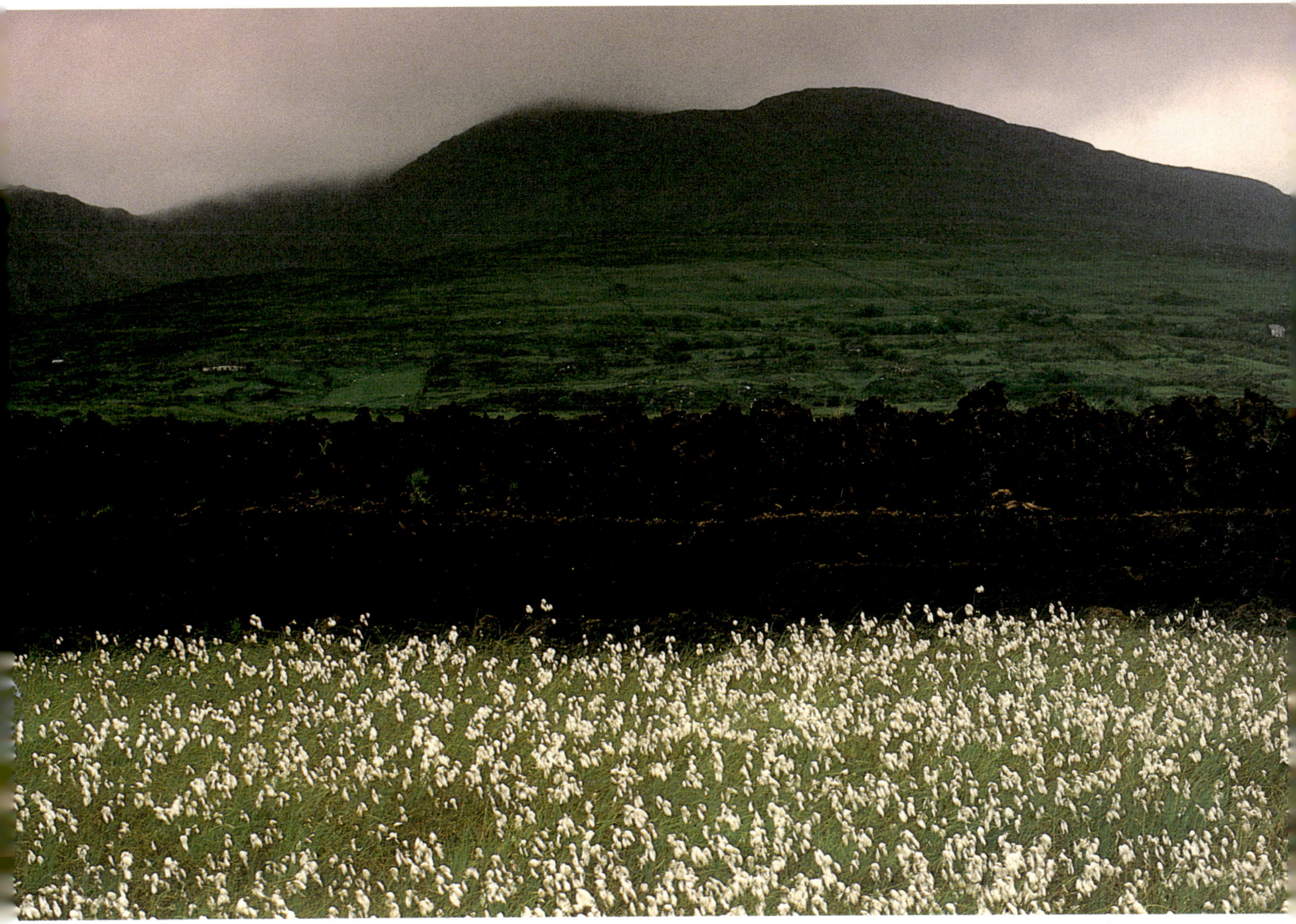

But nature also reflected back to O'Flaherty his own calmer moments of peace and resignation, when he felt at one with creation.

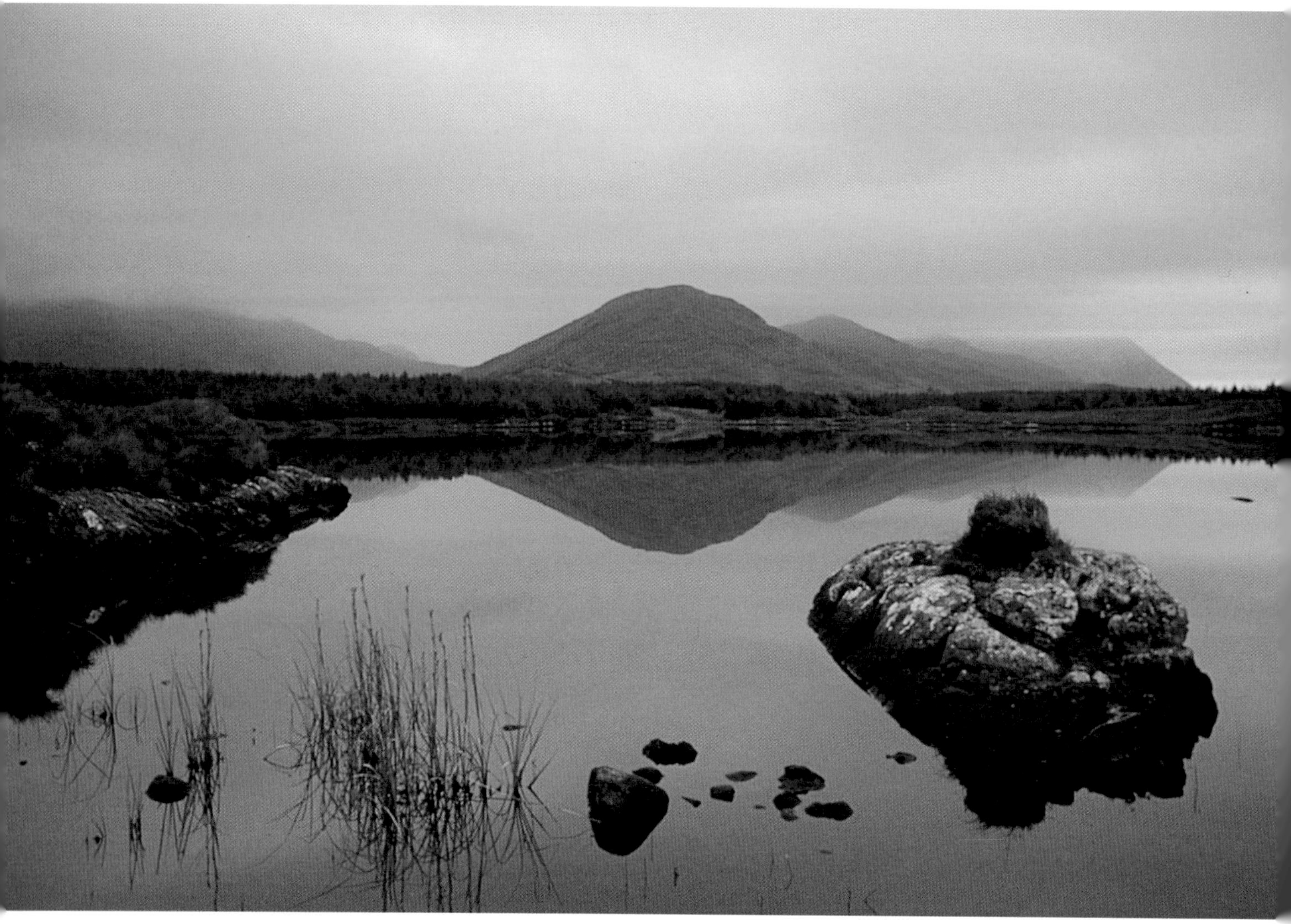

'The Struggle' *by Liam O'Flaherty*

The sea was dead calm. There was no wind. The sun stood high in the heavens. Seamus O'Toole and Michael Halloran were coming from Kilmurrage to Rooruch in a new boat they had just bought. The fresh tar on the boat's canvas sides glistened in the sun, and the polished wooden lathes of the frame emitted a strong smell of pine. The two men were singing snatches of coarse songs as they rowed. They had drunk a lot of whiskey in Kilmurrage. They were both strong young men. Seamus O'Toole rowed in the prow. His cap resting crookedly on the back of his head, showed his white forehead above a ruddy face. His blue eyes were glassy with drink and there was a slight froth around the corners of his thick lips. Michael Halloran rowed in the stern. His bare head was shaped like a cone, shorn to the bone all round with a short glib hanging over the narrow forehead. Sweat discoloured the knees of his white frieze trousers. His shoulder blades twitched convulsively under his grey shirt as he lay forward over the oars and he kept hanging his head sideways, as if he were trying to hit his left knee.

They were passing Coillnamhan harbour about a mile from the shore, when O'Toole stopped rowing suddenly and said, 'Let us have a drink.' 'I'm satisfied,' said Halloran, letting go his oars. The boat flopped ahead with a lapping sound on the eddies of her wake. O'Toole picked up a pint bottle of whiskey that rested on his waistcoat in the prow. He uncorked it and took a swig. The whiskey gurgled going down his throat. Then his lips left the neck of the bottle with a gasp and he passed it in silence to Halloran. Halloran took a long draught and passed it back. 'That's enough for us,' he said thickly. 'Go to the devil,' said O'Toole with a rough laugh and put the bottle to his lips again. Halloran turned round in his seat and snatched the bottle. O'Toole's teeth rasped against the rim as the bottle was wrenched from his mouth. Halloran swallowed his breath hurriedly and tried to put the bottle to his lips with his right hand. He was leaning backwards, his face to the sun, his left hand on the starboard gunwale.

O'Toole cursed, drew in a deep breath, and struck at Halloran's upturned face with his right fist. His upper lip contorted as he struck. He struck Halloran between the eyes. The bottle fell to the bottom of the boat, hit a round granite stone that lay there and broke into pieces. Halloran's head hit the bottom of the boat with a hollow thud and rebounded as he clawed with his hands and legs. His bloodshot eyes glared and he shrieked as he struggled to his feet. O'Toole with his jaws wide open jumped to his feet too and snatched at his waistcoat. He pulled a knife from the pocket. He was opening it when he dropped it suddenly and whirled about. Halloran had yelled again. He was standing athwart his seat, the round stone in his left hand. He drew back his arm to take aim when the boat rolled to port, and he slipped. His right shin struck against the seat. In seizing the gunwales with both hands to steady himself the stone dropped into the sea. Its splash sounded loud in the silence. Hissing, they both stood upright, swaying gracefully with the rocking boat, as agile as acrobats in their drunken madness. They stared into one another's eyes for several seconds, their bodies twitching, their thighs taut. Each felt the other's breath hot on his face. Their breathing was loud. Each stood astride his seat.

Then the boat stopped rocking. With a roar they rushed at one another's throats. They met between the two seats, their feet against the sides, each clasping the other's throat. They stood cheek to cheek, breast to breast. They had moved so lightly that the boat did not rock. The two of them close together looked like

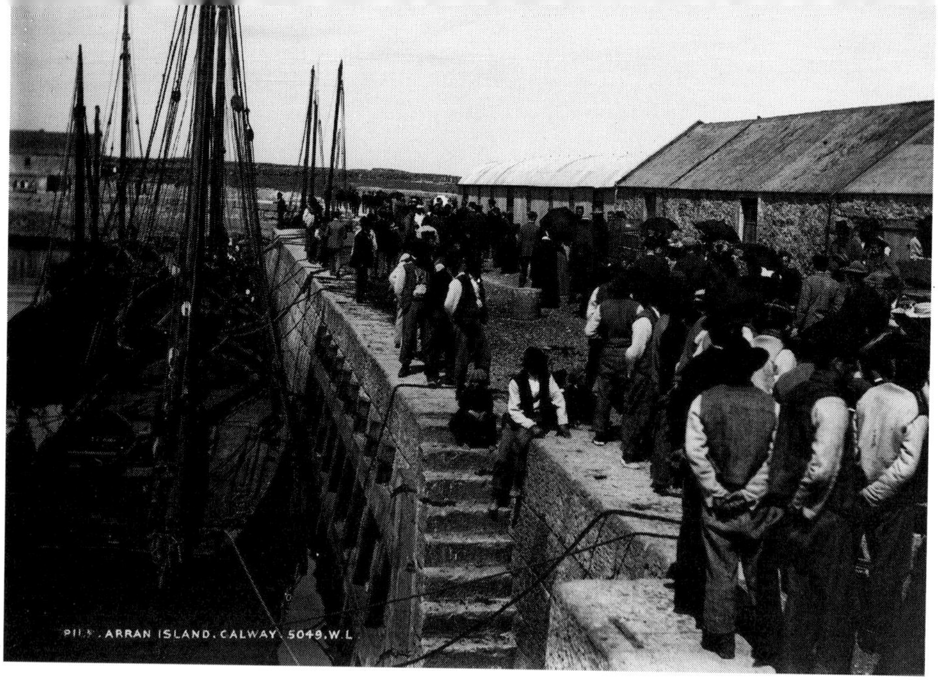

Left: *The island's fishing fleet was an important part of the Aran economy – but the work was often dangerous and dirty.*

Below: *The islanders relished their few hours of relaxation for gossip and story-telling. The high cross is a memorial to Fr O'Donoghue, who founded the fishing co-operative on the islands.*

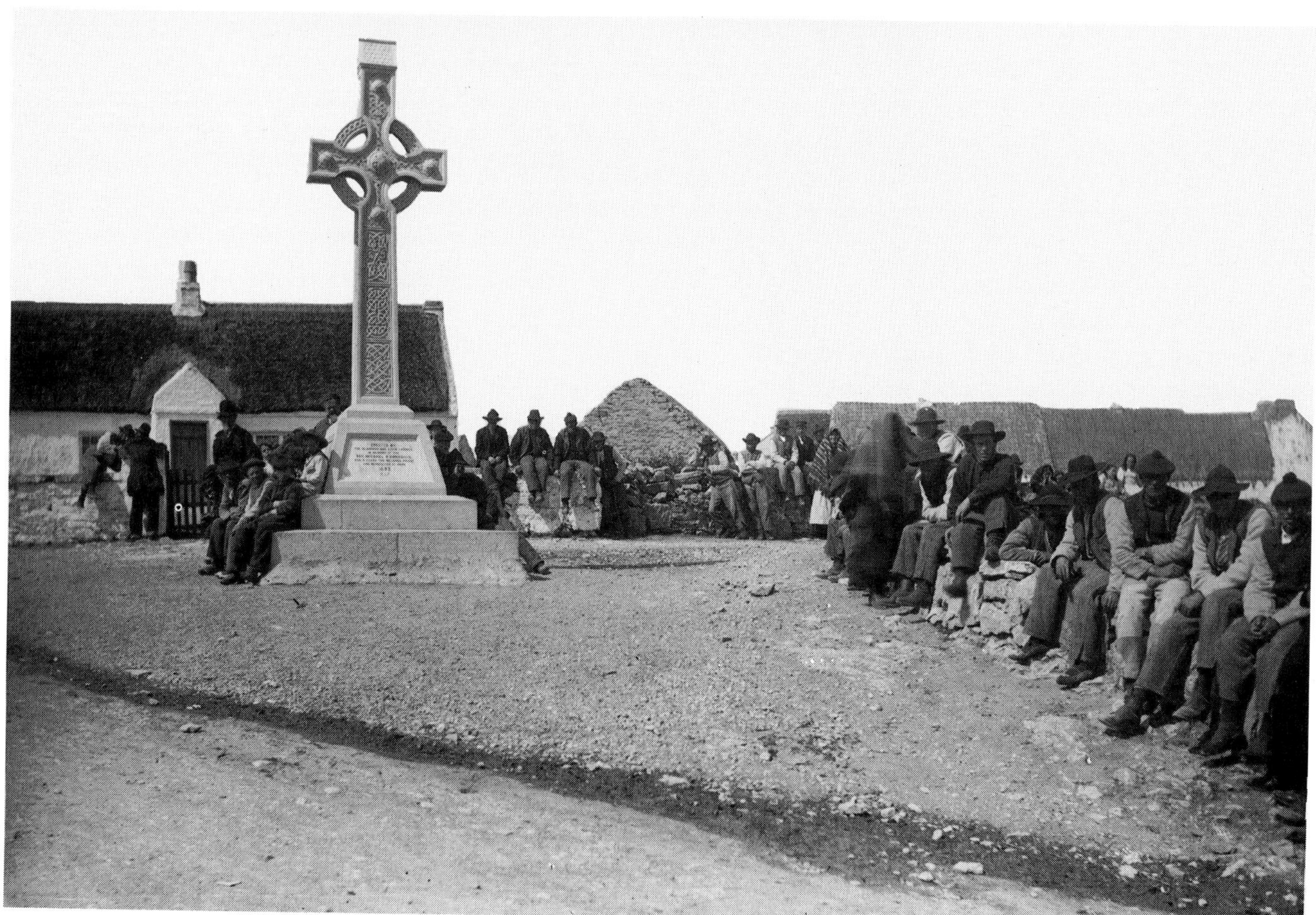

a mast. They stood still.

Then O'Toole raised his left leg and hit Halloran in the stomach. Halloran yelled and doubled up. The boat rocked as O'Toole pressed forward and the two of them tumbled across the second seat, Halloran beneath, O'Toole sprawling on top, his hands still gripping Halloran's throat. Then Halloran heaved and struggled sideways to his knees. He threw O'Toole's legs over the port gunwale. The boat canted ominously to port. The port gunwale was almost under water. They both shrieked. Halloran's body bounded off the boat's bottom as he wrenched himself to starboard and wound his legs about the seat. The boat rocked from side to side madly. Then O'Toole tried to lift his legs on board. They were almost on board when Halloran grasped at his head and seized his ears. They swung out again with a swish. The boat rolled with them, paused for a moment with the gunwale at the water's edge and then it toppled over with a swoop. There was a muffled yell as the two men disappeared beneath the black dome of tarred canvas. Halloran's legs clinging like a vice to the seat, O'Toole's hands gripping Halloran's throat.

For half a minute the boat hopped restlessly. There was a rustling noise of something splashing in water. Then all was still. The sun glistened on the tarred bottom of the boat. A cap floated near.

Then the upturned boat began to drift slowly westwards.

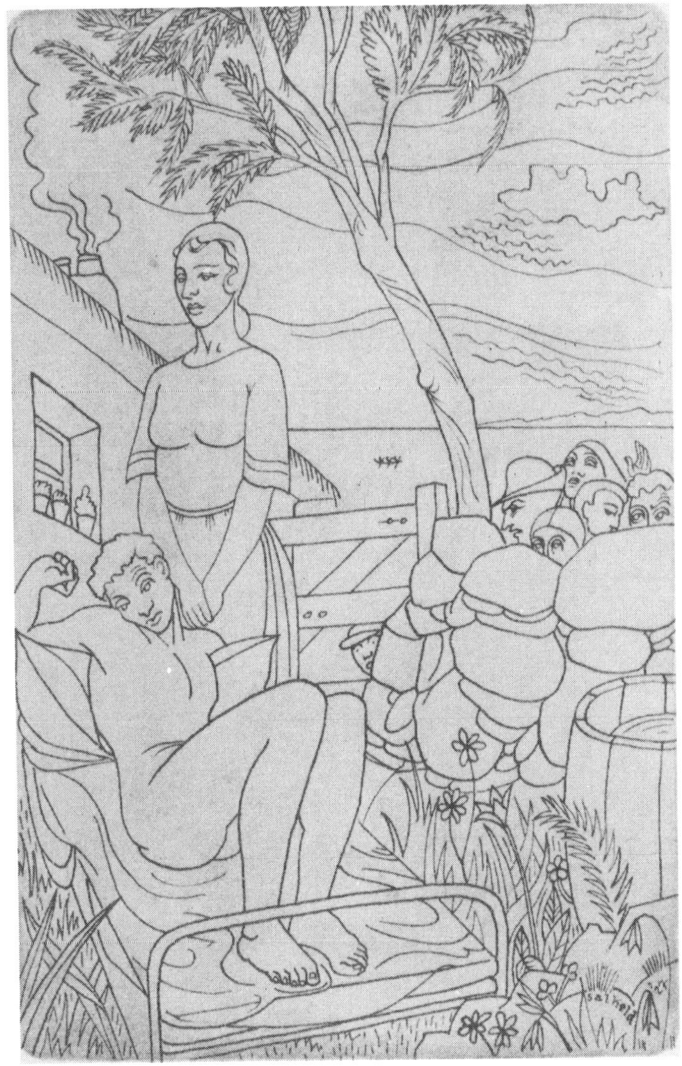

A Cecil Salkeld illustration from Liam O'Flaherty's Red Barbara and Other Stories, *1928*

Right: *Liam O'Flaherty as a schoolboy.*

Below: *Rockwell College in the early years of this century, as it was when Liam O'Flaherty was a student there.*

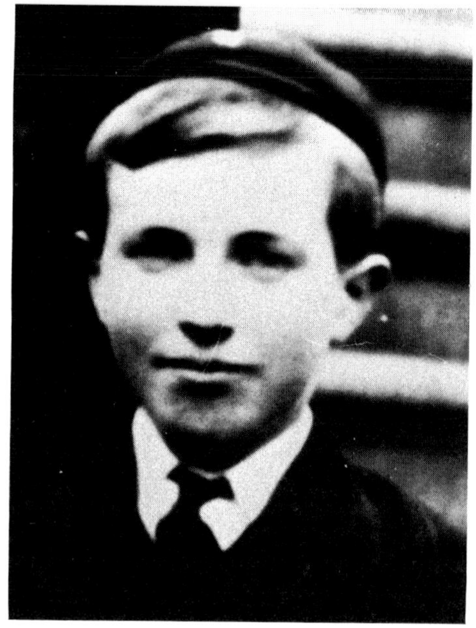

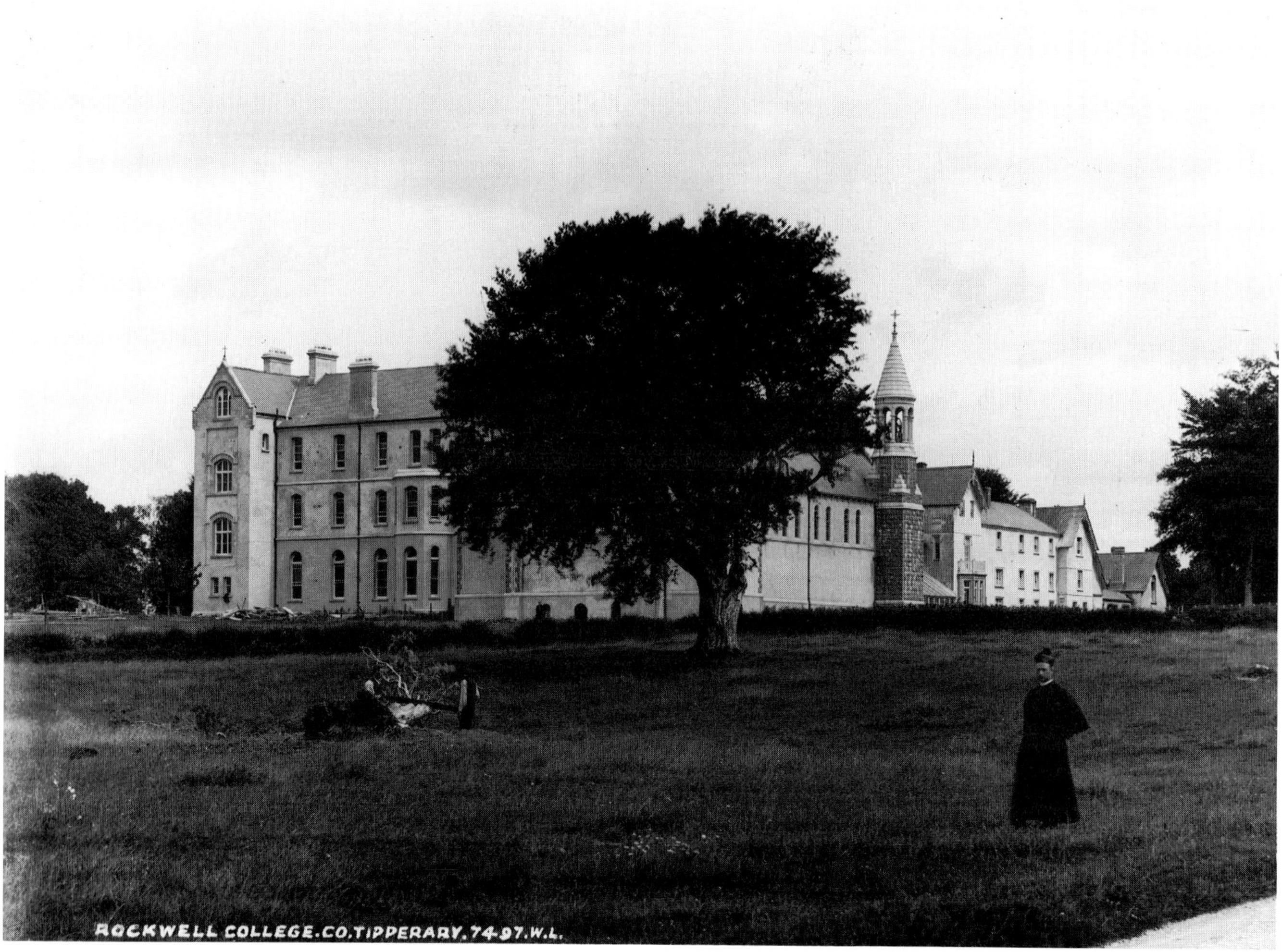

ROCKWELL & BLACKROCK (1908-1914) Despite the family's feelings about their parish priest, Liam's mother had hopes that her bright, handsome younger son would become a priest; for Tom (already a socialist) such an ambition was too late. Through the influence of a Holy Ghost father – Thomas Naughton, a summer visitor to the island and a friend of O'Callaghan's – who was impressed with the boy's abilities, Liam was taken in the autumn of 1908 to study for the entry to the priesthood at Rockwell College. Rockwell lies outside Cashel in green and fertile Tipperary – a great change from the rocky acres of Aran. This is the landscape that haunts the memory of Gypo Nolan as he is hunted through Dublin in the last pages of *The Informer*.

O'Flaherty's surviving relatives think that it was stifling for him as an energetic lad to submit to strict religious discipline – leaving off his childhood petticoat to put on another in the form of the soutane. It must be appreciated, however, that the child had been plucked from a cottage to join the élite of the nation, both in receiving a secondary education and in being groomed to be a priest. The notion of being one of the chosen always lingered with O'Flaherty. At Rockwell the students for the scholasticate were housed separately from the college boys. While four of the staff at Rockwell spoke Gaelic, only one other boy did. Liam's only friend was an English boy – perhaps Paul Leonard, aged thirteen in 1911. Though he may well have been lonely, Liam received great encouragement from a staff member, Fr O'Mahony, who was impressed with his precocious essay-writing. While at Rockwell he won a medal for an essay in Gaelic sponsored by an Irish-American group, which got the boys a half-holiday. But he claimed that he was not settling into his vocation. By the age of fifteen he had become a complete agnostic, and after three years at Rockwell he had to admit he was not suited for the priesthood. The college authorities were angry, feeling that he had gained an education under false pretences – though this was hardly true, as many clerical students did drop away in the course of their preparation.

Academically he did well. In the summer of 1909 he passed the Junior Grade of the Intermediate (a state examination) with honours in Greek, Latin and French – something to celebrate on his thirteenth birthday. In 1910 he passed the Middle Grade with an Exhibition in Classics and Modern Languages, as well as in Irish and Latin Composition.

Meanwhile, back on Aran, in January 1911 Fr Farragher had denounced his rival David O'Callaghan from the altar, and local parents under his influence began a boycott of the school. This did not affect the O'Flahertys so much as they now had only two children at home: Tom, aged twenty, and Agnes, who was twelve. The boycott of the school was raised indirectly in Parliament in April 1911, but the school year ended with the boycott still in effect. At the end of May the Ulster Unionist Charles Craig again raised the matter of the affairs on Aran with the Irish Secretary. But Mr Birrell would not answer, as the matter was now *sub judice*, due to an impending civil action by O'Callaghan against Fr Farragher. The boycott resulted a little later in that summer in the attempted suicide of an islander, and in July and again in the autumn the affairs of the island were raised in the Commons. Once more Birrell temporised, uncritical of the parish priest. It must have left a poor impression in Liam's adolescent mind of the spiritual and temporal powers that governed Ireland.

When his action came to an issue in 1912, O'Callaghan lost his case. He was considered by the

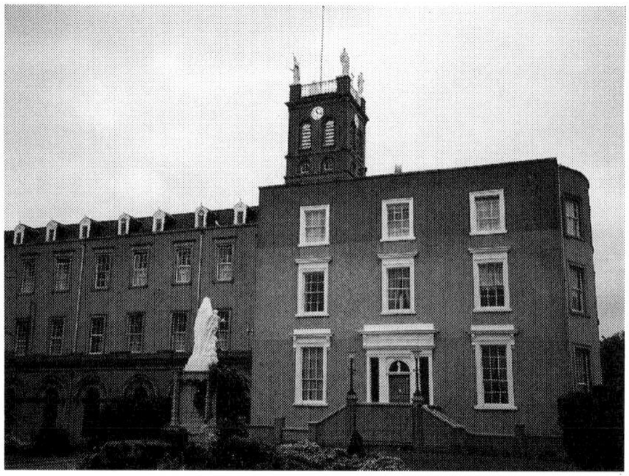

Above: *Blackrock College, O'Flaherty's second school.*
Right: *Liam O'Flaherty as a strangely mature schoolboy.*
Below: *Liam O'Flaherty with his college contemporaries.*

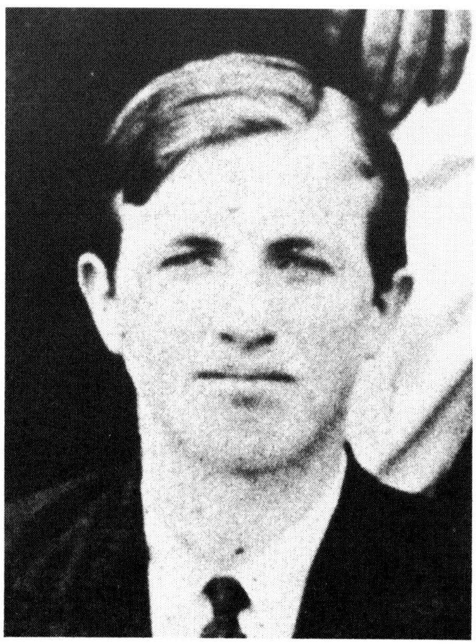

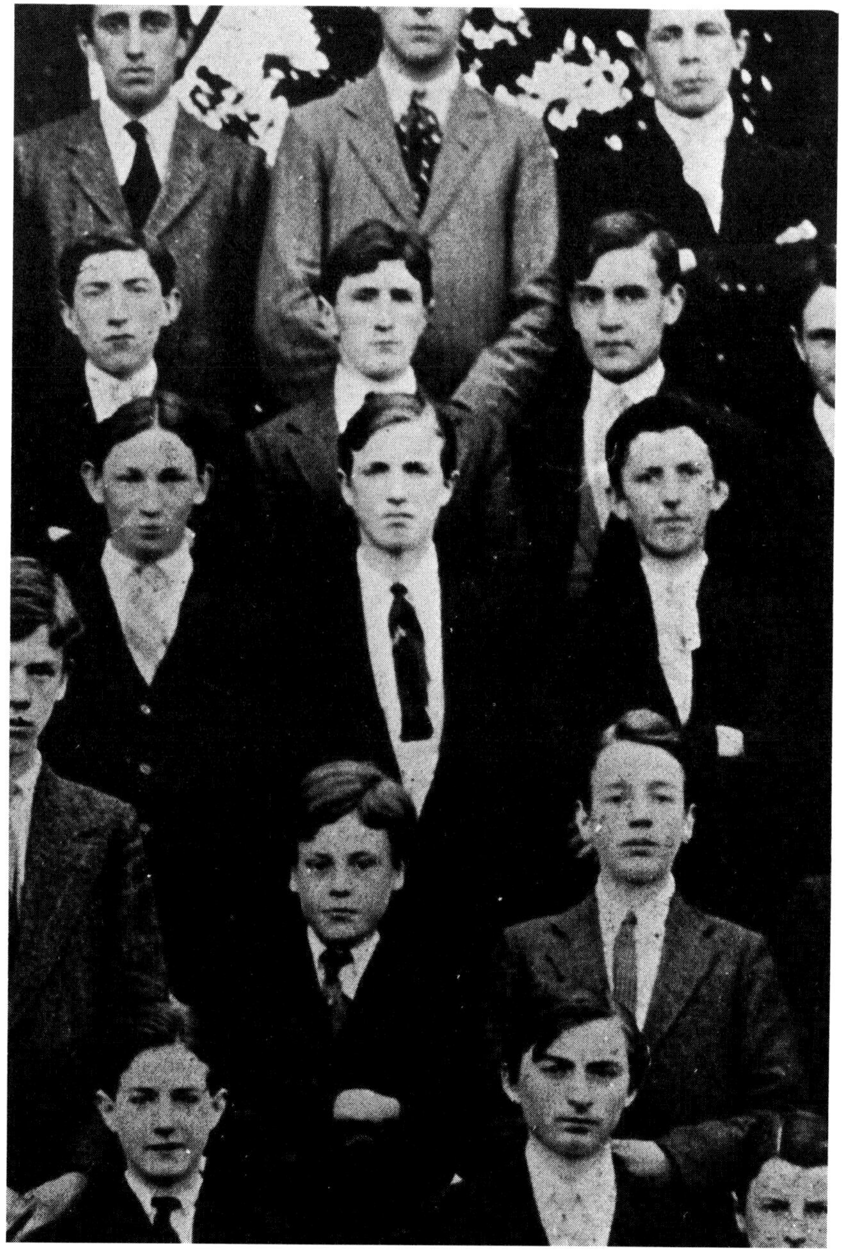

authorities to have 'voluntarily retired', and was granted a pension. And in September (just after Liam's sixteenth birthday) the school at Oatquarter re-opened with a new teacher, and the grants were resumed by the Education Commissioners. O'Callaghan continued, however, to live in the schoolmaster's house.

That summer, in a further public exam, Liam had won a first class Exhibition in Modern Languages and Classics. However, having reached an impasse over his vocation, at the end of the summer of 1913 he left Rockwell. In September, now seventeen years old, he transferred to Blackrock College, just outside Dublin, where Fr Naughton now was. He outlines the reasons for this in a bitter passage in *Shame the Devil*, a volume of reminiscences that he later disowned. At Blackrock, one of the two best schools in Ireland, he continued his academic progress, paying for himself with his money prizes. He was now destined for University College Dublin, and he would matriculate in 1914.

However, during this autumn, the brewing political crisis in Ireland took a new turn. In Ulster, to resist the Home Rule act promised by the government, the Unionists had formed and armed (with imported German rifles) the Ulster Volunteers. What Ulster had begun, the Nationalists could not ignore. On 13 November the first meeting was held in Dublin of the Irish National Volunteers, a meeting attended by 350 students from the university. An article extolling the volunteers appeared in the *National Student* (the College magazine); it was by the editor Denis Gwynn – who would later join the British Army.

Liam wrote to Professor Eoin MacNeill, the leader of the Volunteers, and received his permission to organise a unit among the senior students at Blackrock; he sent Liam Volunteer badges which they wore while strutting round the playground. But this was not well received either by the school or by the other boys, who, like their parents, supported Redmond's National Party. Liam's enthusiasm for the national cause was balanced by writing a school essay railing against nationalism in general, and in favour of individualism. Despite these distractions he took the Senior Grade exam in the summer, gaining honours in Greek, Latin, English, History, Geography, and an entrance scholarship in Classics to University College Dublin. This would be tenable for the academic year 1914-15.

'Benedicamus Domino' *by Liam O'Flaherty*

The college clock struck once. It was five minutes to one. The lay brothers began to march into their refectory from the long hall where they had assembled, the long hall with a stone floor on the left side of the college quadrangle. They moved very slowly, because Brother Silas, the shoemaker, went first and his deformed left leg forced him to go down the four stone steps sideways into the refectory, which Brother Euphronius, the laundryman, said was 'more like a cellar than a refectory.' And in fact it was very bare and sunk into the ground, so that the two windows on the far side from the door only let in a stray ray of sunshine. Sitting at table the brothers' eyes were on a level with the gravel drive that led to the college reception room and very often some of them were scandalized by seeing the legs of lady visitors pass, 'with those shocking silk stockings they wear nowadays,' as Brother Cornelius used to say with a twinkle in his eyes.

They all dipped their fingers in the Holy Water font within the door as they entered and then they filed to their places at the long table in the middle of the room. They all sniffed as they entered and some sneezed, for the gas jet was lit and there was always a leakage at dinner hour, when the light was turned low. But if it were turned on full strength Brother Matthias, the housekeeper, promptly turned it down again, and as it was winter, it was impossible to see without it. So they sniffed and stood behind their covers, with their hands folded within their habit sleeves and their heads bent, shivering with the cold. Brother Silas mounted the rostrum at the rear and turned up the shaded light over it. Then he placed his 'Life of Saint Theresa' on the stand and took up the Martyrology to find the passage. He was the reader for the day.

His life would be perfectly tranquil and happy if he didn't have to read aloud to the brothers at three meals once every eleven days. There were eleven other brothers and they all took turns, except Cornelius, the book-brother, who was the brother-in-charge and was exempt from reading. Old Silas had spent all the forenoon preparing his reading, for there were numerous foreign words and Latin quotations and there was always a titter when he made a mistake. And when Brother Cornelius rang his bell and called out 'Silentium' to reprimand those who tittered, there was still more tittering, for 'Silentium' was Silas's nickname, because of his religious name Silas and his morose and taciturn character. He opened the huge Martyrology and found out those who had been martyred on that date November 25th. 'Gracious me,' he muttered. There were more than half a dozen important people, given to the lions, crucified, and torn by wild horses at various dates and they all had indescribable names in Latin. He lifted his little black round skull cap and scratched his bald head with the little finger of his left hand. He put his wrinkled old face so near the open page that his spectacles touched the book and he could see nothing. So he took them off and began to wipe them with his handkerchief.

Brother Julian, standing at the end of the table beneath the rostrum, looked up at Silas and felt pity for 'the old fool.' For Brother Julian was already tired of wearing a lay brother's habit and looked upon the whole business with disgust. He pitied old Silas because the other brothers poked fun at him. He himself had been but six months in the Order and he had long since recovered from the religious fit that suddenly took possession of him one night in Paris, when he rushed from his studio and went to confession and joined the Order on the advice of the priest to whom he confessed. He was the youngest man in the room, no more than thirty. In fact there was something indecent about his youth, in that assembly of old and withered men; just as if a racehorse in the pride of its youth were sent to stables with a number of worn-out cabhorses. Of course he would not be sent to that college, by the authorities at headquarters in Paris, nor indeed admitted into the Order, for only men past their youth were admitted, but Brother Julian was a good painter and the college required a great deal of painting to be done. And Brother Julian, looking at the round of beef at the far end of the table, waiting to be carved and distributed to the brethen by Brother Cornelius, thought that he had made an unfortunate mistake that night in Paris. All on account of a chit of a girl that didn't care a straw about him. He reflected now that he had chosen a very ridiculous and melodramatic form of revenge for her flirtation with the American sculptor Foster. And he was then almost on the verge of success. Of course they said his painting lacked imagination. But the technique was excellent. See how they exploited him here. Not only had he painted the main chapel, but the Grotto of the Blessed Virgin down by the lake in the grounds, and the priests' refectory. Hundreds of pounds worth. Work that might bring him fame in civilian life. And he could not even claim it. The rules ordered that his work should be unknown. Known only to God. The priests would show it to visitors as work 'done by one of our brothers.' And they treated him as a servant. His ashy pale face went yellow as he thought of it, and Brother John who stood three covers down from him on the right-hand side looked at him and thought that he was struggling with a temptation and murmured a prayer to Saint Joseph to assist him.

THE STUDENT At home again, Liam heard about the eviction of David O'Callaghan from the schoolmaster's house and the other excitements of the continuing island feud. In June Liam entered Holy Cross College at Clonliffe, the diocesan college preparing priests for Dublin, along with four other Blackrock students destined for distinguished Church careers. But his eighteenth birthday and his preparations for going to college were overshadowed by the outbreak of the European war. This put a new perspective on the struggles in Ireland. It was followed by a split in the Irish Volunteers, the great majority of whom decided to follow Redmond and support the Allied cause – the propaganda about martyred Belgium proving effective in Catholic Ireland. A minority broke away, and in a secret meeting in Rutland Square on 9 September 1914, a rebellion was decided upon by the Irish Republican Brotherhood.

The war, which was expected to last only a short time (as had the last real war in 1870), did not at once distract Liam from college. However, he left Holy Cross College on 18 November, finally breaking with any hope or intention of being a priest. He continued at University College. Here, however, annoyed by Fr Tom Finlay's scorn of Karl Marx in his political economy lectures, Liam took himself to the National Library (as countless students before him had done, among them James Joyce) to read *Das Kapital.* This was followed by other books of social revolution by socialists, communists and anarchists.

He was now living in digs at 9 Grantham Street, off Camden Street, with its busy shops and pubs. This was his first real introduction to the bustle and anonymity of city life, which was to be as important to his writing as the scenes of his childhood. Here he made his first

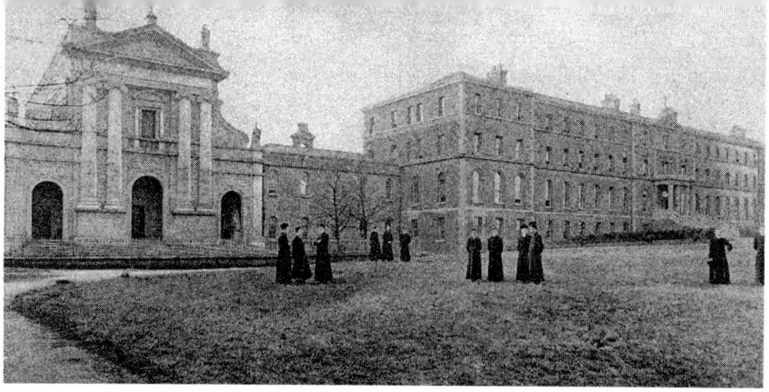

Opposite page: *The lodging house at 34 Lower Gardiner Street (in the area where* The Informer *and* The Puritan *are set), where O'Flaherty was living in 1916 when he enlisted in the army.*

Above: *Holy Cross College, Clonliffe.*
Below: *No. 9 Grantham Street, where Liam had digs in 1915, and where he tried to begin his first adult novel.*

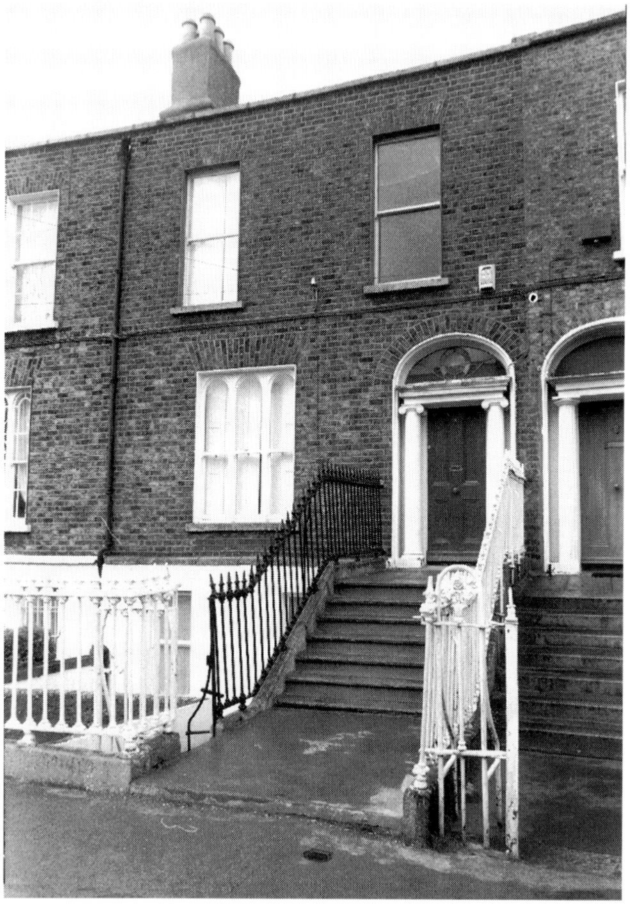

attempt at an adult novel, but he soon gave it up. At college he made his small mark by organising another unit of the National Volunteers, and in May 1915 he ousted Denis Gwynn as editor of the *National Student* in favour of Eimar O'Duffy (later a well-known novelist). He took no part in the debating society, in which many potential politicians and writers first made their names, instead spending a period writing a long, learned paper for the college classical society on the Greek colonies of Asia Minor. In the summer of 1915 he won a first-year scholarship with a Second in Classics, which would be tenable for the year 1915-1916. But by then his own life would have changed completely.

In bed with a cold on the early August morning when his sister brought him the news of the war, Liam had leapt out of bed with delight. Violent action, of any kind, appealed to his nature. Though involved in the Volunteers, he claimed he had grown bored waiting for revolution to break out in Ireland. The Great War had more appeal. But he did not enlist at once. In the summer of 1915 a second battalion of the Irish Guards was raised from reservists and volunteers. Many others in Ireland, and at University College, joined up: by 1915 at least 230 staff, graduates and students had joined; by the end of 1916 it would be 480. There were some 150,000 Irishmen in the army. Indeed, for every Irishman with MacNeill and the Volunteers, there were sixteen with the British.

Liam had left college and was living in lodgings at 34 Lower Gardiner Street, a seedy street on the edge of the notorious Monto, the brothel quarter of Dublin, the district in which *The Informer* and *The Puritan* are set. It may have been at this time that, short of money, he sold the gold medal he had won at school.

'The Spirit of Genius' *by Liam O'Flaherty*

This appreciation of his friend the German film-maker and writer Heinrich Hauser, a free spirit similar to himself, gives some idea of the type of person O'Flaherty admired in his student days.

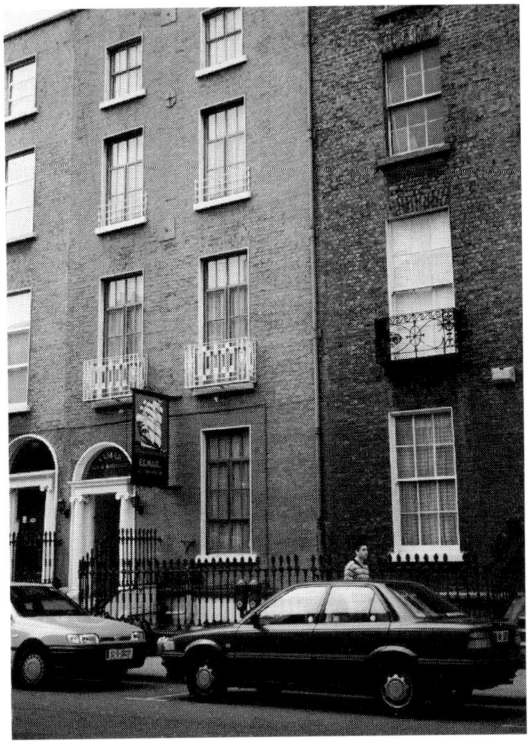

He signed up on 1 February 1916 at the Irish Guards recruiting office just across the Liffey in Great Brunswick Street. He used the name William Ganly, his uncle/godfather's name; in fact he also gave Fr William Ganly (then in Melbourne) as his next of kin. It may well be that his family at home on Aran knew nothing about his intentions at the time.

He was sent for his training to the brigade of Guards barracks at Caterham in Surrey, seven miles south of Croydon. His training continued in the following year, the Rising in Dublin leaving him (and many other Irishmen in the Imperial Army) unmoved. Then on 22 January 1917, now aged twenty, he was sent with his unit to France.

I am always polite to strangers and always suspicious of them. It is a relic of the various wars and revolutions in which I have taken part. Every stranger is a potential enemy, whose capacity for evil is not yet measured. And politeness is the best weapon with an enemy. But almost at once I realised that this was a man in a million that I had met, an extraordinary personality who might have stepped out of those obscure Middle Ages in continental Europe, with that odd expression of eye and that fierce vitality which is so terrifying to those confounded people who are always crying for the normal; because they confuse the normal with the mediocre; with themselves.

He told me about his film. I have no interest in these things. I was disappointed that his wild eyes, with the lust of conquest and creation so strong in them, could conceive of no more fitting thing upon which to spend his strength. He asked me to show him Dublin. I asked him what part of Dublin did he want to see. The intellectuals? The bourgeoisie? The spectacles? No. He had seen all these already. He did not like them. They were only a provincial replica of similar types and scenes in Berlin, London, and Paris, not so vicious, not so interesting, not so pretentious. He wanted to see what was peculiar to Dublin, the amazing slums, with their incomparable collection of human beings, beautiful to the artist, who sees in them models for a thousand hells a thousand times greater than that of Dante. And to the slums we went, with the camera, hunting fine specimens, followed by hordes of children, by ragged harlots, by old men with the itch, by crippled beggars, among herds of goats and asses that fed on waste plots, making pictures that should fill the world with horror, of a ruined city, uniformly unkempt and diseased, from the broken pavements to the souls of its inhabitants.

I don't know what happened to the film we made. Probably it was badly made, that it was no good. I am sure it was no good. That was not important. What was important was that I saw this man reacting to these sights and saw them with him. Any fool can see beauty in pretty things. It is only the man of genius that can see beauty in ugliness. I said to myself that this man was worthy of seeing my island. So I invited him to accompany me thither.

That journey down to the Aran Islands and our stay there were both wonderful. I shall never forget looking down over a precipice near my native village with Hauser. It was the scene of one of my short stories, the one I love best. I felt that if his presence made the scene vulgar, robbed it of its tremendous age or if he reacted in an alien way I could no longer believe in him. But he fitted in.

Then I was certain that he was a genius and that he would do wonderful things. How? I didn't know. As a writer? It was impossible to say.

There are some writers whom one immediately recognises, bookish fellows, whose drawing-room civilisation obtrudes unpleasantly on the senses. They are just writers, no matter how great. But there are others who are great men because they are men and who write because chance turns their energies towards writing as a means of creation. These are the men I love. Out of their speech, out of their eyes, out of the movements of their bodies, joyousness and exuberance flow and they make you feel that it is good to be alive. Women turn their heads when they pass or enter a room. Men like to drink with them, or to go with them on a long, dangerous journey. They cause tumults. Priests denounce them. The dull fear them and say that they are dangerous and disreputable. Critics do not know what to make of their work; and only when they are dead, do the critics come from the caves, where they have been hiding from the hurricane of genius, to write scholarly dissertations on the beauty of the hurricane that has passed, having wasted its beautiful frenzy.

Introduction to Heinrich Hauser's Bitter Waters *(1930).*

THE GREAT WAR For most Europeans, the First World War was a defining moment. In Ireland, living in the shadow of the Easter Rising, this was long denied, but through Liam O'Flaherty's life it is possible to share something of an experience which was suppressed in the memories of many Irish people.

His experiences of the war were re-lived in a later novel, *The Return of the Brute* (1929), which critics and some readers found nasty and crude. His reply to this was one the authors of all Great War books would have made: that the war itself was nasty and crude and vicious. Though he had been an excellent soldier and was intensely proud to have been an Irish Guardsman, the writing of the book would be a purging of emotion for O'Flaherty, releasing him from the war though not the regiment. Finally in France he met a Scot who converted him to socialism, and he lost the narrow nationalism of the Irish Republican. He greatly admired a Catholic aristocrat, Captain Rodekowksi, the commander of his unit, who became his best friend, and whose death in action in October 1917 affected him greatly. At the front he mixed with all kinds and conditions of men, even with the German prisoners of war. Then news of the Russian Revolution broke: first the abdication of the Tsar in March 1917, then the army mutinies and reversals, culminating in the overthrow of Kerensky and the rise of Lenin and Trotsky in November. News of the fall of the empire and the rise of Bolshevism spread like a red wave across the battlefields of Europe and was received with joy by many soldiers.

On the western front where Liam was, the Third Battle of Ypres began on 31 July, and he passed the majority of his war in the mud and squalor of Flanders. In September, while working with a transport unit between the canal at Boesinghe and the front, he was wounded in the head by an exploding shell. Blown up again on the same day, he suffered severe shell-shock. A fearful passage in *Shame the Devil* describes his speechless rage, his violence to the doctors, and his incoherence till a bucket of water was poured over his head. Passchendaele, the village on which the British were advancing, was finally taken in November at the cost of 13,000 casualties; 240,000 had been lost since the summer. This battle was one of the worst disasters of the Great War; and for the rest of his life Liam would remain one of its victims.

Liam was taken up the line, away from further Goyaesque horrors. He was removed first to hospital in Etaples, and from there to England, where he was admitted to hospital on 22 September. Though he was discharged a month later, he was again hospitalised in January 1918; he was sent back to Ireland, where he was treated for shell-shock at King George V Hospital in Dublin (now St Bricin's) at Arbour Hill, close to where the 1916 leaders had been executed. He would then have become aware of a change of feeling in Ireland about the Rising.

Eventually, having been also treated at the Richmond War Hospital in Dublin, he was invalided out of the army into the care of his father on a disability pension on 7 May 1918. The small pension (giving him some background for the gunman in *The Assassin*) was an important help in surviving the post-war years. On his return to civilian life, Liam was awarded his BA (War Service) by the National University of Ireland. During the summer of 1918 he went back to Aran to spend some time at leisure, but he found himself 'regarded as a pariah and a renegade'. By now Ireland had moved away from the support of Redmond. In the khaki election of

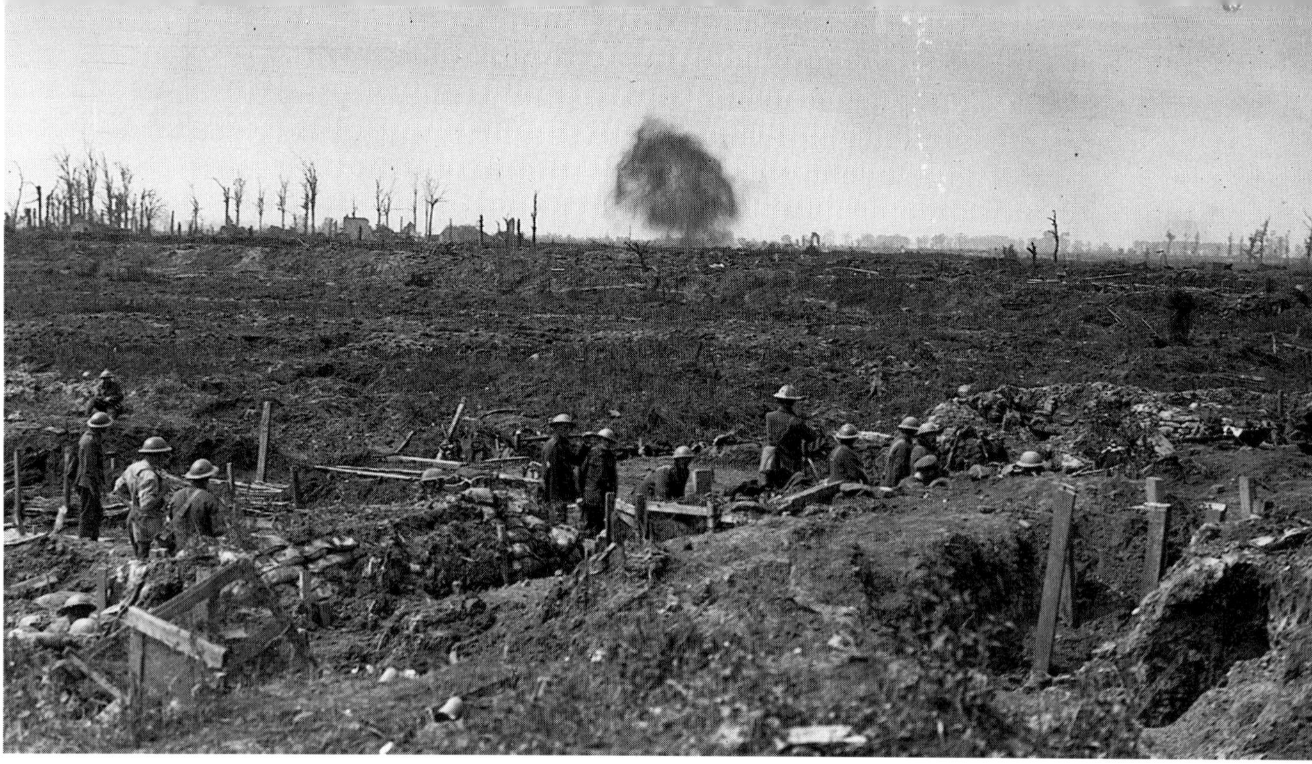

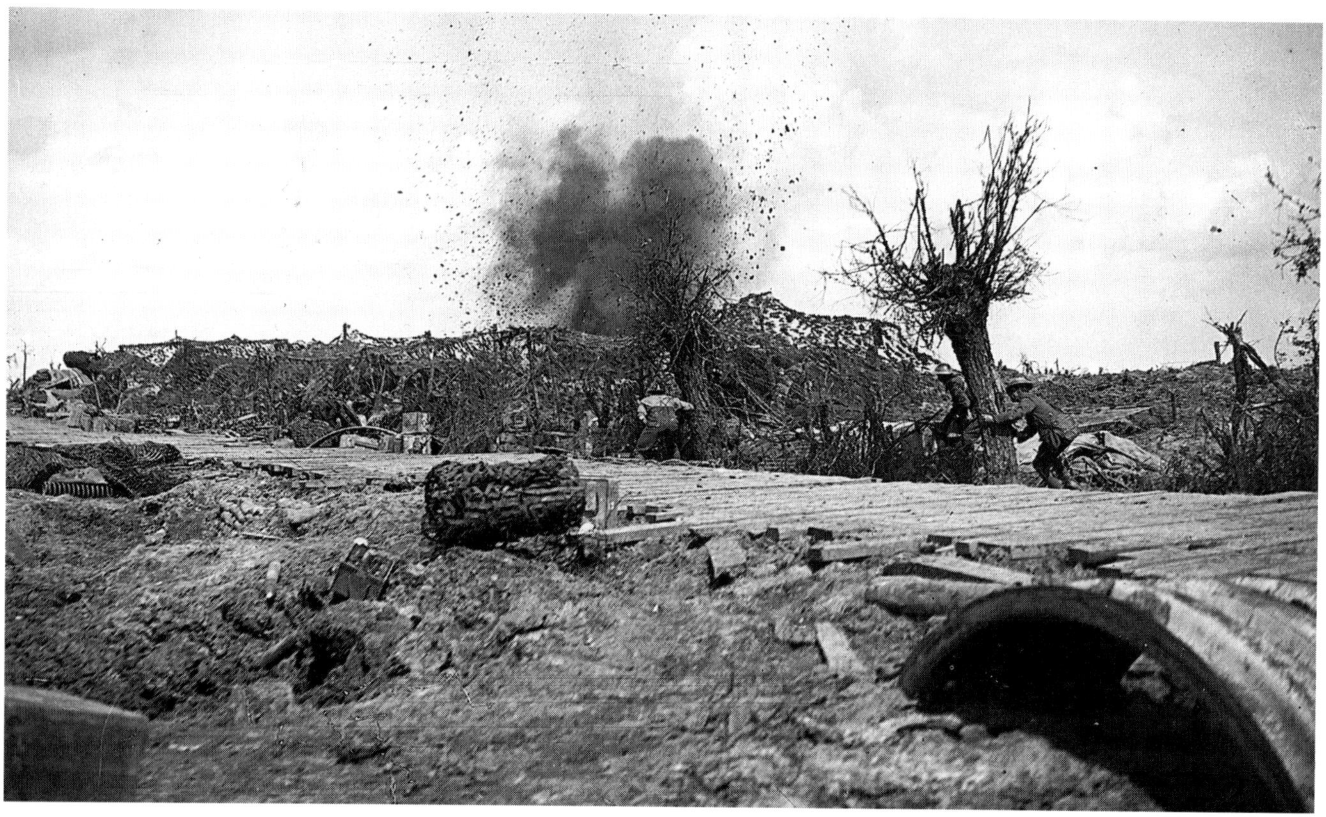

November 1918 the old Parliamentary Party would be swept away into history by the rise from nowhere of Sinn Féin, now a Republican party, seen as the heirs of 1916. Soldiers like O'Flaherty returned from the Great War would play an important part in the coming days. In Ireland, too, a revolution was under way.

Far right above: *The front lines during the early days of the Third Battle of Ypres – scenes which O'Flaherty re-lived in his novel* The Return of the Brute.

Far right below: *Shrapnel from exploding shells was a constant menace along the lines: in September 1917 O'Flaherty was badly injured by such blasts, twice in one day.*

Like all wounded, O'Flaherty was given first aid in a battlefield dressing station (bottom left) *before being removed behind the lines to a hospital* (bottom right) *where doctors saved his life.*

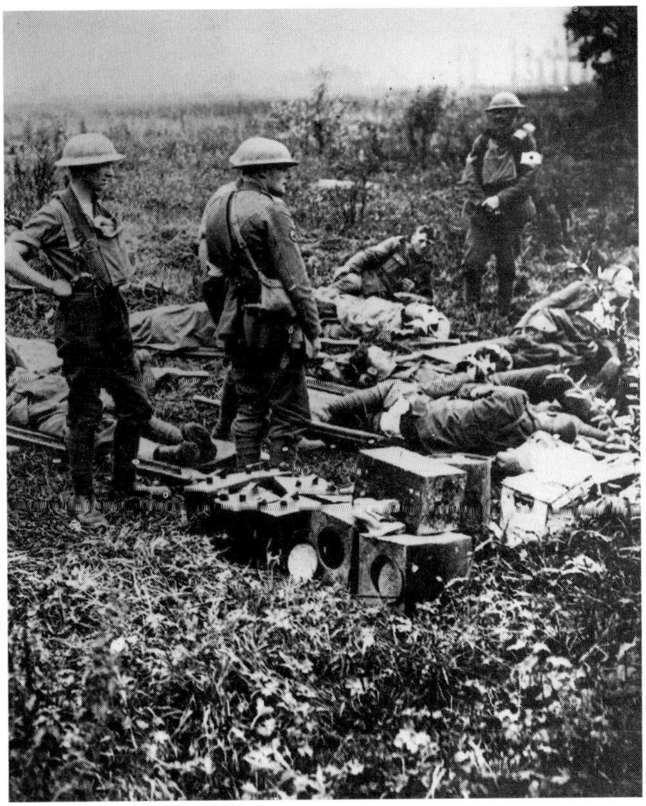

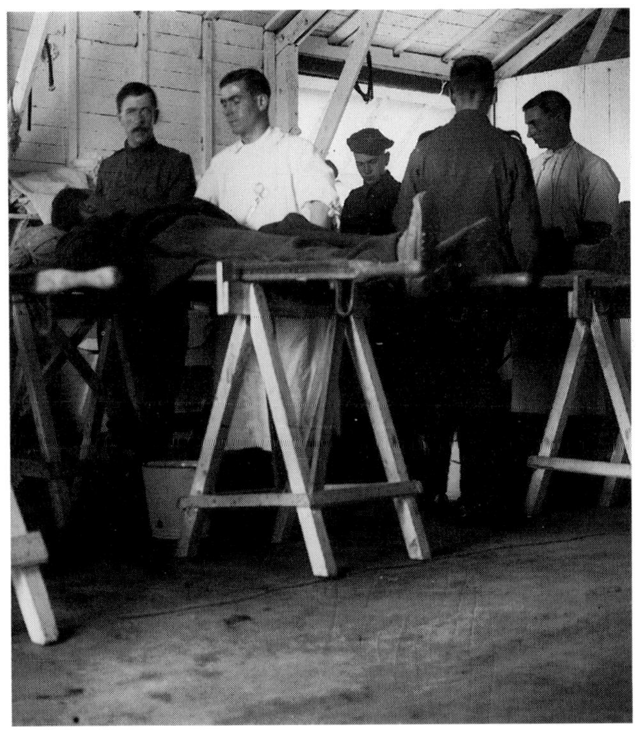

The Return of the Brute *by Liam O'Flaherty*

Extract from O'Flaherty's war novel – a powerful evocation of the Great War through the experiences of a small platoon of men destroyed by the grinding mills of fate.

'You could do me a good turn if you wanted to,' whispered Lamont.

'How d'ye mean? I can't get myself out of it.'

'Give me a blighty one.'

'What?'

'Lots have done it, haven't they?'

'That's enough now,' whispered Gunn, in a voice that was both angry and panic-stricken. 'Pull yourself together. You're a fine mucking-in chum to have. By God!'

Lamont dropped his face on his arms, against the muddy sandbags of the parapet. Gunn took him roughly in his arms and muttered:

'Listen. I know what's the matter with you. I'm going to give you a good punch in the jaw if you're not careful. You're just nagging like a woman. Chuck it.'

'Let me alone,' said Lamont, in a broken whisper. 'Only for mother, I'd do myself in. They'd tell her.'

'You'll do no such thing,' said Gunn. 'I'll see to that. I've no mother, but at your age I could stick this on my own legs, without no mother. Aye! And a double ration of it, boy. Damn this rain! That's the cause of it. Rain. Mud. Lice. Curse it!'

He looked up at the sky and clenched his fist, as if threatening heaven.

He was a huge fellow, so burly that he looked stocky, although he was well over six feet in height. He looked a typical fighter, with a thick neck, square jaws and a body like a full sack. His right ear was battered. There was a scar on his left cheek. He was thirty-two years old and he had laboured for wages since his boyhood, but his body had not become demoralised by enslaved toil. Nature had taken great pains with this seemingly crude and large individual, endowing him with muscles and sinews that refused to be stiffened by monotonous labour, and with a spirit that hardship could not conquer. He had a simple soul, which shone though his great, blue eyes; giving the lie to the cruel strength of his neck, his jaws, his heavy-lipped mouth, his massive shoulders, chest and thighs.

He was like a mastiff, that most ferocious-looking and most gentle of all animals; who, however, when roused or made vicious by brutal treatment, becomes as ferocious as he looks.

He looked down at Lamont and said, 'You'll drive me daft. I'm blowed if I know why I muck in with you. Strike me stiff, if I do. You're like a woman.'

Then he shuddered and looked into the darkness.

'You've been out here now,' he said, 'for three months. You should be getting used to it by now. But you're not.'

'I can't help it,' whispered the youth, 'I'm all in.'

Gunn shuddered again and struck himself a violent blow on the chest. Then he cursed and said with extraordinary anger:

'Now listen to me. I've been out here over two years on this lousy front and I'm as fed up with it as you are. I don't give a curse who wins this rotten war and I'd like to run my bayonet through the fellahs that started it. We're just fighting for a gang of robbers, as '79 Duncan said. I've got my eyes open now, although I hadn't when I enlisted. I came thousands of bloody miles to enlist. Jumped freight all the way from Seattle, Washington, to New York, and then to Liverpool as a trimmer on a liner. See? I walked into it. But if I ever get desperate, same as you are, I'm not going to try and get out of it by wounding myself or running across No Man's Land to bloomin' Fritz with my hands up.'

He spat and added:

'That's a coward's way out of it. I promised to soldier

and soldier I will, though I hate their guts, from the lousiest Lance-Jack to the Skipper.'

He spat again, cursed, looked at Lamont and said almost nervously:

'Jesus! You put the wind up me. I was married once to a woman, way up in Nova Scotia, when I was working on a weekly boat. She was just like you. She had me worn to a ghost. I left her, by Jesus, one night, after giving her a bloody good hiding. I went out west and never saw her again.'

He peered down into the post, towards the corner where Corporal Williams lay asleep under an elephant frame. The Corporal was just a dun blur, from which sounds of snoring came. The dim forms of his comrades lay tossing in their sleep at the bottom of the hole, some of them with their feet in muddy water. Gunn tipped Lamont and whispered, jerking his head towards the Corporal:

'If he heard what you said, d'ye know what you'd get? Eh?'

Lamont shuddered, wiped his face with his sleeve and said:

'I don't care. They can put me up before the firing squad whenever they like. I'm fed up.'

Gunn ground his teeth.

'Then what the hell did you enlist in this mob for?' he said. 'This is the worst regiment in the whole army. Ye knew that. It's the best regiment too! For I've seen our fellahs, by God, go through worse than hell. They're gathered from all corners of the earth, the toughest of the tough. You should have joined the Army Medical Corps.'

'I wish I had no mother,' whimpered Lamont.

'I can't stand this,' growled Gunn to himself. 'As sure as hell I'm going to get into trouble over this kid.'

Lamont had joined the battalion three months previously at a rest camp. When they saw him, the tough soldiers greeted him with jeering laughter. He was a beautiful boy, with pink cheeks, dazzling white teeth like a girl and big blue eyes. He did not swear or drink and it was obvious at once that he had never been used to any hardship. Almost as soon as he arrived he began to receive parcels of food and cigarettes with every post. It became known that his people were well-to-do and that he had a mother who doted on him and that he was an only child.

Gunn took him under his protection and cared for him like a father or a big brother. At first it made Gunn very happy. There had been no gentle influence like this in his rough and nomad life. He almost shed tears when he got a letter from Lamont's mother thanking him for being kind to her boy. 'God will bless you for it. He is the light of my eyes. My heart would break if anything happened to my darling boy.' Gunn had also reached the age when a virile man, who has no children, begins to look upon youth with longing; when the fear of death and old age begins to conquer the arrogant confidence of youth.

But after a while he became aware that the boy was sapping his strength. The boy lived on his nerves. Not only did he have to do the boy's work, but he had to comfort him, to lend him courage.

And now the boy's cowardice was sapping his sense of discipline; that extraordinary religion of the soldier which is proof against the greatest tortures; something that is brutally beautiful.

'Listen,' he said, 'that's the worst act of cowardice a soldier can commit. And what's more, you can't get away with it. If a man could do that without feeling ashamed of himself, d'ye think there'd be a man left on this front? But, ye see, them blokes back there are too cute.' He nodded his head to the rear. 'You can't beat them.' He touched his forehead. 'Up there they've got it. Brains! We're mugs. Look at it that way. Supposing it wasn't a cowardly thing to give yourself a blighty one? Let's say you do it and get back the line. What happens? They'll cop you. Sure as hell. They've got blokes hired specially for copping self-inflicted wounds. They've got smart at it now. At first, you could get into hospital by eating a bar of soap. Now, if you try on any silly stunt, they put you in dock till you get better and then you're for it. I know. I've been out here nearly two years and I've seen many a man, good men too, chancing their arms. Thirty-Nine Townshend tried to wound himself in the head when we were in the straw trenches. The blighter blew his brains out by mistake. Eighty-Four Flynn broke his leg with an entrenching tool at Neuve Chapelle. They copped him. Ginger Moriarty was caught by an officer trying to wound himself in the thigh with his rifle. He got what was coming to him all right. Christ! They've got an hospital away back there for self-inflicted wounds. There's nothing to it.'

He dug his fist into Lamont's back and said:

'Savvy?'

'I'll get out of it somehow,' said Lamont with strange coolness.

Gunn peered at him in the darkness, almost with terror. A stupid fellow, the youth's curious feminine cunning unnerved him, and made him also feel the temptation to do something shameful and desperate. The youth's obstinate determination to save himself from the horrible life of the trenches roused in Gunn a dangerous desire for freedom. This desire was dangerous for Gunn because he was a brave soldier, who knew there was no means of escape, other than death or disablement inflicted by the enemy.

Terrified by the temptation inspired by the boy's words and manner, he instinctively glanced again towards the corner where the Corporal snored.

'Quit that!' he whispered savagely, turning back to Lamont. 'What are ye driving at now? Desertion? 'Fifty-Seven Flood tried that at Armentières. What happened to him? Caught on the wires and riddled with bullets. Disgraced his bloody company. Jerry'd make ye sorry ye came if ye got there. He doesn't want his own men trying that on, so he'd make an example of ye.'

'I'll get out of it somehow,' said Lamont coldly.

'God Almighty!' muttered Gunn.

They became silent, standing side by side, looking out into the darkness over the parapet. With their steel hats and their oil-sheets, which they wore, laced about their throats, over their great coats, they looked like ghouls in the gloom, buried to their waists in a hole; while all round them the earth lay naked, turned into mud, holed, covered with the horrid débris of war, emitting a stench of rotting, unburied corpses.

From the pitch-dark sky the rain fell, unceasing and monotonous, like the droning of brine water falling on a floor of black rocks from the roof of a subterranean cave where moaning seals are hidden and flap about upon their ledges; sounds from a dead world; the mysterious gloom of the primeval earth, where no life had yet arisen; no sap of growing things; nothing but worms and rats feeding on death.

Clods of dislodged mud slipped from the sides of holes, flopped into blood-stained pools, sank and turned into slime.

The silence was horrid.

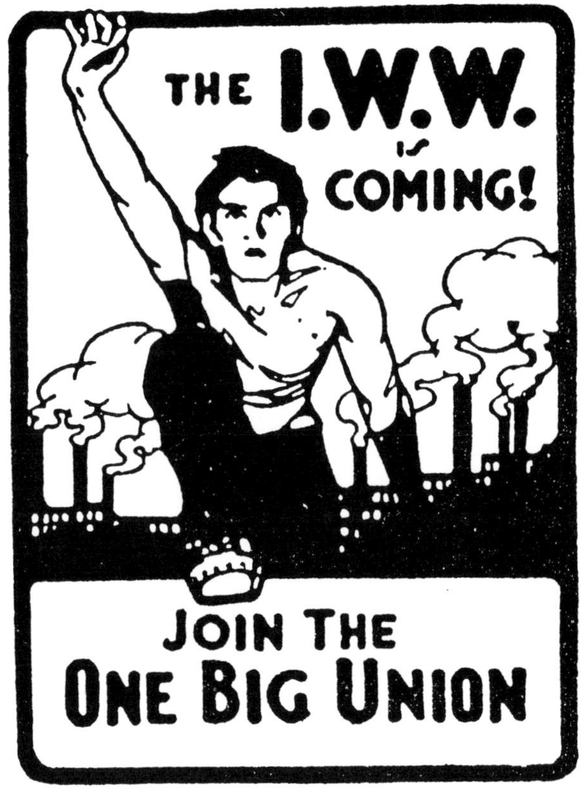

Contemporary poster for the Industrial Workers of the World, the Wobblies, with whom Liam was involved while in America.

THE TRAVELS OF BILL GANLY By August 1918, Liam had left Aran. He had gone to visit his sister, who was teaching in Tyrone, where he passed his twenty-second birthday. On 1 September he was in Dublin, where he began a course at a secretarial college, to prepare for a career as a journalist. He had already written some short stories on Aran to amuse his friends. On the afternoon of 14 September, he made a large coup in the first race at Baldoyle; he immediately left the course, and Dublin too, taking the overnight boat to London. There is a description of such a flight at the end of his later novel *The Assassin.*

He tried various menial jobs, in a brewery and as a night porter in a hotel, but with no great success. He was in London when the Armistice was celebrated on 11 November. Like many ex-soldiers, he was disgusted. He then thought he would sign up as an ordinary seaman as a way of finding adventure. At the end of November he sailed from the Pool of London on a ship bound for Rio di Janeiro in Brazil, using his army papers in the name of Bill Ganly. Arriving in Rio, he stayed on to teach Greek at the Collegio Anglo-Brazileiro.

It was in Rio, in January 1919, that he read of the first sitting of Dáil Éireann, at which the deputies returned at the election established the Irish Republic. That day also marked the opening of the actual war for independence by the IRA. Four years later Liam would be among those who claimed their right as Irishmen to defend the First Dáil and its social programme against the compromises of Collins and Griffith when the Treaty was signed.

Soon after this he sailed from Rio, again as an ordinary seaman, first for Cardiff in Wales, and then from Cardiff to the Levant. The ship first called at Salonika in northern Greece, then occupied by the Allies and by troops of General Venizelos. There they stayed for only five days before going on to Smyrna (now Izmir) on the coast of Turkey. All Liam remembered of the Greek colonies of Asia Minor from his college days came back to him, but that classical heritage was now under threat. The Greek Christians were suffering at the hands of the resurgent Turks, and soon afterwards (in May 1919) the Greek Army occupied a large wedge of Asia Minor. They were eventually driven out in 1922, but Liam was there to see the beginnings of the collapse of a culture which dated back to Homer, and on which much of his early education had been founded. Far more than other Irish writers, O'Flaherty witnessed at first hand the disintegration of civilisation in the twentieth century.

From Smyrna he sailed to Malta, then on to Gibraltar and to Montreal in Canada, which he reached in May. Here he went ashore and took up a wandering life for a time. Liam was sharing an experience of the aftermath of war which dislocated millions – an experience that was closer to the realities of the world than the tribal quarrels in his native Ireland.

He took work in a milk factory, and then travelled along the Canadian railway system into the interior. On this journey he met John Joseph Petersen, of the Industrial Workers of the World ('the Wobblies'), a man whose moral influence on him was great and lasting. The summer was passed at Blind River, in the Algoma District of Northern Ontario, halfway between Sault Ste Marie and Sudbury. Later he lived at Coppertown, moving on to Port Arthur and then to Wild Goose, at Thunder Bay. From there he returned eastward, again by train, to St John's in New Brunswick.

He was twenty-three that summer, a summer marked in the USA by the beginnings of the Red Scare, the Boston police strike and the arrest of the anarchists Sacco and Vanzetti. Though these events suggested there might be trouble for a person of Liam's views, nevertheless in October 1919 he crossed the border from St Stephen to Calais, an easy place to enter the USA without papers. He reached Bangor, Maine, and went on to Boston, where his brother Tom was living with their two elder sisters at Roxbury.

In Boston Liam worked first for Western Union. His brother, however, insisted that he write and bought him a typewriter. What work he produced he sent to the Four Seas Publishing Co, the first publishers of William Faulkner and others, but without success. The brothers then moved to New York, where they became involved with the Connolly Club and with socialist or increasingly communist politics. Liam for a time worked as a porter in the Knickerbocker Hotel. Living in Greenwich Village, he became involved in a love affair, his first serious relationship. Then he worked in Hartford, Connecticut, for the Firestone Rubber Company. This was followed by a move to Philadelphia and work for Dupont. Though he never chose to write about it, Liam had already seen far more of ordinary working life than most Irish writers – on the whole a cosseted, bourgeois lot.

It was in America that he became a member of the Communist Party. In August (when Liam celebrated his twenty-fourth birthday) the Soviet Armies under Trotsky nearly reached Warsaw. It seemed a Red tide would sweep Europe, but the 'Miracle of the Vistula' threw back the invaders, and Poland counter-attacked. To revolutionaries such as Liam had become, it was a disappointment.

Soon after this Liam sailed from New York, again to Rio, by way of Santos, Paraguay, Rio Grande del Sul, Montevideo and Buenos Aires. From there he sailed to Antwerp, Hamburg and Cardiff, living in these open ports the riotous life of a sailor.

‘Rio Bay’ *from* Two Years *by Liam O’Flaherty*

O’Flaherty enjoyed his travels and adventures, but even in Rio de Janeiro the tropical scene was haunted for him by images of home.

I doubt if there is any place in the world as beautiful as Rio de Janeiro. From the moment our ship entered the narrow neck of its gorgeous harbour I was entranced. Across the smooth bay, littered with ships and pretty boats, lay the city, rising in terraces, with majestic mountains behind, and the great sugar-loaf, like a stupendous monument, on the left. Trees and tropical plants everywhere. Everything resplendent with brilliant sunlight. No dirt, no smoke, seemingly no slums. Astonishing, like a fairy tale. Facing this phenomenon of beauty, I forgot that I was penniless, that my nostrils, my eyes, and my finger-nails were blackened with coal dust, that my clothes were shabby, that I was an unknown and unwanted stranger. It seemed to lie before me, waiting for ravishment. I wanted to jump from the ship’s side and swim ashore, lest one extra moment of my life should be wasted before I began the enjoyment of this miraculous city.

I saw a great sign facing the shore: ‘Bebam Antartica.’ Certainly, I was going to drink Antartica, and every other possible drink. I was going to live there in a continual ecstasy of unimaginable pleasures. The whole crew was almost equally excited. Some had been there already, and knew that it is more comfortable to stand in the rain without an overcoat beside the wall of a ruined factory than to stand in golden moonlight on a warm night ouside the brilliantly lit windows of a great house, where there is a riot of merry-making, of wine-drinking, and love-making, and gluttonous feasting. But sailors are easy to please, and they always expect the impossible.

At first we lay at anchor in the harbour, and a fleet of tiny boats came around us, offering to sell us oranges and pineapples. They also had bottles of gashasa, which is a native whiskey of great power. This they offered to us secretly. It was amusing to bargain with them in pidgin Portugese: ‘Quanto costa the oranges? Too much. Quanto the bloody pineapples?’ But we bought nothing. We remained at anchor all that night, greedily watching the brilliant lights of the city. We could hear music from the shore. It was wonderful seeing the seemingly endless row of lights spreading out to the left towards Tres Jardines, or whatever the suburb is called.

Lucy, leaning over the rails by my side, said in a hoarse whisper:

‘It’s all one big whore-house. I wish I were ashore.’

That night in the fo’c’sle, everybody talked of women, women, women. I really felt very exalted, in the same way that I felt when for the first time I saw from the deck of the streamer *Duras* the yellow houses of Salthill drift along as we approached the ancient town of Galway. I was then a little boy at my mother’s side. It was sunset in summer. She pointed ahead over the ship’s prow, and said:

‘Look. There’s Galway. Do you see it?’

I was unable to answer her with excitement. I just clutched at her dress and blushed, and stood on tiptoe, keeping very close to her side, and looked in awe at the dun pile of grey stone houses rising above the shimmering waters of the bay.

That was the first, this was the last time I experienced such a mixed feeling of awe and romance. Now one town is the same as another to me, each country as dull and commonplace as the next, each person intrinsically as disappointing as the previous one I have met. The visible world and the movements of man upon it have both become completely absorbed by my imagination, which has gone farther than reality to create its needed harmony and only looks out upon reality with a frown, and seizes upon its various aspects with remote and critical interest,

Below: *Vaughan's Hotel on Parnell Square today, a mere shadow of its hectic past; and* (overleaf) *as it was soon after the Civil War, when it was garrisoned by O'Flaherty and other members of the Irish Citizens Army.*

merely to imagine harmony more vividly by contrast with disappointing reality. How unhappy that makes one! How pleasant it is to look at the world with the amazed eyes of a child, crowing with glee on sight of a butterfly's wings! How pleasant it is to remain a child, and shout hurrah at the sight of one's country's flag, or to laugh immoderately and sincerely at a bawdy story told by a commercial traveller! The rash ecstasies of the inward-gazing intellect exact a heavy toll in the form of consequent depressions, whereas simplicity and ignorance always look outward, and feed healthily upon the giant stores of the earth's phenomena.

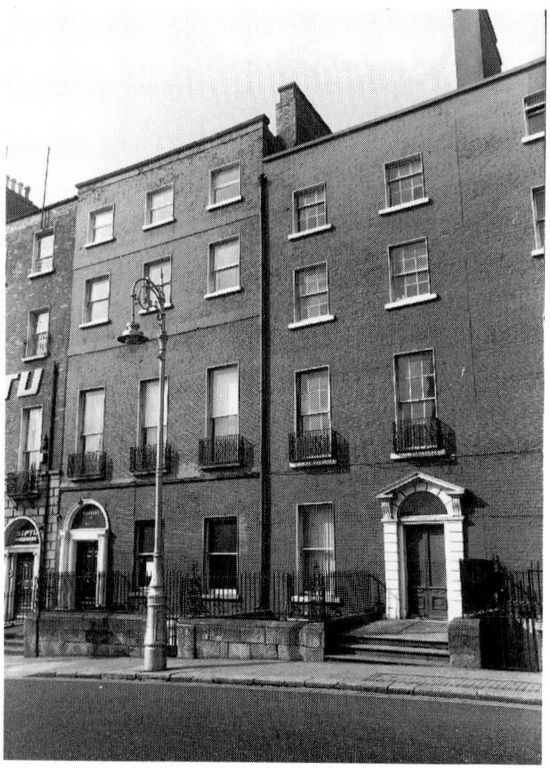

THE HEAT OF REVOLUTION Paid off in Cardiff, Liam returned briefly to Ireland. There in the autumn and spring the IRA war with the Black and Tans was entering a serious stage. But as a communist, he felt that the Tan war did not concern him and he took no part in it. (He was never a member of the IRA, for instance.)

On Aran for some months, he saw himself as a 'godless hermit' isolated from those around him. He went to London to find work as a journalist. This period of his life is obscure, either for reasons of his poverty or for political reasons he later glossed over. In this year (1920) the Communist Party of Great Britain was established, and party leaders in London and Moscow were watching events in Ireland, where the potential for revolution was attractive.

In July a truce was called in Ireland, and after drawn-out negotiations a treaty was signed in London on 6 December 1921. After the truce Liam was back in Ireland as a communist activist. His rousing speeches to the unemployed – mostly ex-soldiers like himself – at Beresford Place (outside Connolly's old headquarters, Liberty Hall) impressed Sean O'Casey and others on the Irish Left. He joined the re-established Irish Citizens Army, which had been founded by Connolly at the time of the 1913 Lockout. At twenty-five he was full of enthusiasm for his new cause and its intrigues.

On 21 November 1921, the Irish Communist Party came into existence when Liam, Roddy Connolly (the son of the executed 1916 leader) and others expelled William O'Brien and Cathal O'Shannon from the central committee of the Irish Socialist Party. But the Communists (supported, it seems, by money from Moscow) found no place beyond an obscure niche in the developing Irish political situation. The revolutionary moment was passing them by.

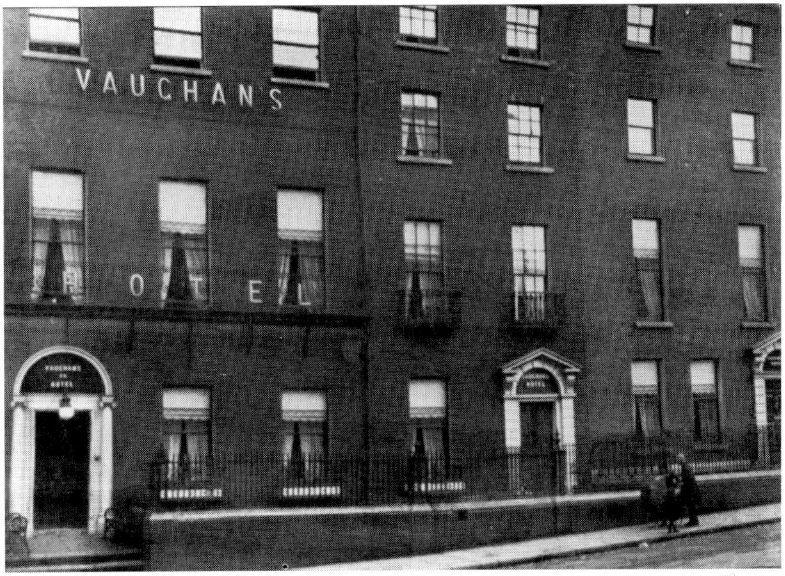

Below: *The Rotunda buildings (today the Gate Theatre) which O'Flaherty occupied with his army of the unemployed in 1922.*

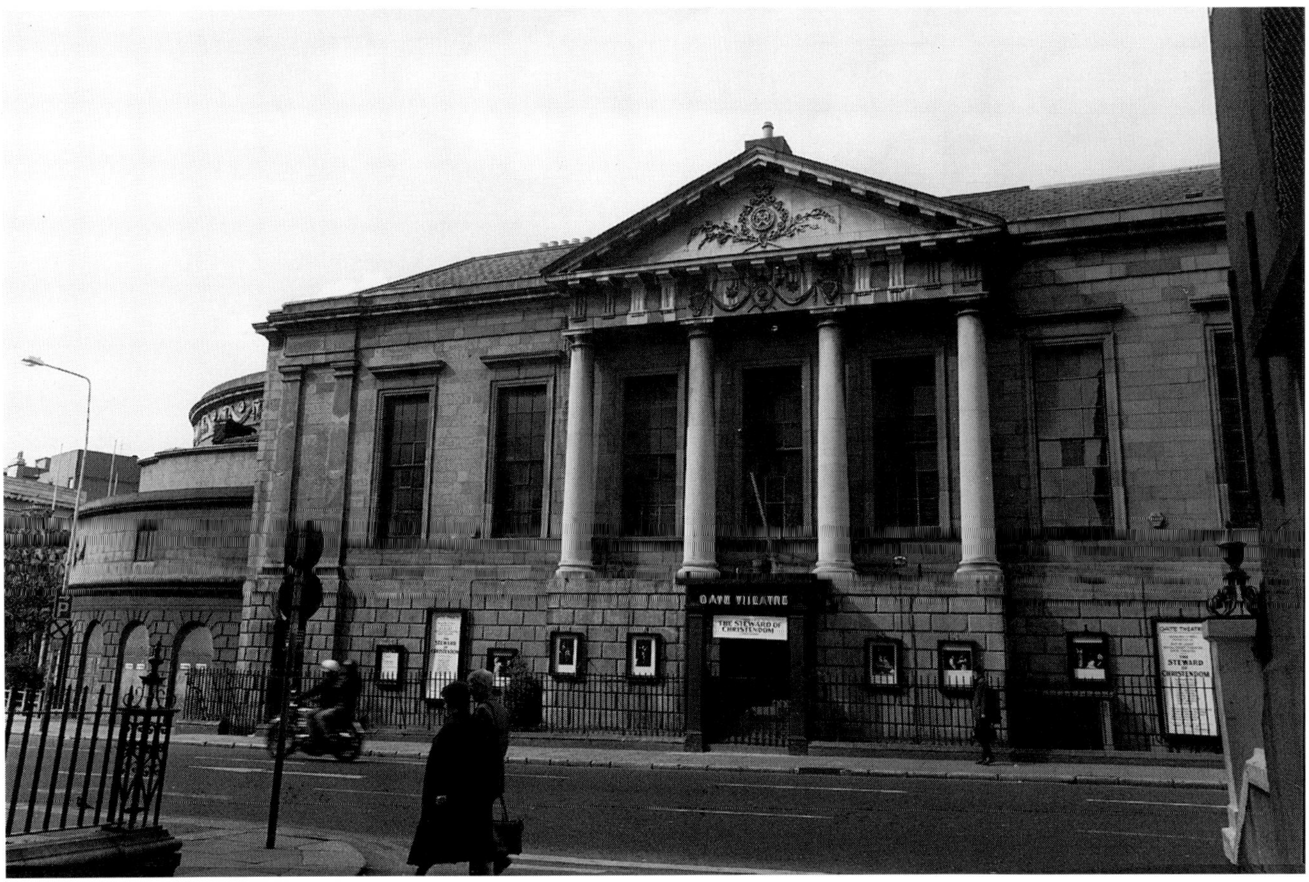

The key factor, it seemed to Liam, was the unemployed, largely ex-soldiers – his kind of people. He clashed with the leadership of the CPI over this. He advocated supporting the workers who were taking over factories in several parts of the country, especially at Cork Harbour and in Limerick. But this suggestion was turned down on the grounds that communists did not lead putsches.

Liam took his case onto the streets. He was already a familiar figure, selling left-wing papers such as *The Workers' Republic* (which he edited) from a stand in O'Connell Street. In January the Treaty was ratified, after divisive debate, in the Dáil; and on 16 January the Provisional Government of the Irish Free State (which many saw as a rejection of the 1916 provisional government of the Irish Republic) was constituted. Two days later, on Wednesday 18 January, Liam, with two hundred of the city's unemployed, seized the Rotunda Concert Hall and Pillar Room (now the Gate Theatre). The crowd's reaction to the red flag flying from the building was unwelcoming. They were held back by a cordon of DMP and Republican Police (the IRA supporting the government). Liam became the sensation of the city, and as Chairman of the Council of the Unemployed was interviewed by the newspapers. The crowds grew uglier and shots were fired over their heads from the building. On Saturday, having held out for four days, Liam and his men left the Rotunda. He fled, with two companions, south to Cork.

This incident was merely one symptom of the general disorder in the country, which was reflected in countless strikes and stoppages of all kinds. In February the new National Army was established by the government, but this soon came into collision with the IRA which opposed the treaty. On 14 April, Rory O'Connor seized the Four Courts; other anti-Treatyites took over other buildings in Dublin. The standoff between the two sides continued. In June Liam returned from the south. He was now writing for Republican papers such as *The Plain People*: an article on Larkin's imprisonment in America (a cause close to Liam's brother Tom) appeared on 18 June. Ten days later, following the murder of General Wilson in London, the government's hand was forced. The new army fired on their former comrades in the Four Courts and the Civil War began in earnest.

The members of the Communist Party were also members of the Irish Citizens Army and joined several of the garrisons in the city supporting O'Connor. Liam was one of those occupying Vaughan's Hotel, a rambling set of houses on the corner of Parnell Square and Granby Row – this had been a haunt of Collins and other Republicans during the earlier troubles. Other Communists were in Moran's Hotel and in the Hammam Hotel in O'Connell Street.

On 30 June, after a tremendous explosion, the Four Courts garrison surrendered. The government was gaining ground in the city. On 4 July Liam's ICA unit was disbanded, and the next day he was able to witness the final drive by the National Army against the Republicans in the city centre hotels. Rumours were flying around the city that he had been shot the day before in Capel Street.

Still with his revolver, he fled the country, taking ship – like his own assassin – through police watches on the trains and ships. On 9 July he arrived in Liverpool, and met up with Jim Phelan. Liam spoke alternately of going to America and of joining the fight in the mountains of the south of Ireland. However, he did neither. In the last week of July he received a letter from a Miss Casey in London, a communist sympathetic to the Republican

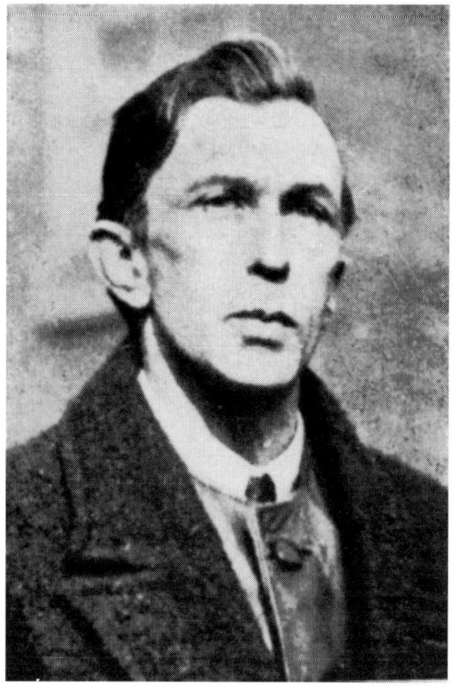

Right: *Rory O'Connor, who commanded the Republican garrison at the Four Courts when the Civil War began.*

Below: *The last day of the Civil War in Dublin: the O'Connell Street hotels occupied by the Republicans are attacked.*

cause, inviting him to stay in her mother's house. So it was to London, still armed, that he went.

In August Griffith died suddenly of a stroke; his death was followed days later by the death in action of Michael Collins. The Civil War went on, becoming increasingly bitter as the Republicans were forced out of the towns and cities and into the hills and valleys of West Cork and Kerry. But in London Liam, whose twenty-sixth birthday fell in that month, was attempting to built a new life. For him, too, the revolutionary moment had passed.

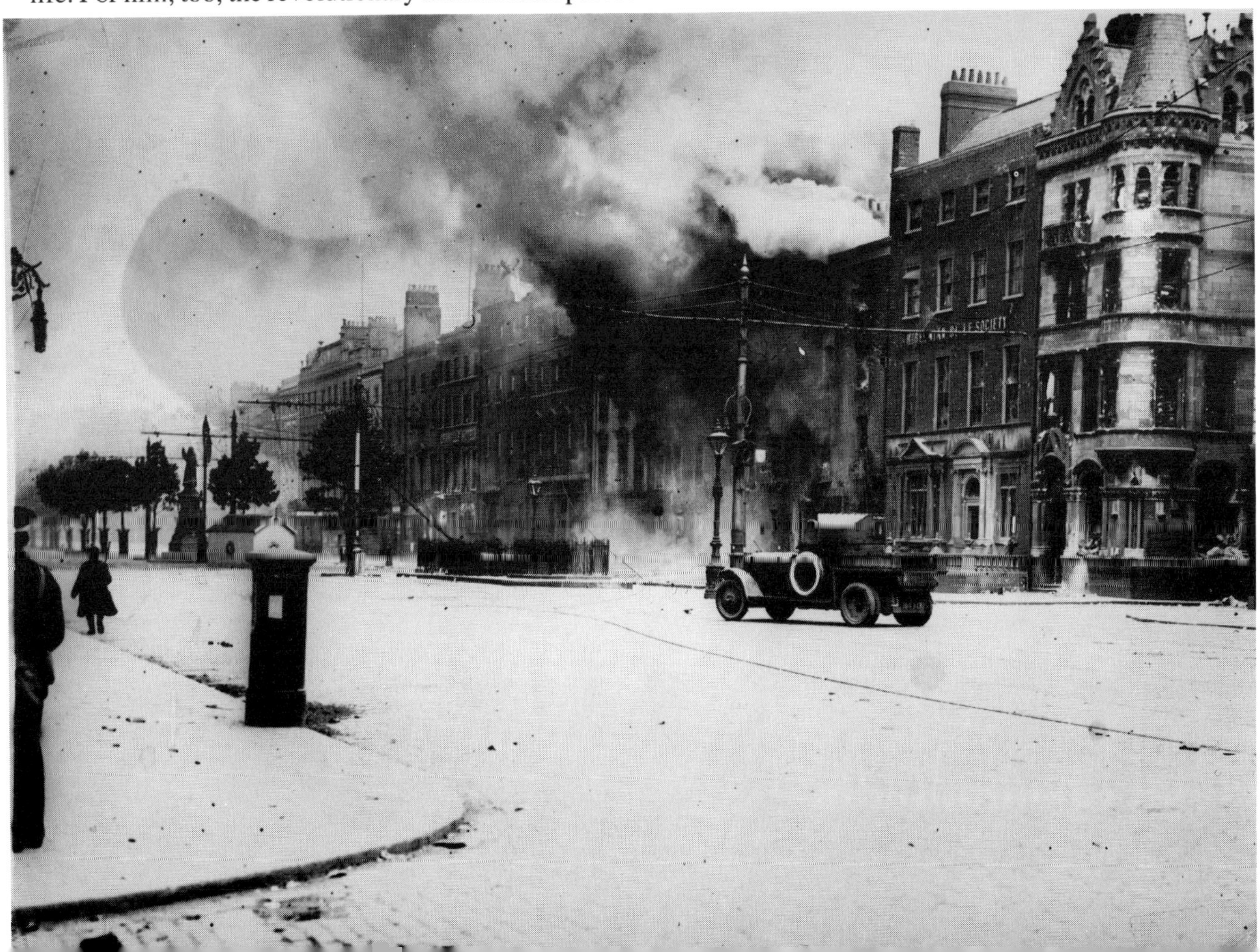

Snipers on both sides played a crucial role in the house-to-house fighting in the centre of Dublin – as described by O'Flaherty in his short stories of the Civil War.

Opposite: *O'Flaherty was lucky not to be arrested in the mopping-up operations by the Government soldiers after the fall of the Four Courts, like this man in a lane off Mary Sreet.*

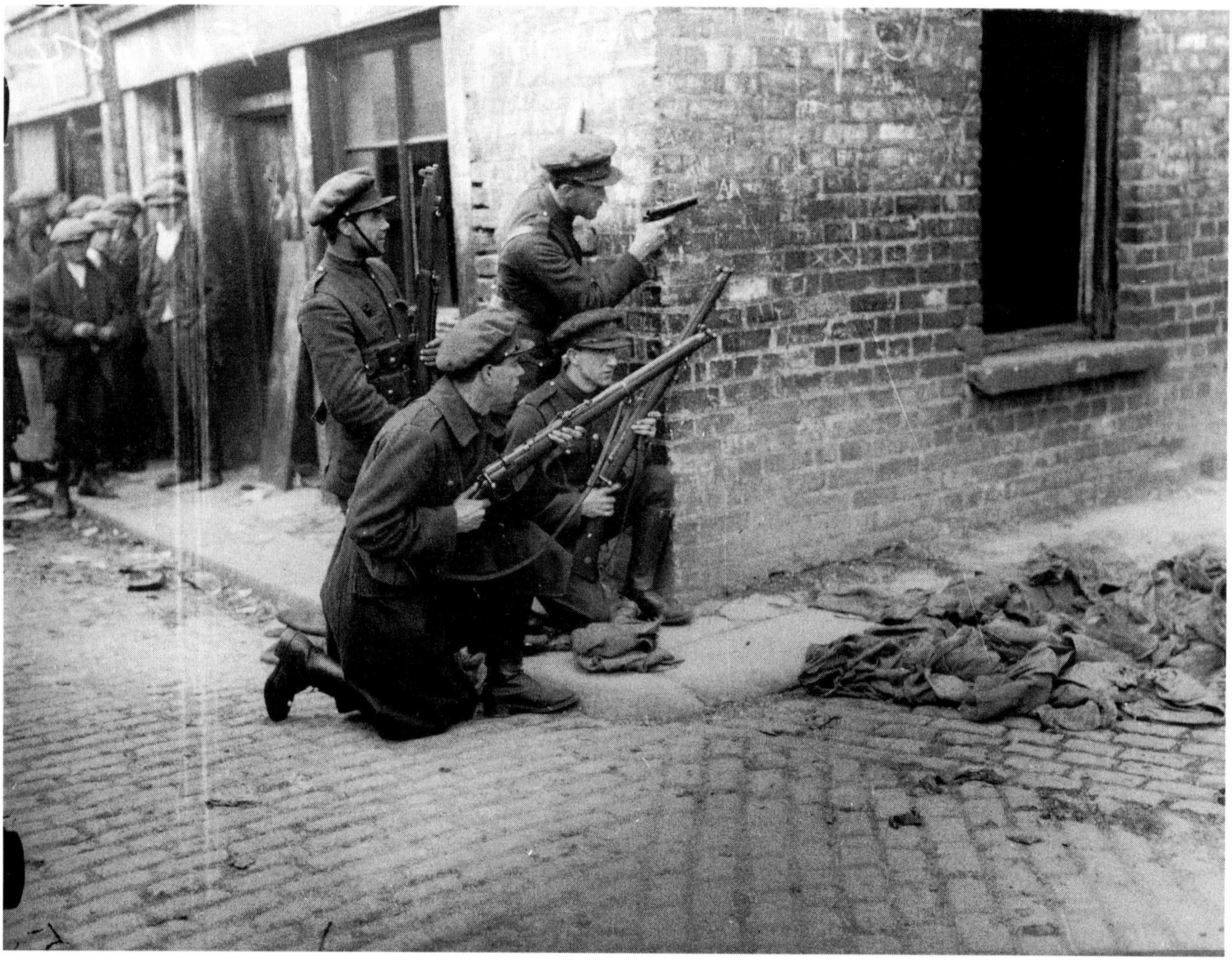

'The Sniper' *by Liam O'Flaherty*

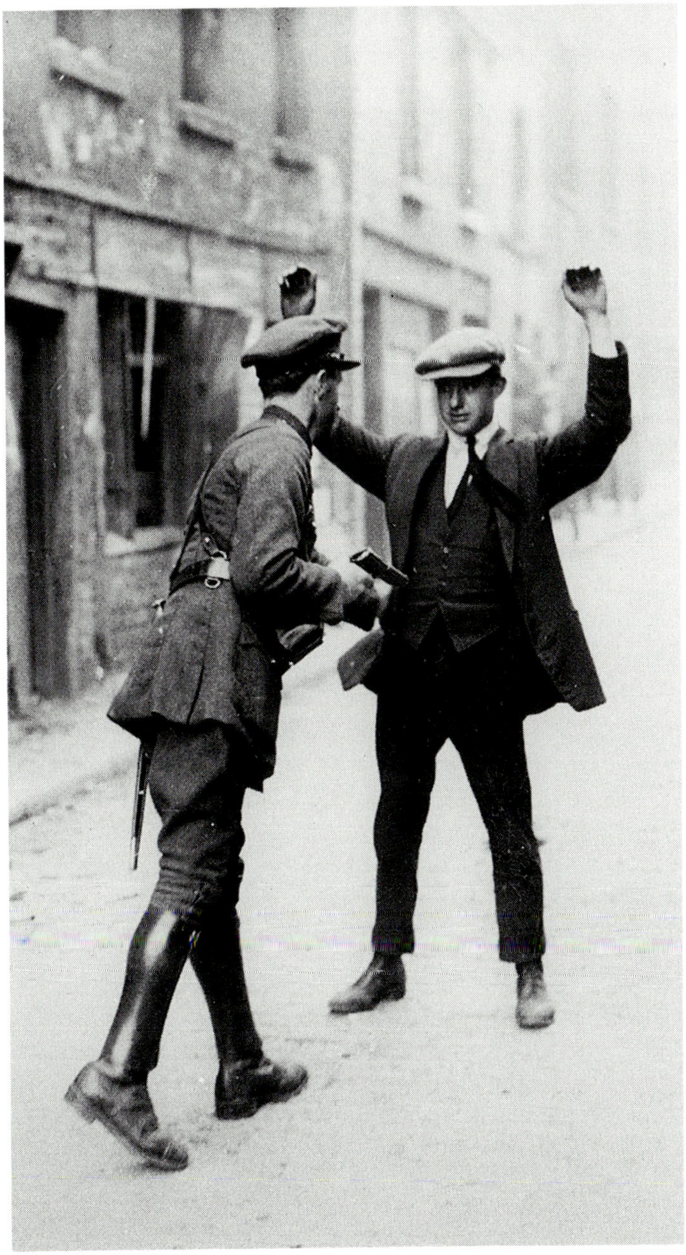

The long June twilight faded into night. Dublin lay enveloped in darkness, but for the dim light of the moon, that shone through fleecy clouds, casting a pale light as of approaching dawn over the streets and the dark waters of the Liffey. Around the beleaguered Four Courts the heavy guns roared. Here and there through the city machine guns and rifles broke the silence of the night, spasmodically, like dogs barking on lone farms. Republicans and Free Staters were waging civil war.

On a roof-top near O'Connell Bridge, a Republican sniper lay watching. Beside him lay his rifle and over his shoulders were slung a pair of field-glasses. His face was the face of a student – thin and ascetic, but his eyes had the cold gleam of the fanatic. They were deep and thoughtful, the eyes of a man who is used to look at death.

He was eating a sandwich hungrily. He had eaten nothing since morning. He had been too excited to eat. He finished the sandwich, and taking a flask of whiskey from his pocket, he took a short draught. Then he returned the flask to his pocket. He paused for a moment, considering whether he should risk a smoke. It was dangerous. The flash might be seen in the darkness and there were enemies watching. He decided to take the risk. Placing a cigarette between his lips, he struck a match, inhaled the smoke hurriedly and put out the light. Almost immediately, a bullet flattened itself against the parapet of the roof. The sniper took another whiff and put out the cigarette. Then he swore softly and crawled away to the left.

Cautiously he raised himself and peered over the parapet. There was a flash and a bullet whizzed over his head. He dropped immediately. He had seen the flash. It came from the opposite side of the street.

He rolled over the roof to a chimney stack in the rear, and slowly drew himself up behind it, until his eyes were level with the top of the parapet. There was nothing to be seen – just the dim outline of the opposite housetop against the blue sky. His enemy was under cover.

Just then an armoured car came across the bridge and advanced slowly up the street. It stopped on the opposite side of the street fifty yards ahead. The sniper could hear the dull panting of the motor. His heart beat faster. It was an enemy car. He wanted to fire, but he knew it was useless. His bullets would never pierce the steel that covered the grey monster.

Then round the corner of a side street came an old woman, her head covered by a tattered shawl. She began to talk to the man in the turret of the car. She was pointing to the roof where the sniper lay. An informer.

The turret opened. A man's head and shoulders appeared, looking towards the sniper. The sniper raised his rifle and fired. The head fell heavily on the turret wall. The woman darted toward the side street. The sniper fired again. The woman whirled round and fell with a shriek into the gutter.

Suddenly from the opposite roof a shot rang out and the sniper dropped his rifle with a curse. The rifle clattered to the roof. The sniper thought the noise would wake the dead. He stopped to pick the rifle up. He couldn't lift it. His fore-arm was dead.

'Christ,' he muttered, 'I'm hit.'

Dropping flat on to the roof, he crawled back to the parapet. With his left hand he felt the injured right fore-arm. The blood was oozing through the sleeve of his coat. There was no pain – just a deadened sensation, as if the arm had been cut off.

Quickly he drew his knife from his pocket, opened it on the breastwork of the parapet and ripped open the sleeve. There was a small hole where the bullet had entered. On the other side there was no hole. The bullet had lodged in the bone. It must have fractured it. He bent the arm below the wound. The arm bent back easily. He ground his teeth to overcome the pain.

Then, taking out his field dressing, he ripped open the packet with his knife. He broke the neck of the iodine bottle and let the bitter fluid drip into the wound. A paroxysm of pain swept through him. He placed the cotton wadding over the wound and wrapped the dressing over it. He tied the end with his teeth.

Then he lay still against the parapet, and closing his eyes, he made an effort of will to overcome the pain.

In the street beneath all was still. The armoured car had retired speedily over the bridge, with the machine gunner's head hanging lifeless over the turret. The woman's corpse lay still in the gutter.

The sniper lay for a long time nursing his wounded arm and planning escape. Morning must not find him wounded on the roof. The enemy on the opposite roof covered his escape. He must kill that enemy and he could not use his rifle. He had only a revolver to do it. Then he thought of a plan.

Taking off his cap, he placed it over the muzzle of his rifle. Then he pushed the rifle slowly upwards over the parapet, until the cap was visible from the opposite side of the street. Almost immediately there was a report, and a bullet pierced the centre of the cap. The sniper slanted the rifle forward. The cap slipped down into the street. Then, catching the rifle in the middle, the sniper dropped his left hand over the roof and let it hang, lifelessly. After a few moments he let the rifle drop to the street. Then he sank to the roof, dragging his hand with him.

Crawling quickly to the left, he peered up at the corner

of the roof. His ruse had succeeded. The other sniper, seeing the cap and rifle fall, thought that he had killed his man. He was now standing before a row of chimney pots, looking across, with his head clearly silhouetted against the western sky.

The Republican sniper smiled and lifted his revolver above the edge of the parapet. The distance was about fifty yards – a hard shot in the dim light, and his right arm was paining him like a thousand devils. He took a steady aim. His hand trembled with eagerness. Pressing his lips together, he took a deep breath through his nostrils and fired. He was almost deafened with the report and his arm shook with the recoil.

Then, when the smoke cleared, he peered across and uttered a cry of joy. His enemy had been hit. He was reeling over the parapet in his death agony. He struggled to keep his feet, but he was slowly falling forward, as if in a dream. The rifle fell from his grasp, hit the parapet, fell over, bounded off the pole of a barber's shop beneath and then clattered on to the pavement.

Then the dying man on the roof crumpled up and fell forward. The body turned over and over in space and hit the ground with a dull thud. Then it lay still.

The sniper looked at his enemy falling and he shuddered. The lust of battle died in him. He became bitten by remorse. The sweat stood out in beads on his forehead. Weakened by his wound and the long summer day of fasting and watching on the roof, he revolted from the sight of the shattered mass of his dead enemy. His teeth chattered. He began to gibber to himself, cursing the war, cursing himself, cursing everybody.

He looked at the smoking revolver in his hand and with an oath he hurled it to the roof at his feet. The revolver went off with the concussion, and the bullet whizzed past the sniper's head. He was frightened back to his senses by the shock. His nerves steadied. The cloud of fear scattered from his mind and he laughed.

Taking the whiskey flask from his pocket, he emptied it at a draught. He felt reckless under the influence of the spirits. He decided to leave the roof and look for his company commander to report. Everywhere around was quiet. There was not much danger in going through the streets. He picked up his revolver and put it in his pocket. Then he crawled down through the sky-light to the house underneath.

When the sniper reached the laneway on the street level, he felt a sudden curiosity as to the identity of the enemy sniper whom he had killed. He decided that he was a good shot whoever he was. He wondered if he knew him. Perhaps he had been in his own company before the split in the army. He decided to risk going over to have a look at him. He peered around the corner into O'Connell Street. In the upper part of the street there was heavy firing, but around here all was quiet.

The sniper darted across the street. A machine gun tore up the ground around him with a hail of bullets, but he escaped. He threw himself face downwards beside the corpse. The machine gun stopped.

Then the sniper turned over the dead body and looked into his brother's face.

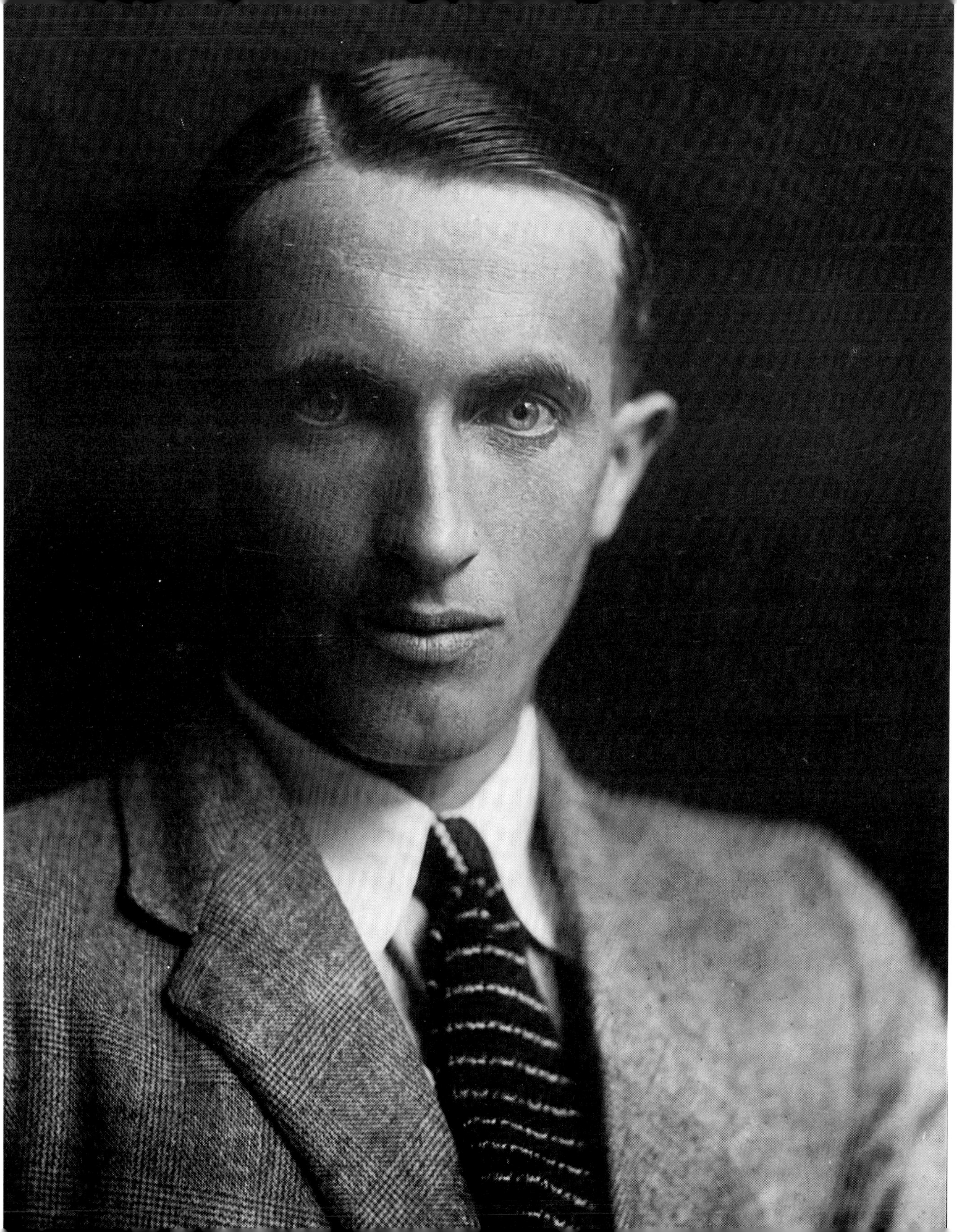

Opposite page: *Liam O'Flaherty, still haunted by war, photographed by E.O. Hoppé in London in 1923.*

THE CHRYSALIS BREAKS September 1922 saw the first meeting of the newly elected Dáil in Dublin. Liam, however, had little time for news: he was trying to write properly at last. He rushed off a 150,000-word novel and some short stories. These were sent to publishers. The stories were returned, as was the novel – which a friend later called 'a West End tale' – by Allen and Unwin. Liam sent it to Tom in America, who told him tartly that a novel must be more than a bar-room yarn. Three days later (it was now the early days of 1923) he began to write *Thy Neighbour's Wife*, set on Aran, in a burst of creative energy.

Mrs Hamilton at the *New Leader*, who was publishing his first short story, 'The Sniper', suggested he send it to Jonathan Cape, then a relatively new publisher. On 12 January his story appeared, under the name William O'Flaherty, and caught the attention of Edward Garnett. He was the reader at Cape and it was into his hands that the novel came in due course. Liam, who had moved out of the Caseys' house into a garret in Fitzroy Street, was walking Fleet Street, trying to find newspaper work: all he achieved was to place one small news item in the left-leaning *Daily Herald.* He thought again that he would go back to America. Ten days later, wanting to retrieve his manuscript before going, he called at Cape's offices at 11 Gower Street. He was asked to wait to see Mr Cape. He suspected a plot to arrest him, but to his astonishment found that his book had been accepted and the firm was prepared to pay a ten-pound advance. He also met Edward Garnett, who was to prove the major influence on his young life. This influence has assumed an importance slightly out of proportion, as it is O'Flaherty's letters to Garnett rather than to other correspondents that have survived in bulk.

Garnett was unimpressed with the West End society novel. Write about what you know, he counselled. But all Liam really knew about, he moaned, was rural life – animals, nature, cows. Write about that then, he was told. And he did, sitting down to write about a bovine suicide. This was 'A Cow's Death', sent first to the *Manchester Guardian,* rejected, but then through Garnett appearing eventually in the *New Statesman.* Both of these publications were in Liam's own political area, as was the *Daily Herald*, to which he was now able to contribute signed pieces.

In the first flush of his success Liam had proposed to the Casey girl. Now he decided against it. His letter received an angry reply from her mother. Liam had now removed himself to a safe haven in the depths of the country in a small house at North Crawley, near Newport Pagnell in Buckinghamshire. He had begun his second novel, *The Black Soul*, and this was completed in August in a room in the King's Road, Chelsea. Liam was not totally out of touch with events, however: he followed the communist uprisings in Germany, especially in Hamburg and Lower Saxony, with interest.

In October – a month which saw the publication of 'First Flight', the story which was to become a perennial favourite among readers of Liam's stories – Cape published *Thy Neighbour's Wife.* At the usual price of 7/6d some 1500 copies were printed. The confidence of his publishers in this story of illicit love on a western island was rewarded with a rave review by AE (the Irish poet George Russell) in the *Irish Statesman*: 'O'Flaherty may be great in Irish literature,' he concluded. O'Flaherty had commented that he wished to save the Irish novel from a music hall joke (that is to say, from the like of Somerville & Ross and Lynn Doyle). Another reviewer, Sylvia Lynd, wondered if he had ever read James Joyce. But of course he had not; for Joyce

‘The Cow’s Death’ *by Liam O’Flaherty*

represented the cerebral and intellectual, everything that O’Flaherty did not want to be.

He had by now completed his third novel under the guidance of Garnett, as well as writing and publishing short stories. The pattern of his work was established.

In March he took ‘Chop Cherry Cottage’, at Chinnor in Oxfordshire, which belonged to another Cape author, A.E. Coppard. Though rural, this was not remote. J.B. Priestley (not yet famous as the author of *The Good Companions*) and Gerard Bullett, writers only a few years older than Liam, lived nearby. From his comments in a later book, however, these were not the sort of English writers that appealed to him.

In America Boni & Liveright, a distinguished literary firm who published Theodore Dreiser and others, brought out *Thy Neighbour’s Wife*. After the publication of *The Black Soul* in April, Cape agreed to provide Liam with financial support to write until September. Sean O’Casey thought that the novel was the best book ever written by a Gaelic speaker – although, alas, it was in English. Though this novel was again admired in Dublin by AE, Garnett claimed that other reviews in London killed it for a decade.

The calf was still-born. It came from the womb tail first. When its red, unwieldy body dropped on the green-sward it was dead. It lay with its head doubled about its neck in a clammy mass. The men stood about it and shook their heads in silence. The wife of the peasant who owned the cow sighed and said, ‘It is God’s will.’ The cow moaned, mad with the pain of birth. Then she wheeled around cumbersomely, her hoofs driving into the soft earth beneath the weight of her body. She stooped over the calf and moaned, again smelling it. Then she licked the still body with her coarse tongue lovingly. The woman rubbed the cow’s matted forehead, and there was a tear in her eye; for she too was a mother.

Then the cow, overcome once more with the pain, moved away from the calf and stood with her head bent low, breathing heavily through her nostrils. The breath came in long pale columns, like sunbeams coming through the window of a darkened church. They drove her away to a corner of the field, and she stood wearily with her head over the fence, lashing her flanks with her tail restlessly.

They seized the calf and dragged it by the feet along the field to the fence, out through the fence into another field, then through another fence, then up the grassy slope that led to the edge of the cliff. They dropped it downwards into the sea. It lay in a pulped mass on the rocks. They rebuilt the gaps in the stone fences carefully and returned to the cow. The woman offered her a hot drink of oatmeal, but she refused it. They seized her and poured the drink down her throat, using a bull’s horn as a funnel. The cow half swallowed the drink, half tossed it away with her champing mouth.

Then they went home, the woman still moaning the dead calf and apologizing to God for her sorrow. The peasant remained with the cow, watching until she should drop the bag. He buried it under a mound of stones. He dug his heel in the ground, and, taking a handful of the brown earth, he made the sign of the cross on the cow's side. Then he too went home.

For a long time the cow stood leaning over the fence, until the pain lessened. She turned around suddenly and lowed and tossed her head. She took a short run forward, the muscles of her legs creaking like new boots. She stopped again, seeing nothing about her in the field. Then she began to run around by the fence, putting her head over it here and there, lowing. She found nothing. Nothing answered her call. She became wilder as the sense of her loss became clearer to her consciousness. Her eyes became red around the rims and fierce like a bull's. She began to smell around on the ground, half running, half walking, stumbling clumsily among the tummocks of grass.

There was where she had lain in travail, on the side of a little slope, the grass compressed and faded by the weight of her body. There was where she had given birth, the ground trampled by many feet and torn here and there, with the brown earth showing through. Then she smelt where the calf had lain. There were wet stains on the grass. She looked around her fiercely, and then she put her nose to the ground and started to follow the trail where they had draggged the calf to the fence. At the fence she stopped and smelt a long time, wondering with her stupid brain whither the trail led. And then stupidly she pressed with her great bulk against the fence. The stones cut her breast, but she pressed harder in terror and the fence fell before her. She stumbled through the gap and cut her left thigh near the udder. She did not heed the pain, but pressed forward, smelling the trail and snorting.

Faster she went, and now and again she raised her head and lowed – a long, mournful low that ended in a fierce *crescendo*, like a squall of wind coming around a corner. At the second fence she paused again. Again she pressed against it, and again it fell before her. Going through the gap she got caught, and in the struggle to get through she cut both her sides along the flanks. The blood trickled through jaggedly, discolouring the white streak on the left flank.

She came at a run up the grassy slope to the cliff. She shuddered and jerked aside when she suddenly saw the sea and heard it rumbling distantly below – the waves seething on the rocks and the sea birds calling dismally with their noisome cackle. She smelt the air in wonder. Then she slowly advanced, inch by inch, trembling. When she reached the summit, where the grass ended in a gravel belt that dropped down to the sheer slope of rock, she rushed backwards and circled around wildly, lowing. Again she came up, and planting her feet carefully on the gravel, she looked down. The trail of her calf ended there. She could follow it no further. It was lost in the emptiness beyond that gravel ledge. She tried to smell the air, but nothing reached her nostrils but the salt smell of the sea. She moaned and her sides heaved with the outrush of her breath. Then she looked down, straining out her neck. She saw the body of her calf on the rocks below.

She uttered a joyful cry and ran backwards, seeking a path to descend. Up and down the summit of the cliff she went, smelling here and there, looking out over the edge, going on her knees and looking down and finding nowhere a path that led to the object on the rocks below. She came back again, her hind legs clashing as she ran, to the point where the body had been dropped over the precipice.

She strained out and tapped with her fore hoof,

scratching the gravel and trying to descend, but there was nothing upon which she could place her feet – just a sheer drop of one hundred feet of cliff and her calf lay on the rocks below.

She stood stupidly looking at it a long time, without moving a muscle. Then she lowed, calling to her calf, but no answer came. She saw the water coming in with the tide, circling around the calf on the rocks. She lowed again, warning it. Wave after wave came in, eddying around the body. She lowed again and tossed her head wildly as if she wanted to buffet the waves with her horns.

And then a great wave came towering in, and catching up the calf on its crest swept it from the rocks.

And the cow, uttering a loud bellow, jumped headlong down.

THE LAND OF TIM HEALY Liam returned to Dublin, taking a cottage at Killakee, below the Hell Fire Club. He got to know the younger writers grouped around AE's *Irish Statesman*, to which he was soon contributing reviews and articles, and Seumas O'Sullivan's *Dublin Magazine*, which began to appear in 1924. Among the younger writers associated with that magazine was Margaret Barrington, the young wife of Edmund Curtis, a history don at Trinity College. Liam visited Sean O'Casey, soon after his success with *Shadow of a Gunman,* and wrote about him for the *Daily Herald.* He also met Cecil Salkeld, the artist, and Francis Stuart, who was married to Iseult Gonne, daughter of the beautiful Maud Gonne, to whom Yeats had once proposed. He also met Padraic Ó Conaire (a fellow old boy of Blackrock), and with him planned to write plays in Gaelic, meanwhile placing his first Gaelic short story in the *Dublin Magazine.*

It was in Dublin, a city still seething with discontent and intrigue from factional elements of the left and right, in April 1924 that he conceived the plot of *The Informer.* The fictional events take place in March 1924, the actual shooting for which Frankie McPhillip is sought by the police having occurred in November 1923. The newspapers of the day were filled with shootings, murders and other crimes, especially among rural farm labourers, which the history books, but not the novelist, have forgotten about.

Liam visited Aran briefly, where he found his sister Agnes mortally ill, and stayed a few days with his father. His mother had died in 1922, soon after the Rotunda escapade: she collapsed with a massive heart-attack in front of her husband and died in ten minutes. Liam's father had now suffered a stroke, and was dying on his feet, his mind clouded.

The writing of his new novel did not prevent Liam from intrigues of his own. With Francis Stuart, Salkeld and others he wanted to form a Radical Club, to actively oppose the views and schemes of Yeats. That, at least, was the impression of Sean O'Casey, who refused to become involved. Liam, O'Casey claimed, disliked Yeats for some reason. This dislike of the Nobel laureate and Free State senator was, however, shared by many of O'Flaherty's Catholic background, though Yeats's political views as an admirer of Mussolini would have been enough. Liam, from a review he wrote at this time, saw himself as a sort of De Maupassant, whom he admired as a story writer – though he admitted the Frenchman could not write a novel (a criticism often made of O'Flaherty).

The plans of Liam and his friends matured into the idea of publishing a journal to be called *To-Morrow.* Whatever they may really have thought about Yeats, they recruited his support for this venture. He wrote them an editorial, and with stories by Lennox Robinson and others the magazine burst controversially upon Dublin in September. It caused a scandal, the reverberations of which were still echoing decades later. Though another issue did appear, the first lost Robinson his job and, in the eyes of obscurantist Catholics such as those associated with the *Catholic Bulletin,* earned Liam and the others black marks.

That month Liam's first collection of short stories – appropriately named *Spring Sowing* – appeared. In this book of limpid, beautiful snapshots of life in Ireland a distinctive new voice was finally established. Whatever George Moore or Joyce had hoped to achieve through their short story collections, *The Untilled Field* and *Dubliners*, here was a new master of the form. Its title redolent of a new beginning, it contained thirty-two

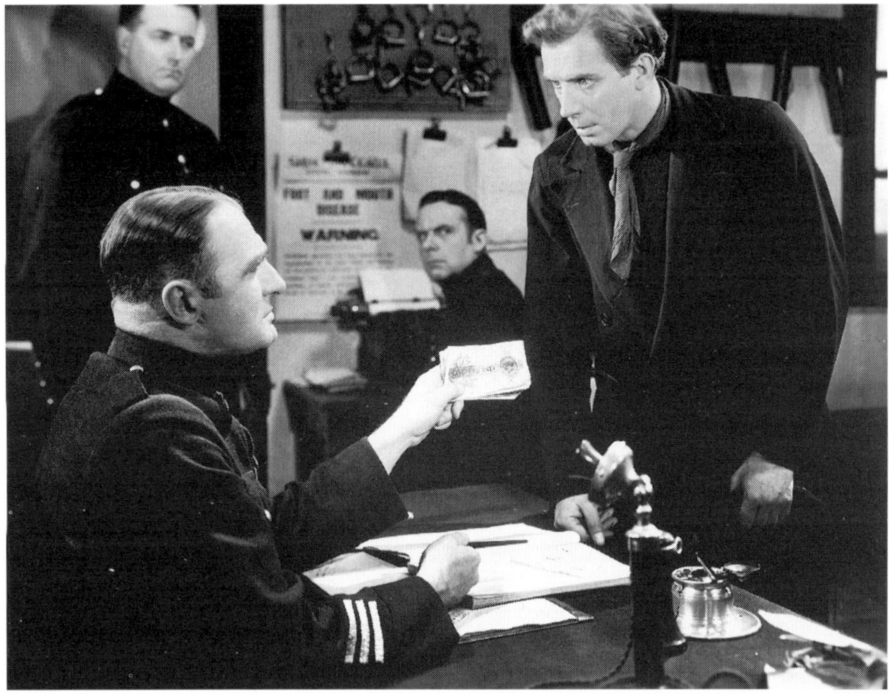

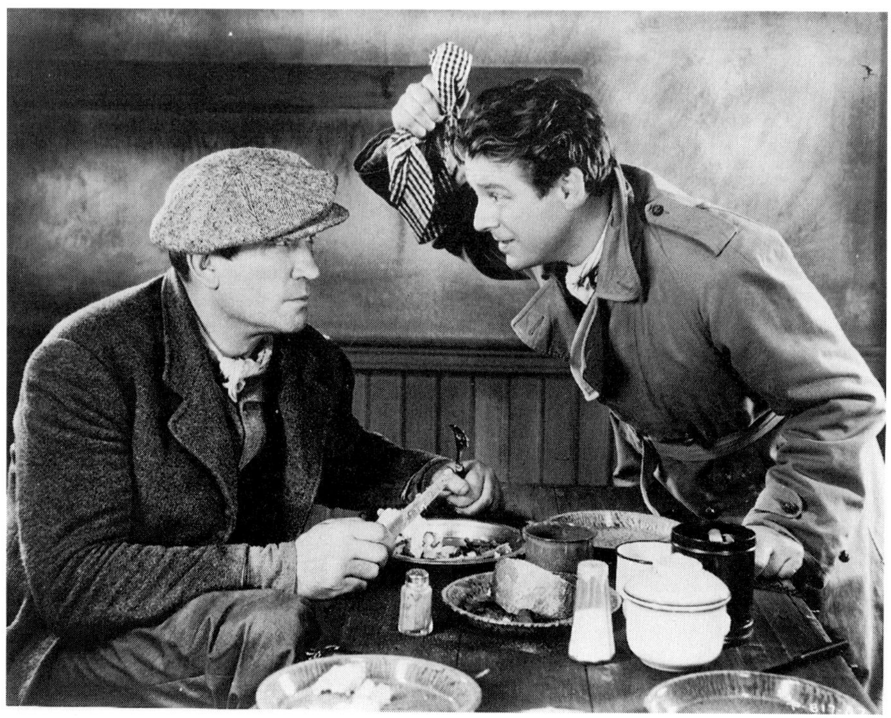

Top right: *Gypo Nolan (Victor McLaglen) and Frankie McPhillip (Wallace Ford) in the opening scenes of John Ford's version of* The Informer, *when Gypo decides to betray his comrade.*

Bottom right: *Gypo Nolan (Lars Hansen) collecting the reward for Frankie McPhillip from the Dublin Metropolitan Police at Store St. police station, from Artur Robison's version of* The Informer.

Far right: *Gypo Nolan (Lars Hansen), on the run from the Organisation in the stews and brothels of Dublin, finds friendship with the prostitute Katie Fox (Lya de Putti), who eventually betrays him.*

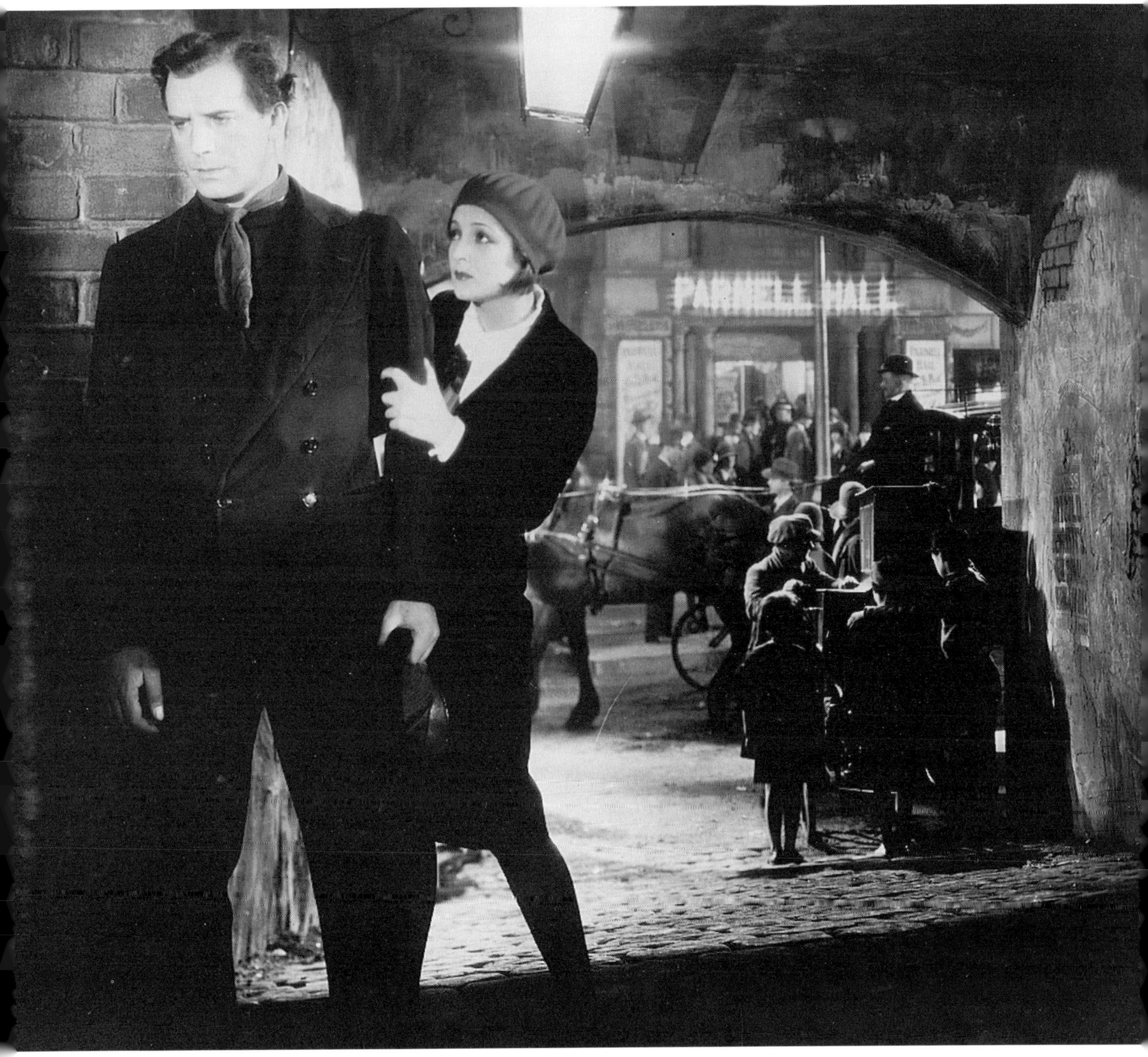
PARNELL HALL

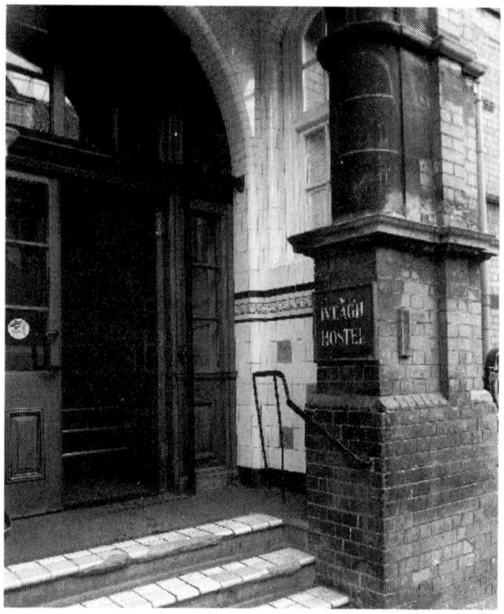

Above: *The entrance to the Iveagh Hostel in Bride Street, the men's lodging house, where the first chapter of* The Informer *is set.*

Right: *The dying Gypo (Victor MacLaglen), having been shot by the communists hunting him down, begs forgiveness in the local church from Frankie McPhillip's mother (Una O'Connor).*

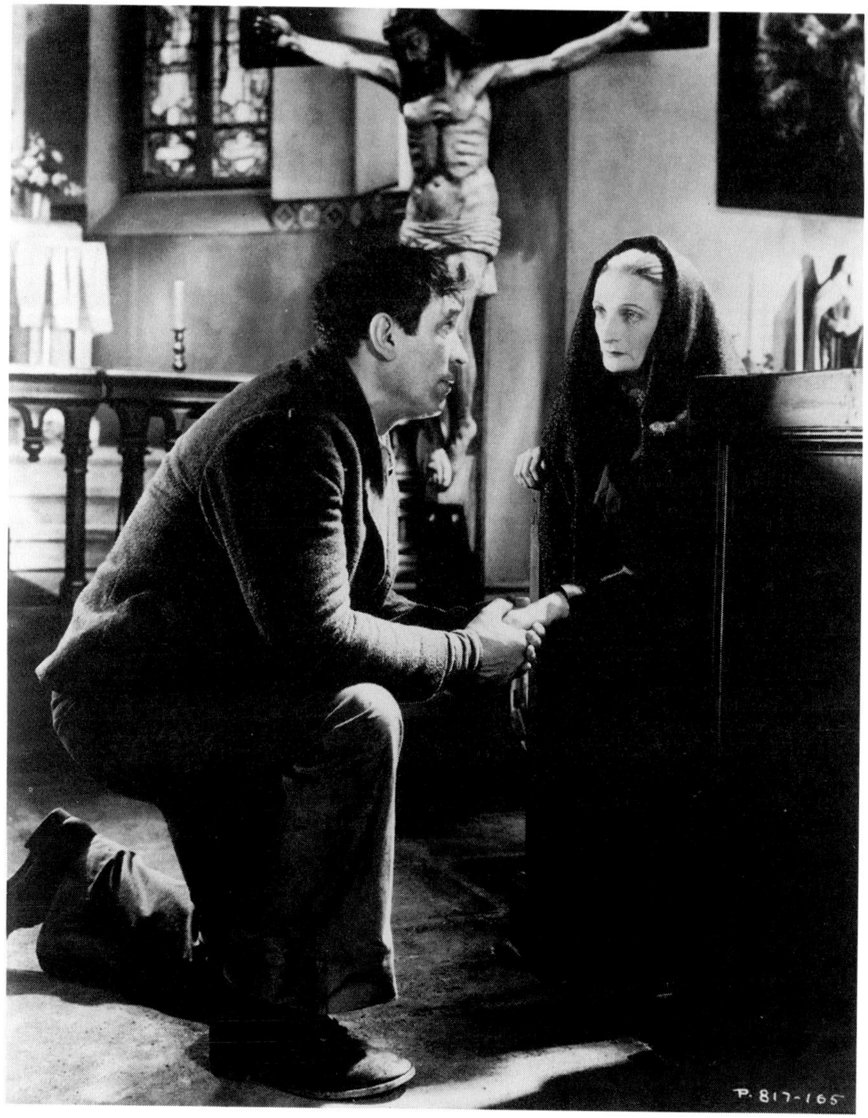

stories, all written since the start of 1923 – a remarkable achievement.

Liam crowned the scandal caused by *To-Morrow* by running away with Margaret Curtis, the professor's wife, who had fallen in love with him. Born Margaret Barrington – the name she used for her writings – she was the daughter of an RIC inspector in Donegal. Four years older than Liam, she had been educated in Dungannon and had taken a degree in modern languages at Trinity in 1918. Her marriage to Curtis in 1922 was a *marriage blanc* (so I have been told by a friend of Curtis's): there was no great passion on either side. But with Liam there was passion. They spent some time in London and then visited T.F. Powys on the south coast at East Chaldon, where they slept on the beach at Lulworth Cove below his house. Liam was soon after to review Powys's new novel *Mr Tasker's Gods*, and Powys was one of the few writers of the day whom he admired.

The writing of *The Informer* was well advanced when Liam suffered a nervous collapse, which lasted six months. The book was eventually finished; the contract was made on 5 November 1924, while Liam and Margaret were living at Sunnybank Cottage in Great Milton, Oxfordshire. The beginning of 1925 found Liam and Topsy (as he called her) in dire straits back in Dublin. Through the influence of Garnett, they received some £200 from the Royal Literary Fund in February. Margaret was seeking a divorce from Curtis – then a troublesome business, as was reflected in one of her own short stories. A decree *nisi* on grounds of her adultery with O'Flaherty was granted in London in July 1925. But there were other troubles. *The Black Soul* was brought out in New York by Boni & Liveright, but in that month a row arose over the publication date of Liam's new novel of the Dublin underworld. He was anxious for money, but Cape – who had already developed a reputation for being stingy – wished to delay the London publication to coincide with the issue of the book by Alfred A. Knopf in New York.

By the summer Liam and Margaret were established in a house at Ballybawn, above Kilmacanogue in Wicklow. Here Sean O'Casey spent a day with Liam, where he heard him read 'The Fireman's Death'. At this time Sean was working on *The Plough and the Stars*, and he may have discussed it with Liam. A little later David Garnett, Edward's son, on a visit to Ireland, was taken by Liam to visit Sean O'Casey in his Dorset Street tenement room. If O'Casey was brooding on the Troubles, so was Liam. He completed his story 'Civil War', which he sent to Charles Lahr – the anarchist owner of Red Lion Books, a left-wing bookshop in London which Liam frequented – for publication as a pamphlet.

In July Liam published a translation of his early story 'The Cow's Death' in *Fainne an Lae*; it was admired by Padraic Ó Conaire and the two became friendly. Liam published a version of Ó Conaire's story 'The Agony of the World' in *The Adelphi* in September. They still hoped to work on Gaelic plays together, but they got little support. One play of Liam's, *Dorchadas*, was produced by a Gaelic language group who produced plays in the Abbey on Sunday evenings, but Liam was not paid for it – an experience which soured him against the enthusiasms of language revivalists.

In August Liam and Topsy agreed with the poet Joseph Campbell to lease his cottage and forty-three acres at Lackan Darragh in Glencree, from 1 October for a period of two years, for twenty pounds a year.

In September Cape and Knopf finally published *The*

Informer, for which Liam came to London. In London it quickly went through two impressions, selling over two hundred thousand copies in a short period, and it had an equal success in America. Knopf was a keen admirer of advanced European writing, and he published *Spring Sowing* a little later, but the connection was not to last. The success of the book may have helped to pay not only for Liam's day-to-day life, but also for his horse-racing debts. He often went, with Francis Stuart, and at times with Gordon and Beatrice Campbell (later Lord and Lady Glenavy).

Lahr published Liam's signed edition of *Civil War* in September. On publication in November he told Lahr he was trying to interest the Dublin booksellers in it, but 'the priests have the whole country collared'.

All the difficulties and delays over *The Informer* were rewarded when it was nominated in December 1925 for the James Tait Black Memorial Prize, and then won the prize in the spring of 1926.

A further limited edition came from Charles Lahr in February 1926. Liam saw these as a way of making more money, from collectors of first editions. But they really produced no substantial funds compared with a bestseller. Liam was planning to visit London, but the early part of the year was taken up with controversy.

Sean O'Casey's play *The Plough and the Stars* opened at the Abbey on 8 February 1926, and was greeted with an orchestrated chorus of disapproval. Among the critics were Liam O'Flaherty and his friends Austin Clarke and F.R. Higgins, the writers of a new generation. O'Casey, it must be realised, was sixteen years older than Liam, older even than Joyce. The young Turks had in him an easy target for creating their own reputations. Liam attended not only on the first night, but also on 12 February (as recorded by Joseph Holloway). On 20 February, letters attacking O'Casey began to appear in the *Irish Statesman.* O'Casey suspected his critics of having political or hidden motives, and spoke in a letter to Gabriel Fallon of Liam's 'funny sense of humour' – a trait he shared with many Aran Islanders.

In London Liam's play *Darkness* was given a reading in an artists' studio to secure copyright and was published by Lahr on 27 April, with a portrait of Liam by William Roberts.

Liam's own political motivations were strong at this time. He published, in the *Irish Statesman,* an article on communism and fascism – meaning, of course, Mussolini, who had many admirers in Ireland. The publication in June of a new collection of short stories, *The Tent*, was followed by another impression of *The Informer.* It was during this summer that Sean O'Faolain came to meet O'Flaherty (perhaps through the AE connection). He was, O'Faolain recalled decades later, after Liam's death, the handsomest man he had ever seen, and he was amazed at Liam's muscular strength: he seemed to be bursting with energy. Liam advised Sean to send his first true story, 'The Bomb Shop', to Edward Garnett. This he did before on 15 August he left for the USA. Eventually he too would become a Cape author. Another young writer was on his way. Liam's advice to O'Faolain was that he should murder Alfred O'Rahilly of Cork University, an enemy of them both, and write a story about it. He also advised him, 'Don't write home. Be a scoundrel': it was advice he would often take himself. O'Faolain visited the cottage, and admired the Kerry goats which Liam was keeping on his hillside acres. These had also been much admired by Edward Garnett. Rearing goats and playing the melodeon were actually listed by Liam as his hobbies

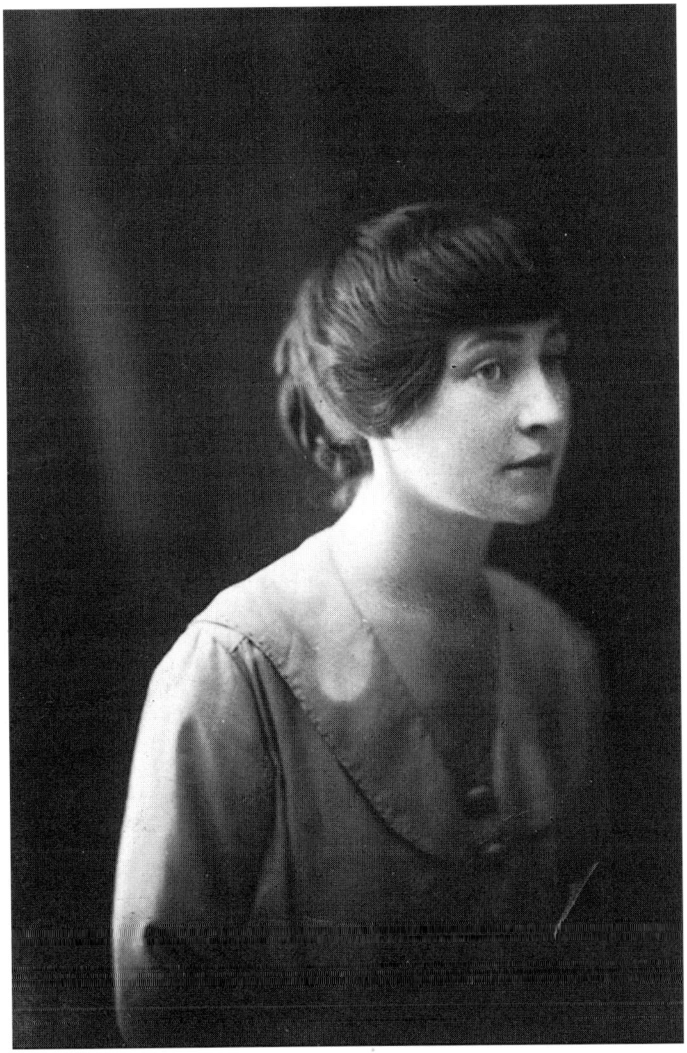

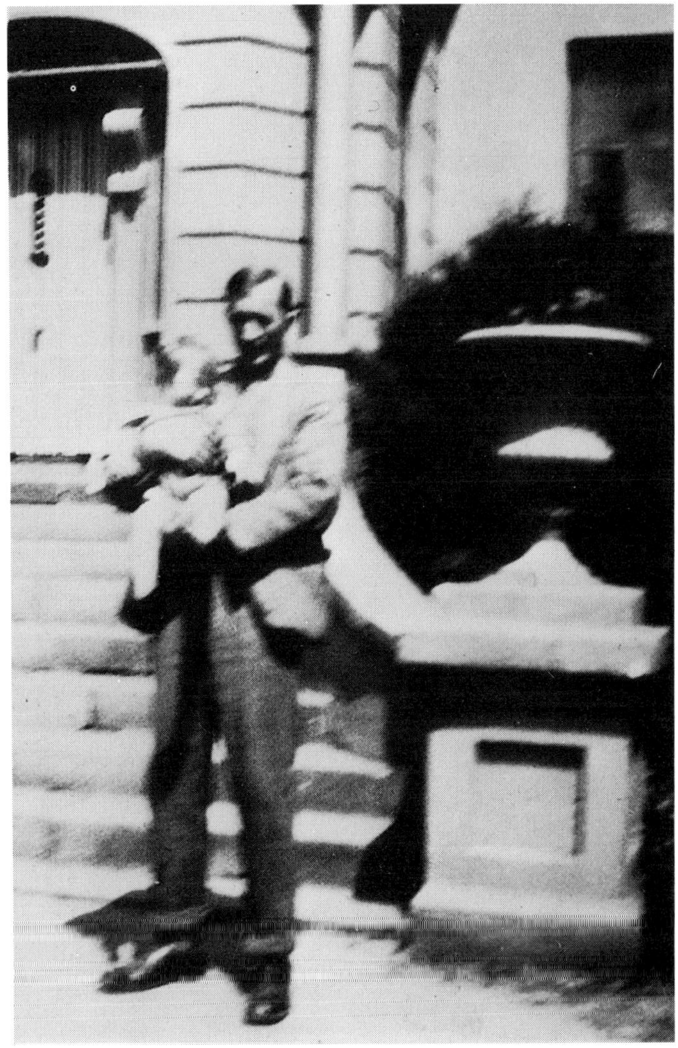

Above left: *Margaret Barrington (then Mrs Edmund Curtis) about the time she met O'Flaherty.*

Above right: *Liam O'Flaherty with their daughter Pegeen on the steps of Hazelbrook, where they took a flat in the autumn of 1926.*

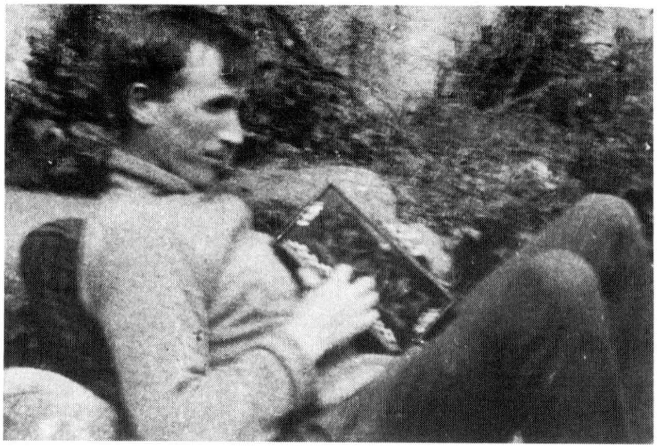

when he filled in his form for his entry in *Who's Who.*

The goats – along with his melodeon playing – belonged with Liam's rural visions; but the life of the city in the early years of the Free State also had its animal attractions for him. In October he published *Mr Gilhooley,* a novel of the seedier side of Dublin life, featuring the passion of an older man for a young girl, and her eventual murder. At this time the book was as well-known, even as notorious, as Joyce's *Ulysses.* The text caused concern at his publishers, and later editions were expurgated. A third edition of *The Informer* did little to assuage his annoyance at some of the reviews. He thought *Mr Gilhooley* would get a bad press in Dublin, as he wrote to Lahr, though 'curiously the Dublin booksellers are placarding him though they boycotted my other books as obscene'. That month it was nominated, with *Adam's Breed* and *Lolly Willows*, for the Femina – Vie Heureuse Prize for the best work of fiction published between June 1925 and June 1926. The nomination was in itself a distinction, though the prize went in April 1927 to another Cape author, the lesbian Radclyffe Hall, for *Adam's Breed.* At Christmas time Lahr published *The Child of God* in a limited edition.

Liam had finally unravelled his matrimonial affairs. The Curtises' divorce having been made absolute in February, Liam and Margaret Barrington were finally married, a few weeks before the birth of their daughter Pegeen. He asked Garnett if he would like to be the godfather, though this was in a purely secular way, as the infant was not baptised at that time – she was later by members of his family.

Winter and the arrival of the baby had brought the family down from the hills to take a place nearer Dublin, at Hazelbrook in Kimmage to the south-west of the city. This combined the rural aspect of a dairy farm with nearness to the city; the Glenavys lived opposite. Here Liam wrote a new novel, *The Wilderness* – inspired by his mountain acres at Lackan Darragh, and his own feelings for nature – which was serialised in the *Humanist.* He imported the special atmosphere of Lackan and its woods into his story of a modern saint.

In January Cape published *Spring Sowing* as no. 26 in their new pocket series, the Travellers' Library, as distinctive of the 20s as Penguins would be of the 30s. (Joyce's *Dubliners* was no. 14, and George Moore would be no. 79. They and O'Flaherty were the only Irish authors in the series.) *Mr Gilhooley* was published in an expurgated edition, which Cape also brought out. Liam was still astute enough in generating controversy for publicity, as when in March he attacked Gogarty in a letter to the *Irish Statesman* in which he claimed that the conditions in the western Gaeltacht regions were the fault of the British. A month later the British Broadcasting Corporation invited him to read a story over their Belfast station. Liam shared the ambivalence of so many Irish writers about British cultural influences on Ireland.

In June his biography of Tim Healy was published, both in London and in New York. Many (among them Sean O'Casey) thought this to be an odd venture for O'Flaherty. Healy had been Governor-General of the Free State since December 1922, and was due to retire at the end of the year. Healy himself was undismayed. He told Max Beaverbrook that only fools would buy a book about him by a man he had never met, though it would now enable him to publish his own memoirs. Through his part in the downfall of Parnell, Healy had become an object of scorn to many of his countrymen (notably Joyce). O'Flaherty was less interested in the biographical exactness of his account than in capturing a certain sense of the nature of the Irish Free State which Healy seemed to epitomise. Liam had the help of a Republican friend, M.J. McManus ('My Fellow Worker' to whom the book is dedicated, later literary editor of de Valera's paper *The Irish Press),* and of A.J. Leventhal of TCD. They provided the background and research (from an antagonistic point of view), but the text was completely Liam's.

The conclusion of this, for him, off-beat book left him, according to Topsy, depressed – though he was lively enough to write about going to the new dog tracks at Shelbourne Park for the *Irish Statesman* in July.

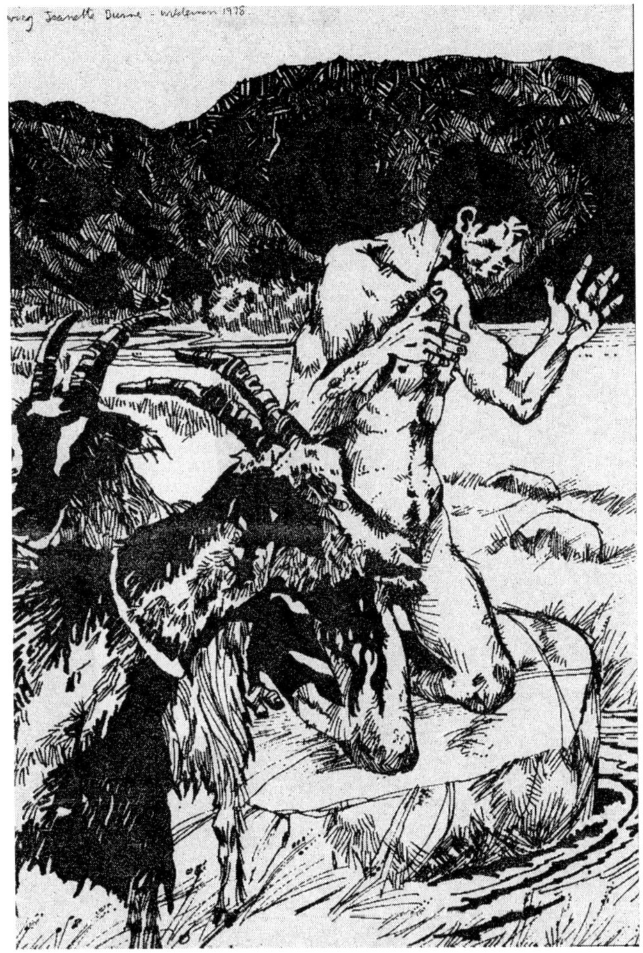

Above: *The goats Liam reared at his cottage inspired the background to his novel* The Wilderness. *Illustrated here by Jeanette Dunne from the 1978 Wolfhound edition.*

Opposite: *Liam playing his melodeon outside the cottage at Lackan Darragh in the Wicklow mountains.*

'Wolf Lanigan's Death' *by Liam O'Flaherty*

It was a frosty January night about ten o'clock. A large barge drawn by two horses was coming slowly down the canal nearing its destination at Portobello Bridge, Dublin. There was no moon, but now and again glaring lights from the tramcars that rattled over the Bridge lit up the dark waters of the Canal, the grey bulk of the barge, the taut rope, the narrow gravel path and the two lean horses walking slowly in single file with their heads drooping.

Then as the barge drew closer to the bank, Wolf Lanigan raised his head and shoulders behind the windlass in the bows and looked about him cautiously. 'Jump, towny,' cried the helmsman in a whisper. Wolf stood up suddenly, jumped on to the tarpaulin that covered the cargo, stooped and took a flying leap to the bank. He landed on his hands and knees, jumped to his feet, waved his hand to the barge and vaulted over the low concrete wall into the street beyond. He landed ankle deep in the mud beside the wall with a loud thud. The noise made him stiffen with his hands and back gripping the concrete wall. He listened for several seconds without breathing. Not a sound in the dark street but the squelching of the displaced mud. He ran crouching across the street and into a dark alleyway between two houses. At the far end there was a heap of rubbish and an upturned cart in a little wooden shed. He went on his hands and knees in the shed behind the cart, took an electric torch from the pocket of his loose raincoat and flashed it about. There was nothing but a heap of straw, a torn black hat lying in a corner, and an empty sack.

He switched off the torch and placed it in the cart. Then he took off his raincoat, a blue serge coat and a leather jacket. Lying between his shoulder blades on his white shirt was a Colt automatic pistol, bound by leather thongs around his neck and waist.

He loosed the thongs, placed the pistol in the cart, and dressed hurriedly. Then he switched on the torch again and placed it in the cart with the light towards him. He took the pistol, released the cartridge case, emptied the cartridges, wiped each one with a handkerchief, notched their heads with a clasp knife, returned them to the case and returned the case to the pistol. Then he switched off the light, put it in his pocket and jumped to his feet. He put the pistol in his left breast pocket, and with right hand on the butt he walked back into the street with stooping shoulders.

He crossed Dublin without stopping, following dark side streets, going under arches and through by-lanes. He passed over the Liffey at Butt Bridge and then hurried through a maze of slum streets until he reached Dublin's brothel quarter, north of Amiens Street. There he slackened his pace and went cautiously, stopping at every corner and convulsively pressing the butt of his pistol when anybody passed. At last he crossed a waste patch of ground that was strewn with bricks, heaps of debris and old pots and he came to the corner of Divis Street.

Peering around the corner of a deserted house at the end of the street a blaze of light struck him, running low to the ground in parallel lines until it ended in a dark lane at the far end. The light streamed from the open doorways of the two-storied brothels, shebeens, and dens of criminals on either side, while the second stories were in darkness, or with only a dim light showing through heavy blinds. The street was crowded with men and women, walking up and down and standing at the doorways, some drunk, staggering and quarrelling, others singing with clasped hands, others walking silently in couples with the measured tread of policemen. Strains of music and the sound of wild singing and still wilder laughter rose from the street in a strange inhuman melancholy roar to the still sky overhead. And yet in spite of the noise there seemed to be a deadly silence. The music, the singing, the banging of doors, the obscene curses, the drunken lascivious laughter came like a casual murmur heard from the bottom of a dark abyss.

The Wolf waited over five minutes, motionless, with his body pressed against the brick wall, watching the street. He could not move while those silent couples were pacing up and down steadily, seemingly intent on nothing but their thoughts. He knew their eyes would catch him slinking past, that guns would flash out, and deep voices bellow out 'hands up!'...

Then from the far end a young woman came staggering down the street, hanging on the arm of a young man. Her long, black hair flowed down about her shoulders. A loose dressing-gown was open to below her breasts. She laughed hysterically as she tried to brandish a bottle over her head. Then suddenly another woman rushed out at her from an open doorway. 'Let him go, you b –, he's mine.' A shriek, a sudden rush and the two women were at one another's throats. The whole street gathered around, shouting. 'Now's my chance,' muttered the Wolf.

He darted along the side of the street, passed the crowd and dived into a dark doorway at the far end. On tiptoe he passed a door on the right of the hall. Sounds of drunken revelry came through the door, sounds packed close together as of a pot boiling furiously. In the hall there was the silence and darkness of death. The Wolf drew his pistol and groped for the wall with his left hand. He couldn't see his hand. At last he found the wall. He slid along it, holding the pistol behind him, facing the street. His foot came in contact with a stairway. Noiselessly he mounted step after step, sideways, with the pistol behind. He reached a landing. The roof was so low that he had to stoop. Opposite him there was a gleam of light coming through the keyhole of a door. Catlike, lifting each foot carefully and planting it flat, he reached the door. He put his ear to the keyhole and listened. Then he knocked quietly, two double knocks. There was a noise of a bed creaking and then of slippers shuffling along a boarded floor. The door opened slightly and a woman's head appeared. 'Rosie,' hissed the Wolf.

'God!' ejaculated the woman, stepping back.

The Wolf darted in after her and closed the door gently and put his back to it. Turning the key with one hand, with his gun levelled, his eyes darted around the room. It was bare, low roofed, garret-like, with a table in the centre of the bare boarded floor. On the table was a white cloth with dirty crockery in a pile at one end. In the corner was a wide bed with the yellow quilt crushed, evidently where the woman had been lying on top of it. A coal fire burned brightly in the open grate. A lamp with a broken chimney hung on a nail on the wall. Not a sound was heard in the room but the lazy crackling of the fire and the distant heavy murmur from the street coming through the heavy blinds on the window. The air was heavy and thick.

The Wolf stood with his legs wide apart, crouching forward from the hips. His sallow face was contorted with excitement. A thick growth of black beard covered his square jaws and his lips. There was a patch of clotted blood over his right eye. His boots were caked with mud and there was a large rent in his right trouser leg below the raincoat, that covered his body from there to the throat. A grey tweed cap was pulled far down over his head. A bony hand covered with dirt gripped the pistol close to his hip. He stood squat, broad-shouldered, leaning forward, as if he were ready to jump through the window at the slightest sound.

The woman stood by the table staring at him with an expression of horror on her pale beautiful face. It was deadly pale. Even the open lips were pale and her large eyes were glassy and lifeless. A long plait of black hair was hanging over her right shoulder, trailing down the breast of her loose grey dressing-gown. Her hands clutched at the end of the plait. Her bare feet were stuck into a pair of heelless slippers. She stood, tall and motionless, staring wildly and intently at the Wolf's face, with compressed lips, as if hypnotized.

For several seconds they stood that way, the two of them, in the silent room. Then suddenly the Wolf spoke.

'Anybody been here?' His voice came in a hoarse, cracked whisper, the voice of a man who has spent sleepless nights in the winter air.

The woman tried to speak, swallowed something and shook her head.

'What the h-ll is the matter with ye?' hissed the Wolf through his yellow teeth. 'Aren't ye glad to see me? Eh! Has anybody been here? Ye know who I mean?'

He advanced towards her noiselessly and stood with the muzzle of his pistol pointed within an inch of her breast. But the woman, without a movement of her body and without taking her eyes from his face, just shook her head once more. Then she gasped, shivered, put her right hand to her forehead, and sank to a chair by the table, still looking at the Wolf, as if drawn by a magnet.

'Afraid of me? Eh?' said the Wolf opening his mouth wide and bursting into a noiseless laugh. His head and shoulders shook, but he made no sound. 'Do I look funny? Eh? Come on, move, an' get me somethin' t' eat. I'm starved. D'ye hear? Didn't eat this two days. Move, blast ye.'

He watched the woman get to her feet and walk to the cupboard near the fireplace. Then he moved on the flat of his feet to a chair by the table facing the door. He laid the pistol in front of him. The woman was putting a kettle on the fire.

'Don't mind that kettle, I tell ye,' he said. 'Give me somethin' t' eat. I don't want any tea. Haven't ye got any grub?'

Without a word she dropped the kettle and went back again to the cupboard. The Wolf took off his cap. His forehead was bald and sloped straight back from the eyes. There was another large patch of congealed blood where the bald spot met the hair near the top of his skull. He put his fingers to it and ground his teeth with pain. The woman put a pork pie, bread, butter and milk on the table. She moved mechanically, using only one hand, as if driven by an alien will to do something hateful. And all the time her lifeless eyes strayed to the Wolf's face. Without looking at her the Wolf began to eat ravenously. Every time a shout came from the street, he started, looked around wildly and grabbed his pistol. The woman stood by the fireplace, with her hands folded on her breast, motionless, her eyes fixed on his face.

Then he finished eating, licked his fingers and looked at the woman. His small grey eyes roamed over her face and his under lip protruded.

'Why the h-ll don't ye say somethin'?' he snarled. 'Ye heard about the racket in Mullingar, didn't ye?'

The woman's lips quivered, but she didn't speak. He jumped up, and gripped her by the right shoulder and pointed the gun at her breast.

'Listen to what I'm goin' to tell ye. I'm goin' to tell ye somethin' that'll wake ye up, dosey. D'ye know where I went four days ago? Eh? Well, me an' Chris

Moloney an' the Bull Kelly went to raid a bank in Mullingar. The cops followed us from here, see? Somebody gev the game away. Chris an' the Bull got pinched, an' I'd have got pinched too, only I plugged a cop. I plugged a man, Rosie, d'ye hear? Shot him dead. Been two days comin' down in a canal boat. I'm wanted for murder, d'ye hear?'

The woman nodded her head several times and pointed to a newspaper that lay in the coal-scuttle. The Wolf darted over and picked it up. On the front page in large headlines it ran:

MULLINGAR BANK HELD UP

DETECTIVE SERGEANT CARNEY SHOT DEAD.

And underneath was the Wolf's photograph.

The Wolf swore softly, crushed the paper into a ball and stamped on it. Then he turned once more to the woman. His nostrils were expanding and contracting.

'Listen. They aren't goin' to get me by – ' He pulled out the cartridge case from the pistol. 'They are all dum-dum. An' one is for mesel' and another for you. See? The rest is for the gang that comes to take me. Un'erstan'?'

There were beads of sweat on his swarthy forehead. The woman never moved or spoke. But her eyes became larger and the skin around her lips tightened. Swearing frightfully the Wolf took a bottle of whiskey from the cupboard and held it up to the light. It was nearly full. He wrenched out the cork with his teeth and drank deeply. Then he sat down again at the table facing the door, his left hand clutching the bottle, his right on his pistol butt. The woman drew a chair to the fire and sat down, still watching him.

The Wolf began to drink, starting at every noise; and between drinks he stared at the table, his eyes narrowed, his forehead wrinkled into deep furrows; as if his brain were struggling with some intricate problem. The silence in the room was intense. Then gradually the Wolf's face relaxed. He began to move his limbs and nod his head. Then he struck the table with his fist, put the bottle to his head and emptied it and got to his feet. His body swayed slightly and there was a slight mist before his eyes. With his foot he drew his chair beside the woman's. He was careless now about making a noise. He sat down with a flop. He still had the gun in his hand. He put his arm around her waist. She looked into the fire and shivered.

'Say, Rosie.' His voice was loud and hoarse and there was an attempt at merriment in it. 'Be nice to me. Won't ye? Ain't I been a good pal to ye? Eh? Be the lumpin' Moses didn't I pick ye up in O'Connell Street, half starved, after that sojer friend o' yours deserted ye? Amn't I after keepin' ye here two months, an' ye never had to go out once an' bring in any money same as any other girl. Eh? Ain't ye goin' to kiss me, Rosie?'

The woman never moved. He staggered against her and pressed his lips to her white cheek. She shuddered.

'Divil take ye. Yer like a dead thing. Is it how ye think I haven't got any money?' He fumbled at his shirt and pulled out a wad of bank-notes tied with a string. 'There's three hundred there. See? It takes the Wolf to get away with 'em. See? We're goin' to have a good time on them, Rosie. Me an' you, Rosie. See? Soon as these cops are off the hunt, we'll ship across t' England. See? They ain't goin' to get me. See?' He jumped to his feet, suddenly furious. 'Who's goin' to get me?' His voice came like a hiss between his teeth. Then he growled like a wild animal and stalked about the room with his gun levelled. 'See? I'm the Wolf Lanigan. The Wolf. D'ye hear?'

Suddenly he staggered and put his hand to his head.

'Blast it, my head is goin' round. Must have a sleep.' He moved over to the woman and whispered, 'Rosie, I'm goin' to lie down. See? You keep watch.'

He tumbled on to the bed and lay on his back with the pistol in his right hand across his chest. The woman's eyes were fixed on the fire. She sat immovable. The Wolf's eyes began to shut, but as soon as a noise came from outside, he started up and grabbed his pistol. Then gradually a weariness seized his limbs. They became listless. The weariness crept up into his head. His eyes shut. His mouth fell open. The hand slipped off the butt of the pistol. He began to snore. He was asleep.

Then slowly the woman turned her head around towards the bed and looked at him. Her eyes opened wide like the eyes of a child brought face to face with something strange and tremendous. Gradually a look of wonder spread over her face. Her lips were parted, showing her white teeth. She stood up with her hands down by her sides. The dressing-gown slipped from her shoulders. Mechanically she slipped her hands from the sleeves and let it fall to the ground. She stood in her nightdress, her hair plaited, white like an apparition. She walked over to the bed, moving straight and stiff. She stood over the bed looking down at the Wolf's face.

Then a strange, ghastly smile crept over her lips and cheeks without touching the eyes. The eyes became cold and glassy; two large discs lit with an immeasurable hatred, while her lips smiled. Her right hand moved forward slowly until it reached the pistol. Slowly the fingers crept around the butt. Then the smile faded from her lips. Her eyeballs started from the sockets. Her teeth bared. She drew in a deep breath, pressed the pistol to the Wolf's chest and pressed the trigger.

There was a deafening roar as bullet after bullet crashed through the sleeper's breast. Then in the silence that followed, the rattling of the window, the fragments of the lamp falling to the floor sounded like the dying echo of a thunder-clap. The woman turned, dropped the smoking pistol to the floor and burst into a wild shriek of insane laughter. Then there was silence again. Little clouds of smoke roamed about the ceiling. The figure on the bed was still.

O'Flaherty did not often pause to be painted – this sympathetic portrait is by his friend Harry Kernoff, himself a man of radical views. He shows the O'Flaherty of the late 1930s, at the height of his fame, with an insignia of the Republican movement on his lapel, and a black beret that nods to his support of Republican Spain.

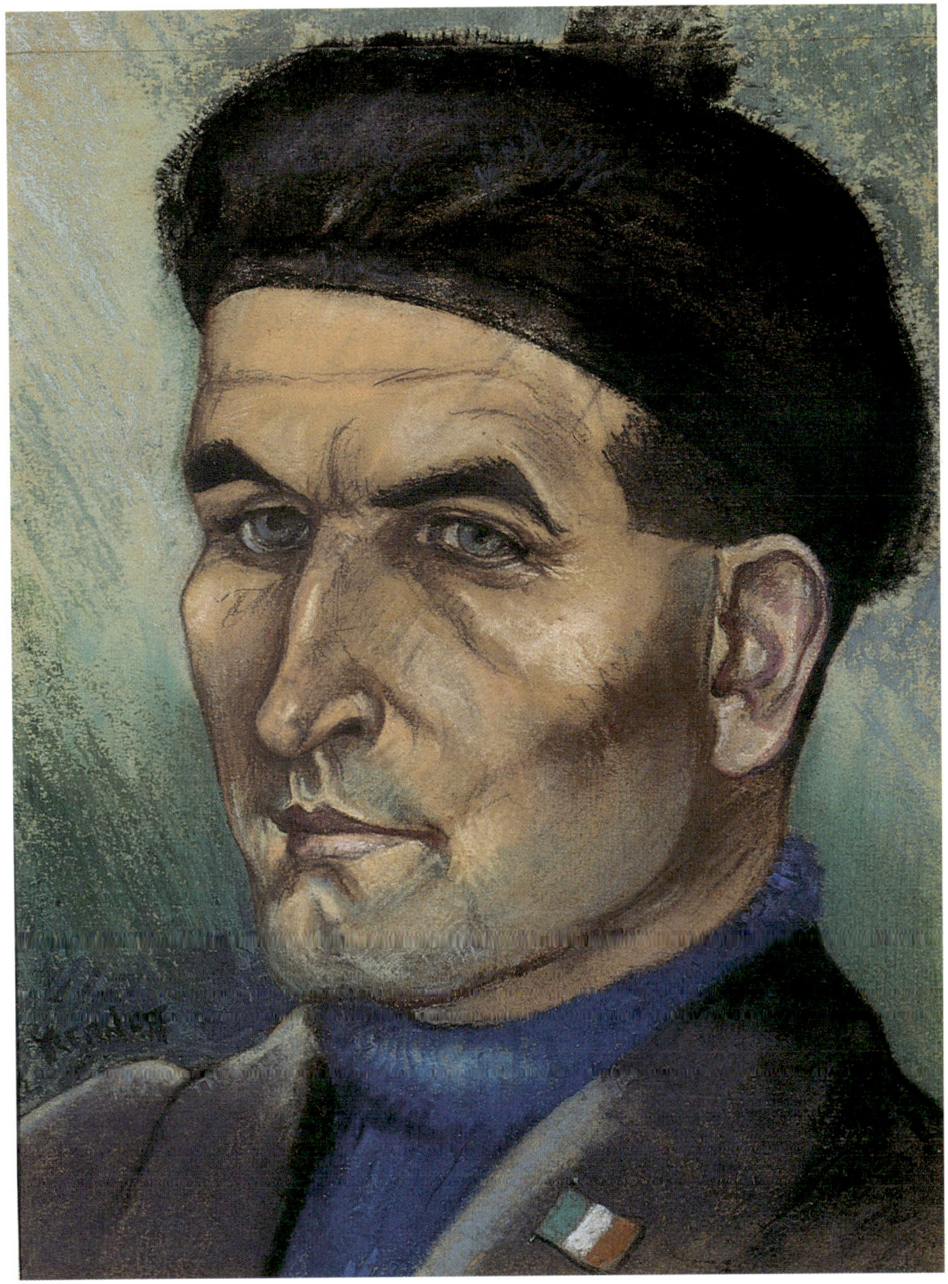

At last she appeared noiselessly at the door, clad like a nun, all in white. But as she advanced across the floor, it appeared that her feet were bare. And then through his mist-covered eyes, he saw that she wore nothing but the veil, that her body, as she moved, showed through its folds, like something passing behind a curtain. She came towards him dancing, moving the folds of the veil, so that they unfolded slowly, as she danced. He did not see her dance and did not know whether it was beautiful or not. He only watched the gradual disclosure of her beautiful body, appearing from beneath the veil. Then with a cry, she dropped the veil and stood quite naked before him, shielding her eyes with her hands.

from *Mr Gilhooly*

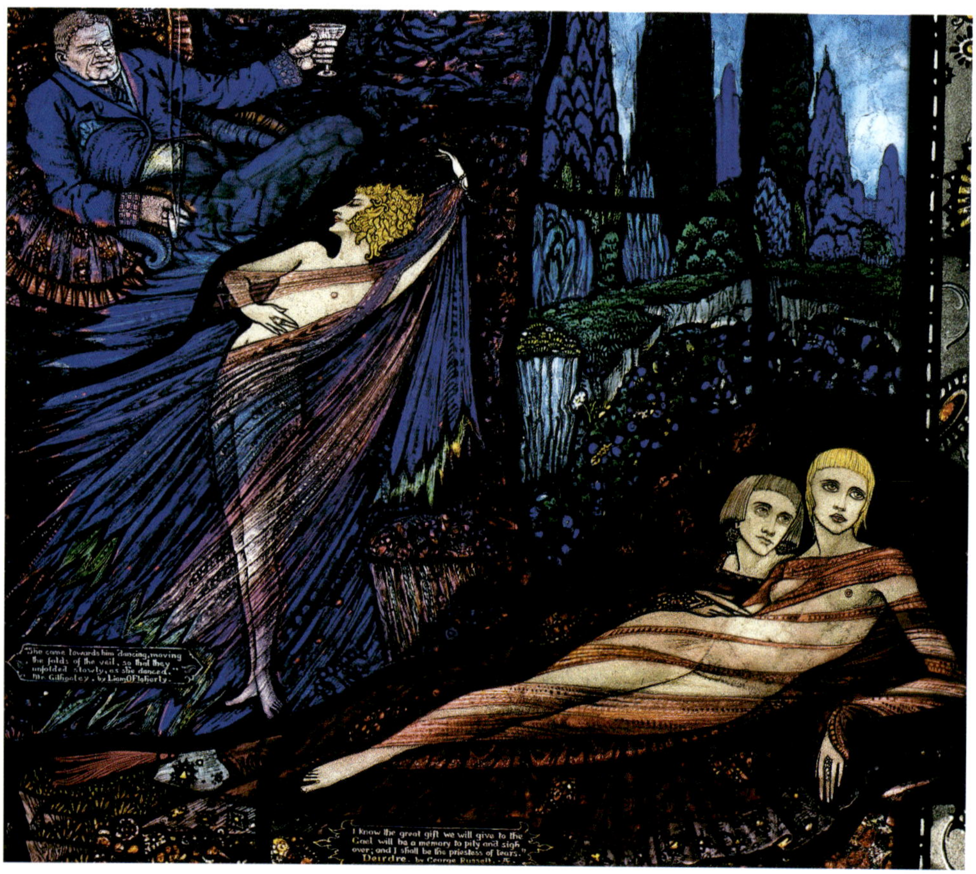

Right: *O'Flaherty's grim novel of Dublin life,* Mr Gilhooly, *inspired one of the panels of Harry Clarke's great masterpiece originally intended to be Ireland's gift to the League of Nations – but this scene was thought to provide the wrong image of Irish life! (see page 74). On the right is a scene from James Stephens' novel* Deirdre, *which must also have added to official concern.*

Left: *The clashes of cultures in Ireland often provided O'Flaherty with moments of comedy. By the 1950s the invading culture had become American – here Hollywood disturbs the life and emotions of a small western village in a contemporary illustration of his story 'The Post Office'.*

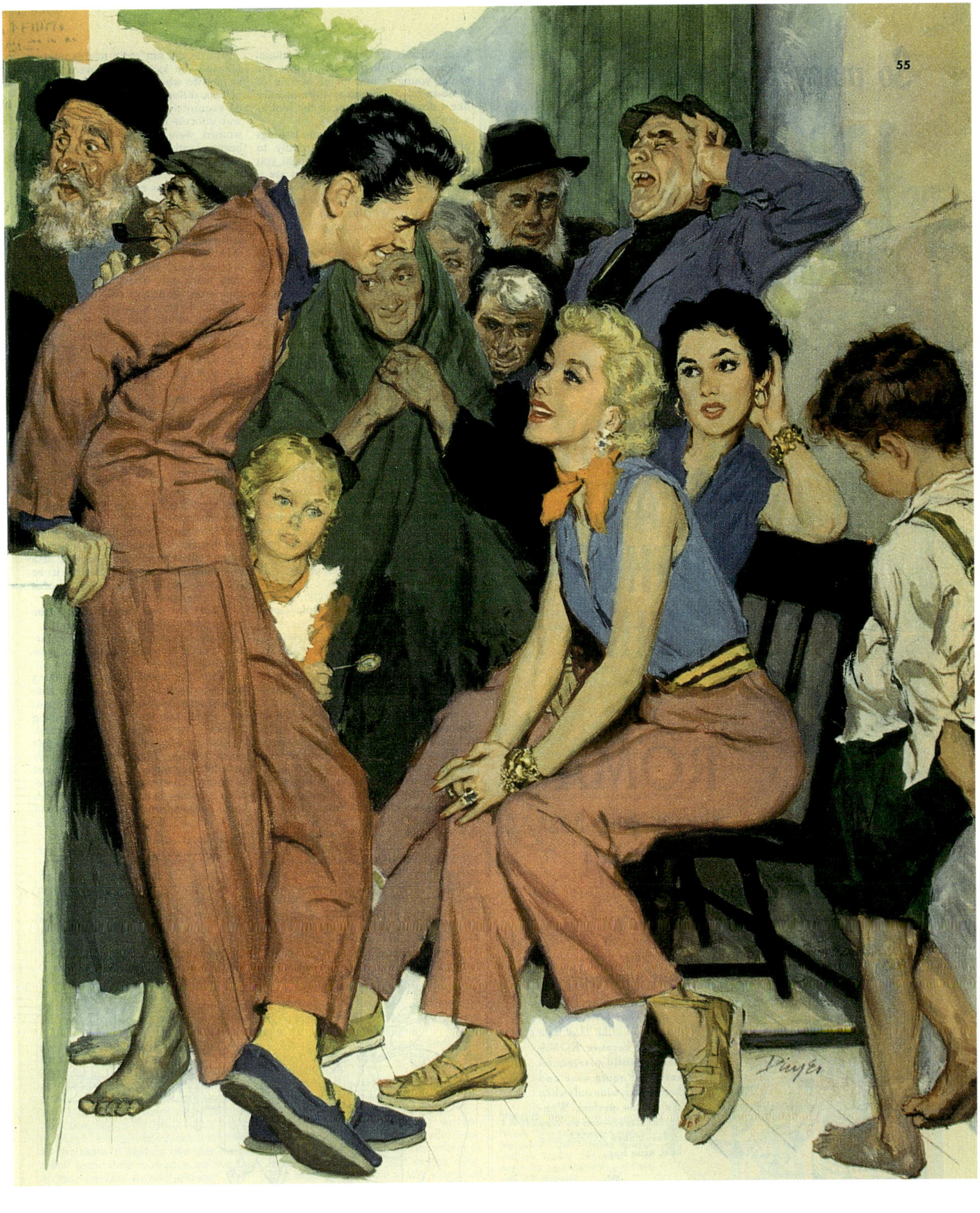

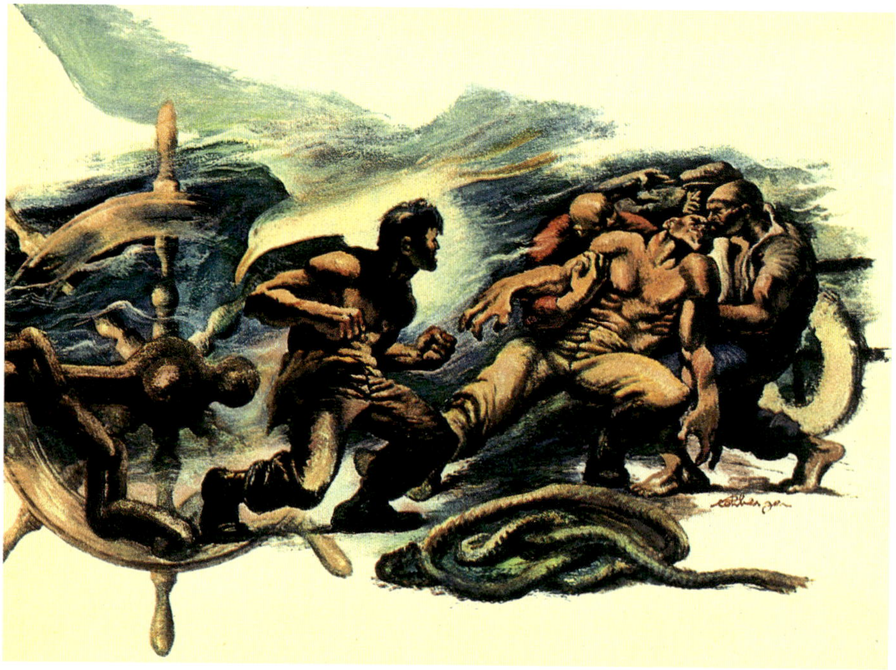

Top: *His stories reflect themes of male violence – here (illustrated for him by an American artist) the savage life of sailors too long at sea, which he had experienced for himself in his world-wide wanderings in the 1920s.*

Below: *But he recognised that violence, often casual, can also change in a moment to love, as here in his story of the charged relationship of a boy and his father on a pig buying trip in 'The Blow'.*

Opposite: *Religion once entered into every aspect of Irish life, especially on Aran. Below, almost from a Sean Keating painting, Aran Islanders crowd into the chapel – but O'Flaherty reacted violently against this aspect of the life of the people he loved.*

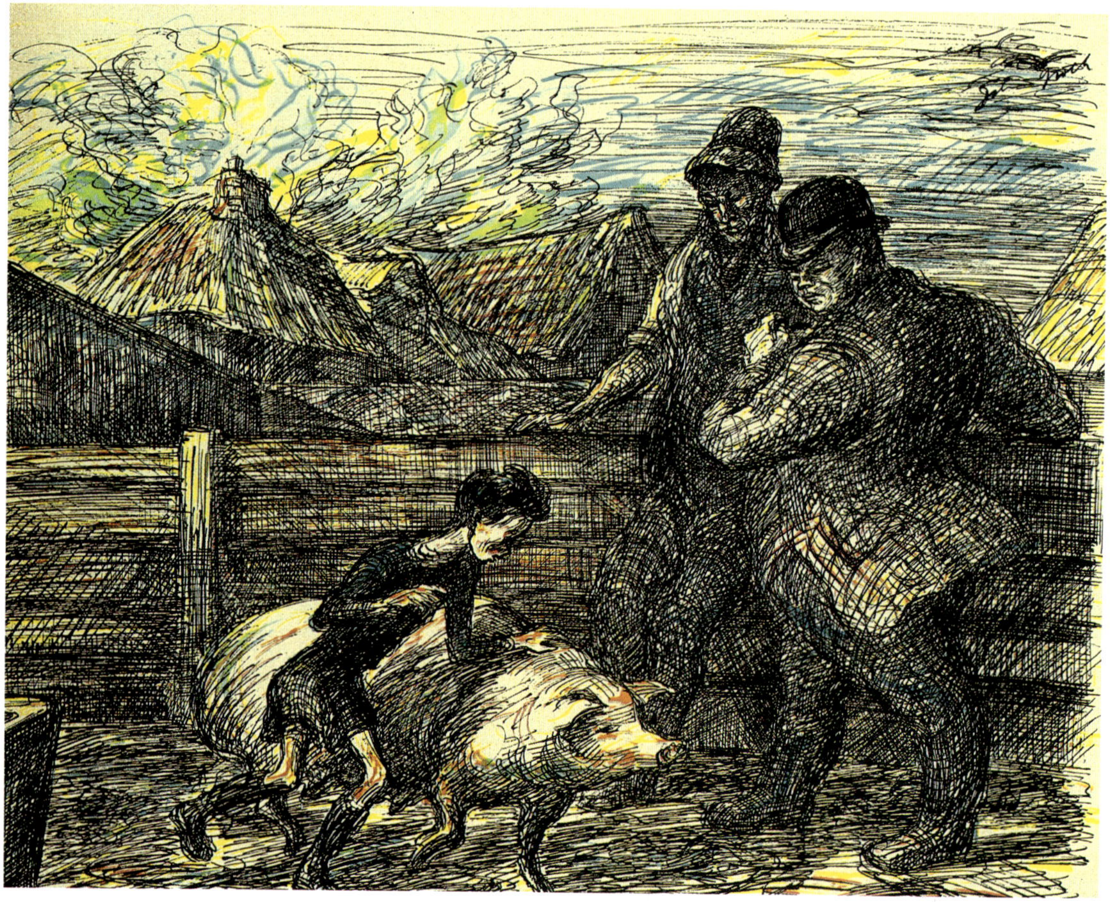

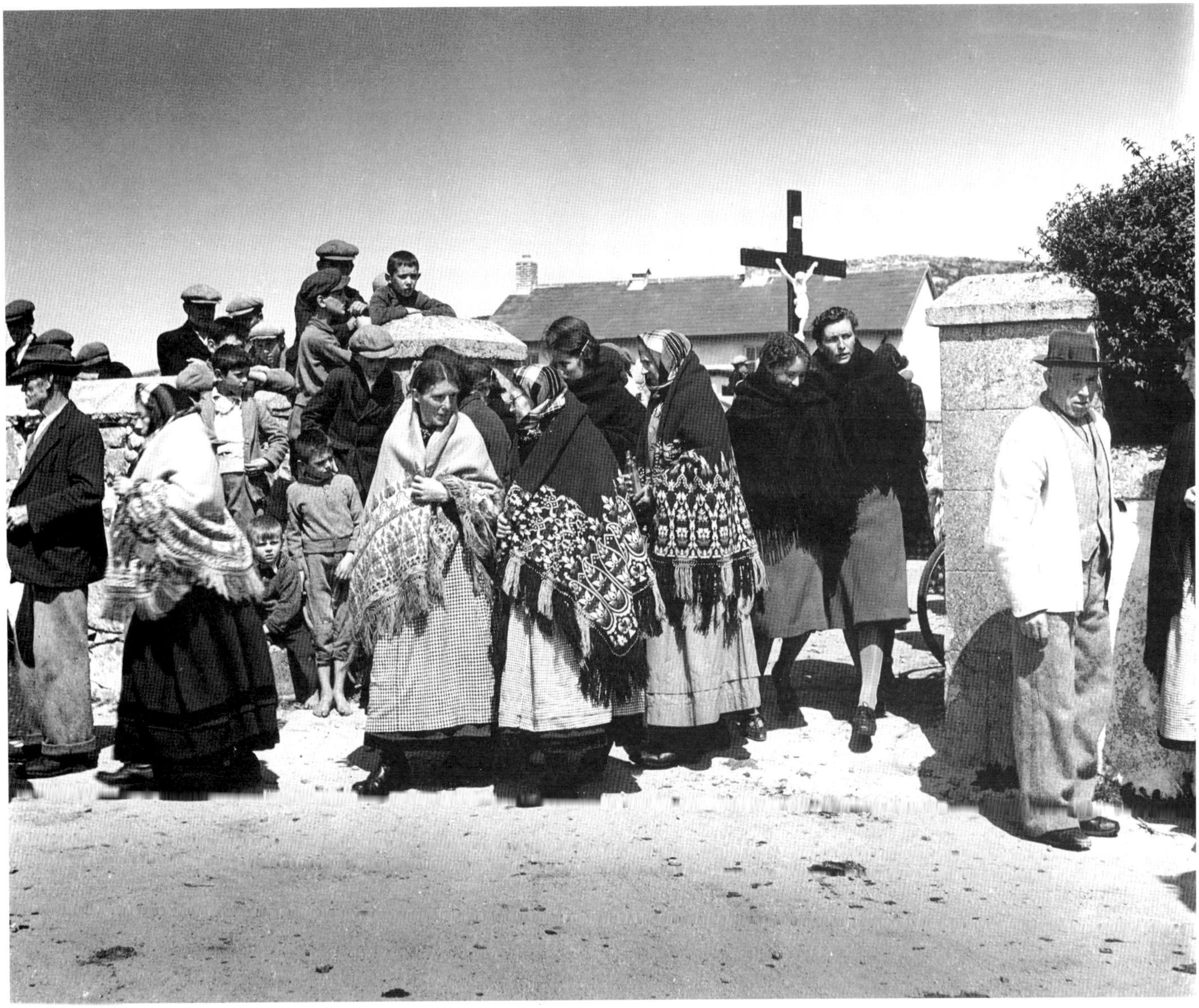

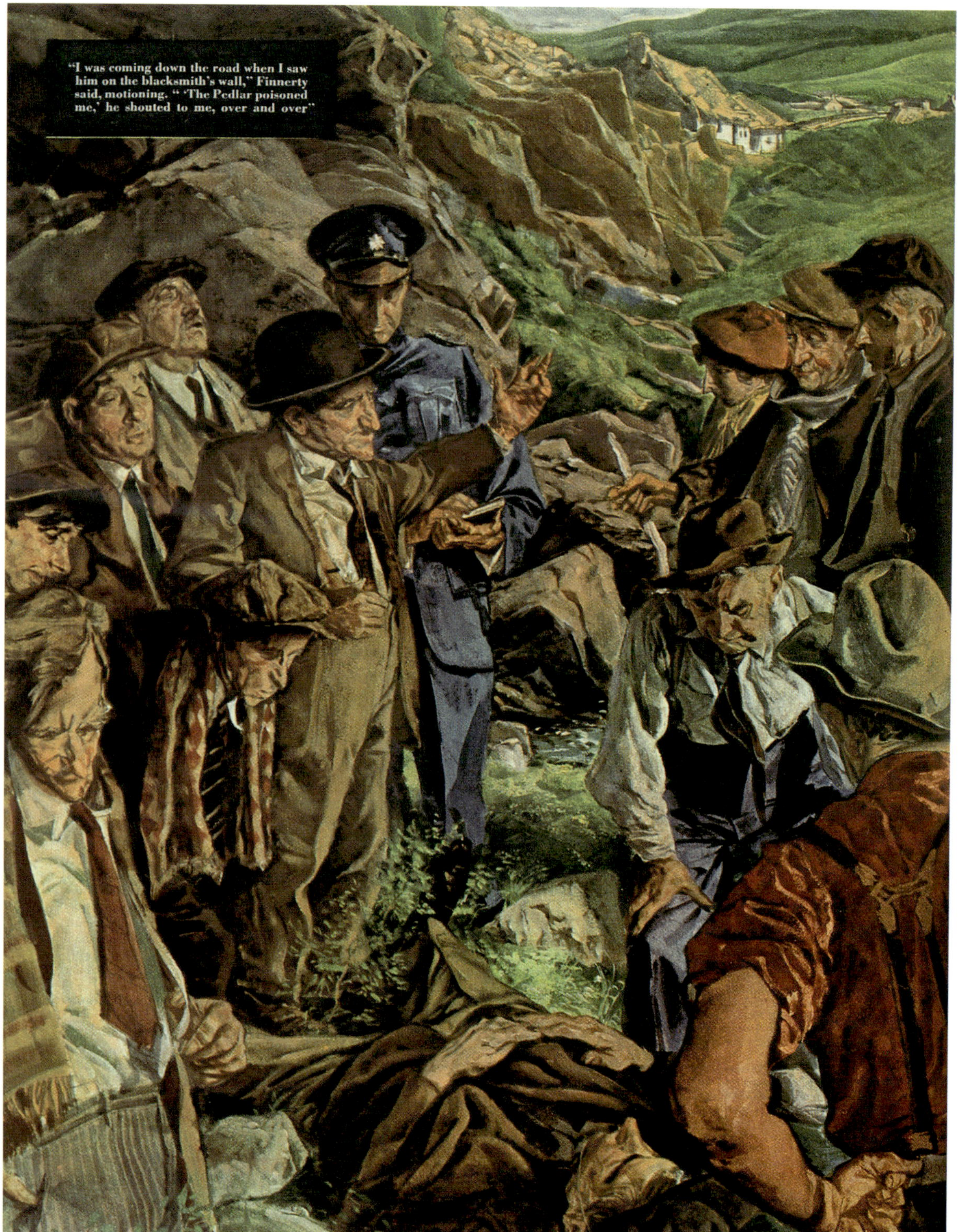

"I was coming down the road when I saw him on the blacksmith's wall," Finnerty said, motioning. " 'The Pedlar poisoned me,' he shouted to me, over and over"

Left: *Feuds and violent revenge – themes common throughout O'Flaherty's writings – are here illustrated in a late story, 'The Pedlar's Revenge'. For O'Flaherty, death, even murder, had a natural place in the landscape of Irish life.*

Below: *The great passions and small triumphs of O'Flaherty's men and women were played out against a landscape filled with reminders of past loss and failure, of death and emigration, themes which O'Flaherty movingly treated in his last historical novels, especially in his great masterpiece* Famine.

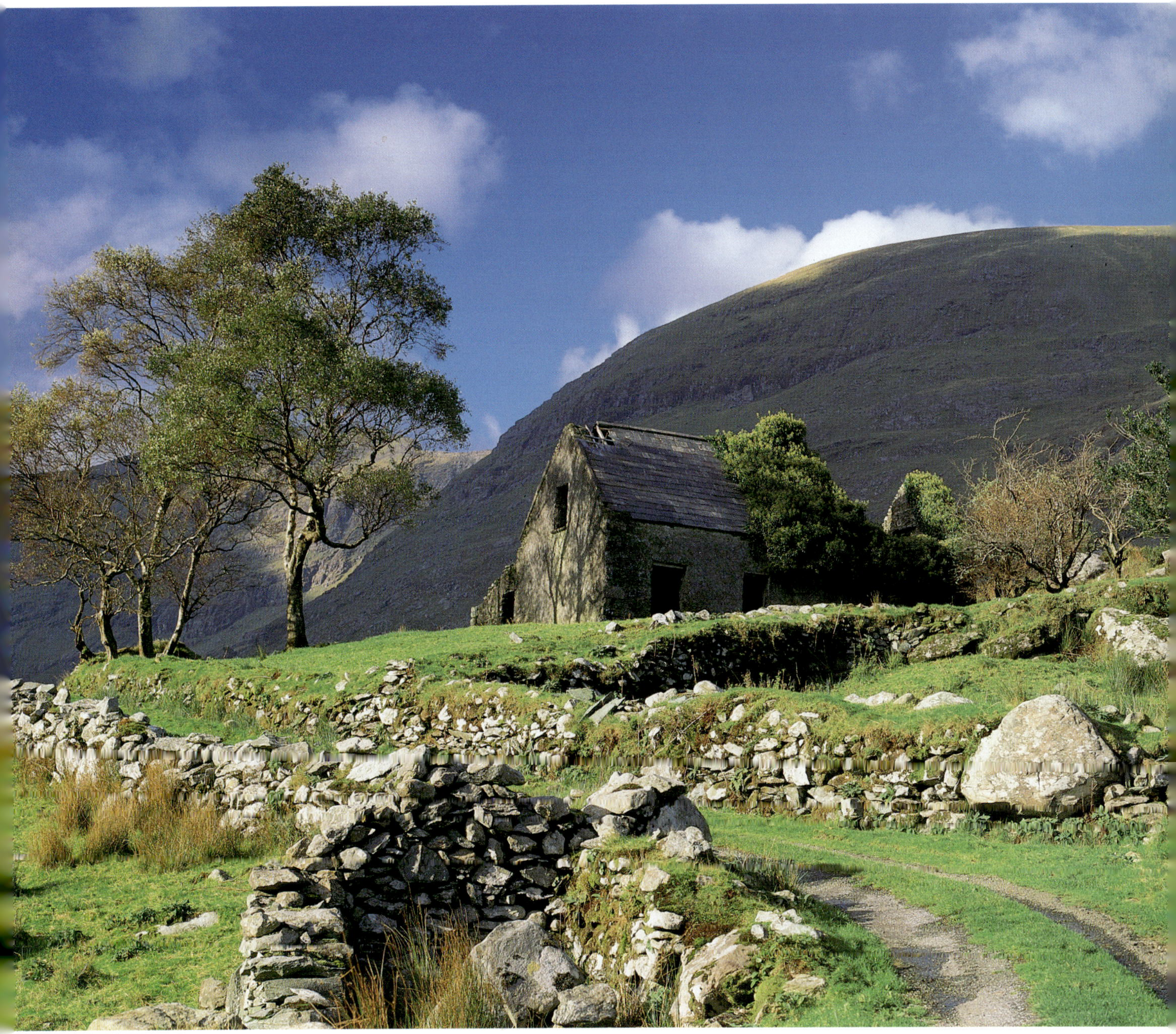

Suddenly the form of the two trees gripped his soul. Something rushed from every corner of his body, from his legs, stomach, head, hands and heart, to the centre of his chest and then straightforward to the trees. For a moment he was spellbound. Then his brain cleared. It seemed to make a noise like a screen being swept hurriedly from a window. He saw the two trees stand out against the background of blue sky, with darkness between him and the trees, and between the trees and the sky. He forgot they were trees. They appeared to be alive ... Then his eyes smiled tenderly and sadly. He tiptoed up to the right tree. He put his arms around the dark dewy trunk. He kissed it. Then he rushed headlong back to his fiancée.

From 'Beauty' in *Spring Sowing*

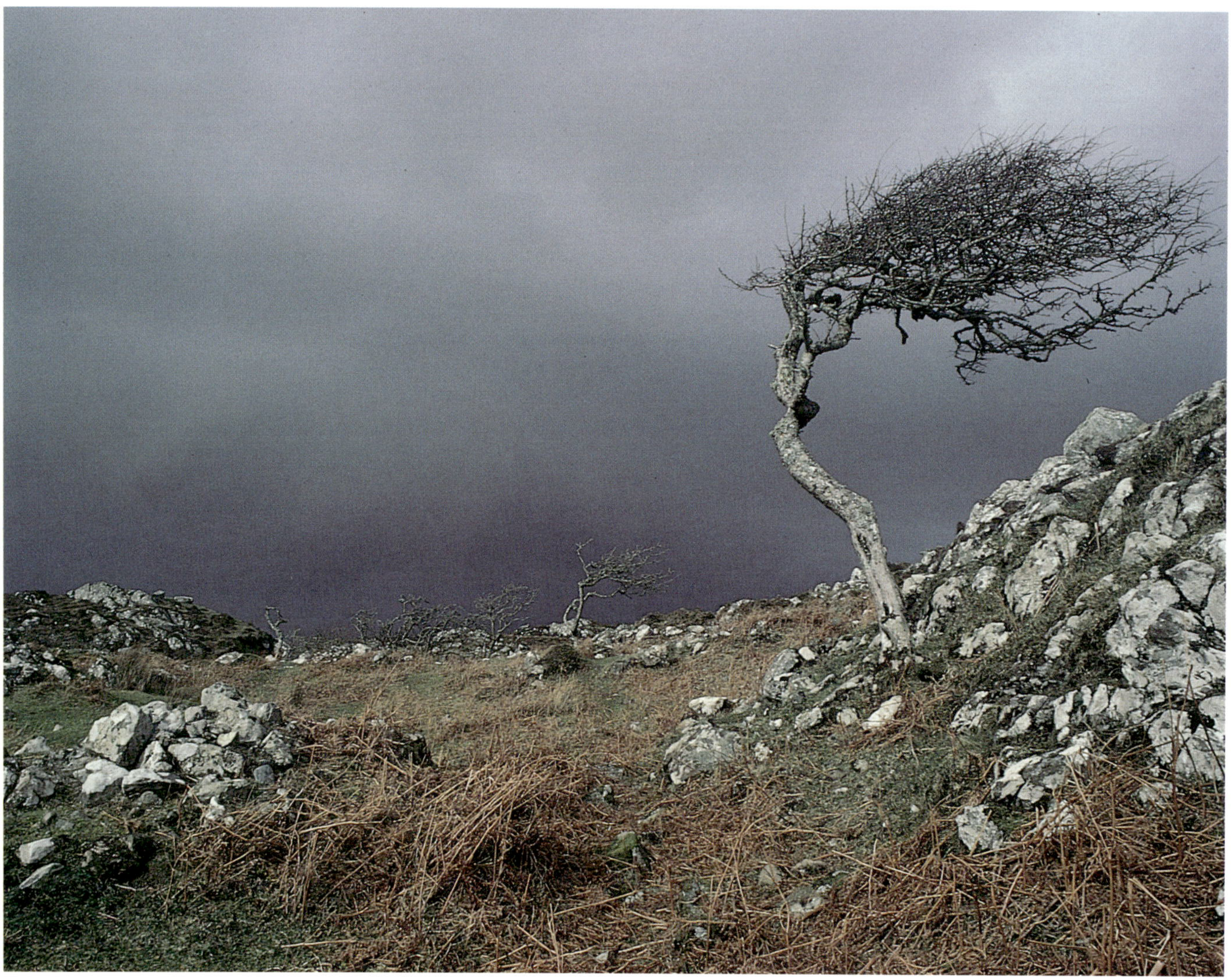

THE BRUTAL PART OF LIFE The Free State was severely shocked when, on 10 July, Kevin O'Higgins – Healy's nephew – was murdered by gunmen while walking to mass near his home in Booterstown. This was widely thought to be revenge by Republicans for his exaggerated role in the executions of the Civil War four years before. The government responded with an Act that forced de Valera to take up his Dáil seats won at the election in August. The state funeral was a great occasion, at which many groups in the national life of the country turned out (including, ominously, a party of Fascists from the Italian community wearing their black shirts).

Liam spent his usual August break in Aran. Then he and his wife visited the Garnetts at Pond Street. Garnett now had an opportunity to read Liam's new novel, which had been inspired by the O'Higgins murder, and Liam was grateful for his trenchant criticism. But he could still put work aside so as not to miss the visit to Ireland of the New Zealand rugby team. Rugby was a passion from his schooldays at Blackrock which lasted to the the end of his life. The final version of *The Assassin* was begun in December, a month which also saw the publication from Crosby Gaige of another of their limited editions – *The Fairy Goose*. Twelve copies were printed on green paper, in honour of the author's motherland.

His relations with that motherland had been called into question by Una Dix and Padraic Colum, and Liam publicly explained in a letter to the *Irish Statesman* why it was he did not write in Gaelic. He and Ó Conaire had indeed wanted to write plays in Gaelic but had been defeated by the money question. Money was always a problem for Liam. In the new year there was talk of selling film rights, and of writing a satirical guide to Ireland. When his novel appeared it was dedicated not, as promised, to Edward Garnett, but 'To my creditors'. Though it was to have two British impressions, as well as an American edition, Liam felt that Cape were not pushing his work. He explained to a reporter for the *Daily Mail* at the time, 'I must keep very quiet here, work to pay my debts and then get back home next spring in time for Punchestown.'

His friend Cecil Salkeld provided illustrations for *Red Barbara* when it was published in an expensive limited edition in August. The three stories ranged over themes of sex, civil war, the sea and nature – the key themes of all Liam's writing. But in fact he gained more by such things as the publication of *The Black Soul* as no. 99 in the Travellers' Library, and by the appearance of translations of his books in French and German. The German version of *The Informer* was done by a new friend, Heinrich Hauser, whom Liam had met in Dublin through an old army friend, Patrick Kirwan, and whom he had helped with the making of a film report on the social conditions of Dublin and the Free State.

The film rights to *The Informer* were finally sold for £750 to British International, who saw the film as one of their most ambitious. There were now feelings at Cape that Liam was a difficult author. They had persuaded him not to publish one book, and to make cuts in others, and a new contract would have to reflect this, they told his agent in September 1928.

Liam, however, had departed for France, where Stock were publishing *Le Denonciateur*. There, with Sean O'Faolain, he met James Joyce. He attended a party at the Joyces' with Caresse and Harry Crosby, who were publishing a fragment of 'Work in Progress'. Hauser was also present (though Caresse described him as Swedish). To Nino Franck Liam described Joyce as 'the Playboy of the Western World'. It may have been at this

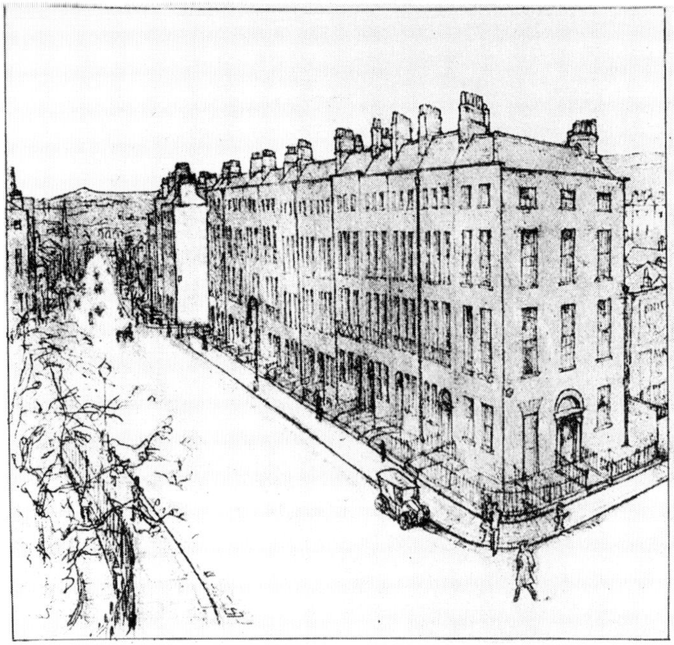

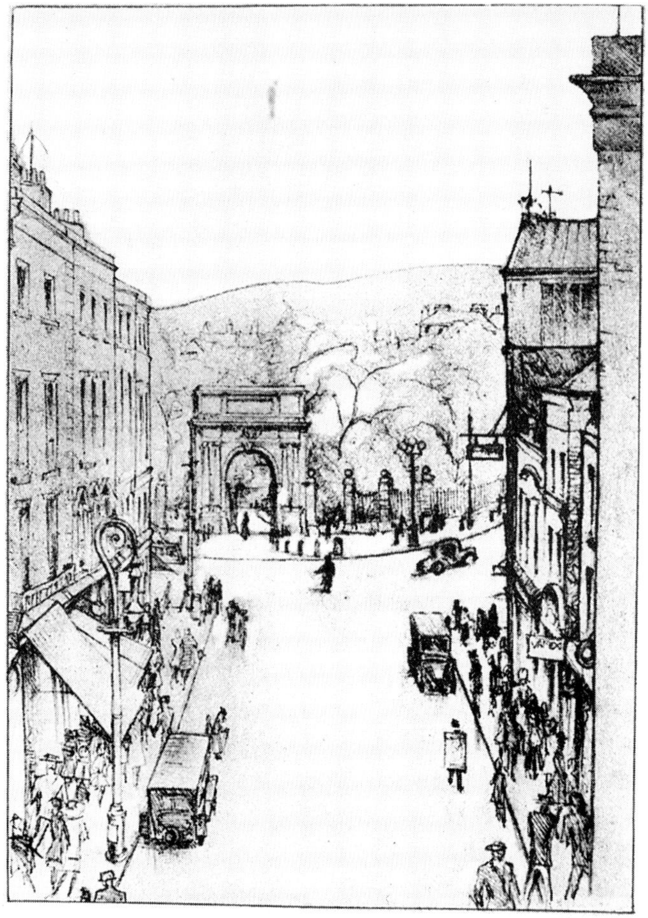

The two sides of Dublin life, reflected in O'Flaherty's novels Mr Gilhooley *and* The Puritan, *drawn by Hilda Roberts in 1927: fashionable Grafton St.* (top right), *and the slums of Gardiner St.* (top left) *and Mountjoy Square.*

Kevin O'Higgins (bottom left) *whose murder in 1927 inspired O'Flaherty's novel* The Assassin *(1928). AE, the poet George Russell* (bottom right), *an early and influential admirer of O'Flaherty's work. The poet and novelist Austin Clarke* (bottom centre), *one of the group who protested along with O'Flaherty against Sean O'Casey's play* The Plough and the Stars.

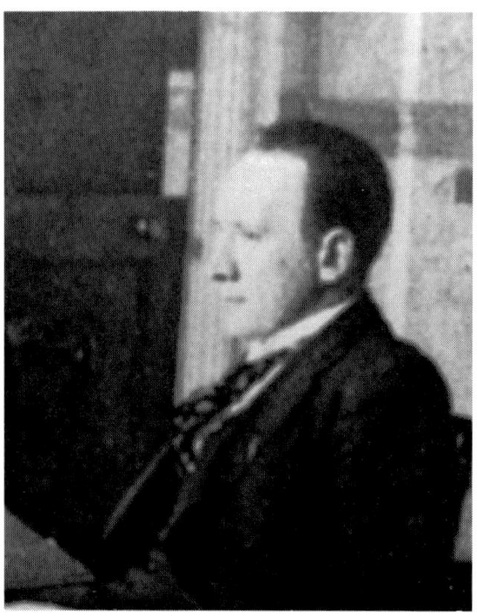

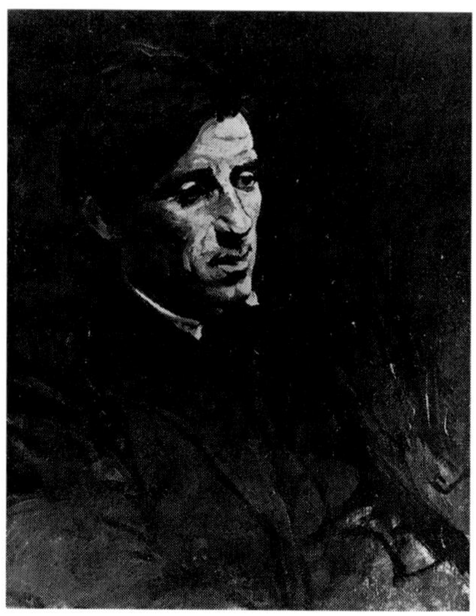

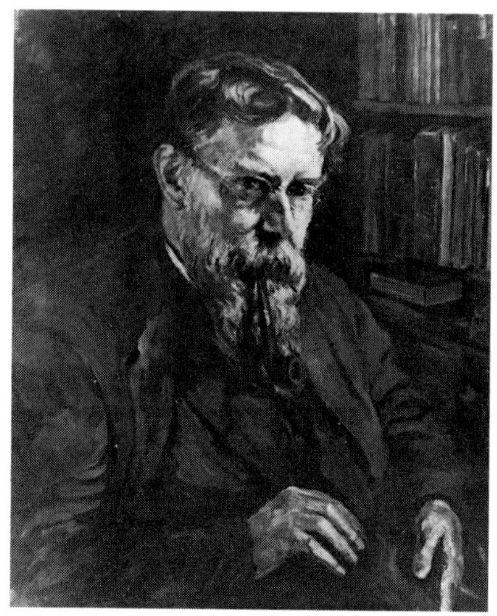

Introduction by Liam O'Flaherty to D.C. Grant's The Back-to-Backs *(1930)*

This is a terrifying novel. It is the first one published by the author, of whom I know nothing, except that his name is Grant. And the *milieu* of the novel is almost as vague as the identity of the author. As it were, from out a gloomy valley, where there is no sun, no song, no laughter, overcast by clouds, dripping with fog, comes suddenly a voice crying out a prophecy of desolate doom. That makes it still more sinister.

It is a terrible warning to every thinking man. For if this abject slavery exists among us, if we allow vast hordes of our people to live in such a manner, more corrupt, more filthy, more bestial than cave-dwellers in primeval times, then the crash of our civilization can only be avoided by an immediate revolution.

When I read of these miners and am forced to look at their nakedness by the power of this writer's work, I feel overwhelmed by the ugliness of our civilization and I feel that I too am responsible for such misery, since I do not take a stone and hurl it into the machinery of the social organism that wills such slavery. I feel that I can never again escape from the consciousness that such abject slavery exists, that I am dragged down by it into a black despair, hopelessness, death. So that its ugliness and its bestiality corrupts and darkens the glittering vanity of the cultured rich who live in idleness on its proceeds. Ascot, Cowes, Mayfair, the Riviera, gambling, expensive drunkenness, tables to load which the world has been scoured, gilded Eros twisting in the grip of perverse passions, all these are stripped and shown to be rotten, foetid, barren of joy. For the brute bellowing of the doomed slaves comes rumbling all the while, threatening.

Calvin did not speak of hell with equal force, for in his time there was no earthly hell of equal torments. In his time the world still contained untrodden places, to which slaves could escape. Now there is no escape but through the bloody doors of revolution.

What will the purse-proud hypocrites who revelled in the exposure of Indian barbarism by such books as *Mother India* make of *Back-to-Backs*, which is an exposure of more loathsome barbarism in hedge-rowed, lawned and Christian England? Those people who roll their sanctimonious eyes in horror when they read of slavery abroad should be forced to read this book, which shows them the fruits of their 'humanity.'

If one could only believe that such denunciation is exaggerated it would be well. But alas! it smells terribly of truth. It is the truth. It seems that every honest man, taking up a pen to write, must now tell in brutal fashion of the brutality of our economic governance. D.H. Lawrence, T.F. Powys, Rhys Davies, James Hanley, all our best writers of the present day have done what Grant is beginning to do. They cry out against the tyranny of ugliness.

Critics will go on arguing that beauty cannot come from ugliness; that literature, if it is art, must eschew a preponderance of gloomy scenes, crudity, violence and all manner of lewd excess. But literature in all ages must concern itself with life. The sincere writer must be truthful to the urge that makes him write, and if his world is ugly, let the critics remodel it so that they may get novels as pretty as their tastes.

In any case what do the critics know of life? How do they live, those cynical, superior fellows who always sneer at realism, unless it be the realism of the boudoir and studio variety, the psycho-analytic tosh that preoccupies the majority of our intellectuals? Let them quit their cottages in Sussex, their villas in France, their flats in St. John's Wood. Let them go among the masses, in factory towns, in docks, mines, army barracks, ships, jails, workhouses, asylums. Then they will realize that the vitality of this modern world has fled the cottage, the villa and the boudoir. Power is in the shrieking, smoking machine. It is a rough power, gaunt, raucous, bellowing, a spitting, swearing, violent power, but even so, it is more admirable in spite of its barbaric violence than the languid homosexuality and lesbianism which is the sole stock-in-trade of its alternatives.

'Where is England going?' said Trotsky.

This young writer seems to me to answer:

'England is doomed unless –'

And yet if she continues to produce artists of such promise, of such vigour and courage, there is hope that she will rise from her apathy, from her subterranean prisons, from her smoke-belching factories, from her teeming slums, and that she will shake off the languid decadents who loll upon her back.

party that Liam asked Arthur Power who a girl on the other side of the room was: she had agreed to met him at the Gare Saint-Lazare. Power was shocked: did O'Flaherty not realise that the girl was Joyce's daughter, Lucia? Liam also met James Stephens, again with Joyce, and Stephens repeated to him Villiers de l'Isle Adam's remark from *Axel* that 'as for living, our servants would do that'. This was not a maxim of Liam's. Joyce, however, must have been curious to meet the biographer of Tim Healy, about whom he had composed his first published work in 1892. With the appearance of *Le Denonciateur* and *Monsieur Gilhooley* Liam had become a well-known, even celebrated Irish novelist in France.

Liam travelled south – in October he was in the Alpes Maritimes. In Nice he met with R.P. Stephensen (later owner of the Mandrake Press, publisher of several of Liam's books), then trying to interest Aldous Huxley and D. H. Lawrence in a radical paper to be called *The Red Rag*. It may have been at this time, too, that Liam visited Roy Campbell at Martigues. It seems likely that they had already met in London, as Campbell later recalled how he and Liam had inveigled two girls away from a nightclub and got them into a taxi, in which they had forgotten they had already stowed their wives.

Possibly, too, it was then or even earlier that Liam met D.H. Lawrence – who alludes to him in a letter to the Glenavys. Lawrence was musing on visiting Ireland, among the attractions of which were not only the Glenavys but also Liam O'Flaherty.

Hauser had translated Liam's work into German; Liam now returned the favour by providing a preface for *Bitter Waters* when it appeared in America and in London (from a communist publisher, in a translation by their friend Patrick Kirwan). *The Assassin*, too, had appeared in German. A collection of stories was in progress; it would appear as *The Mountain Tavern* in April. The agreement for the satirical guide to Ireland was signed and the book duly appeared in June 1929. It

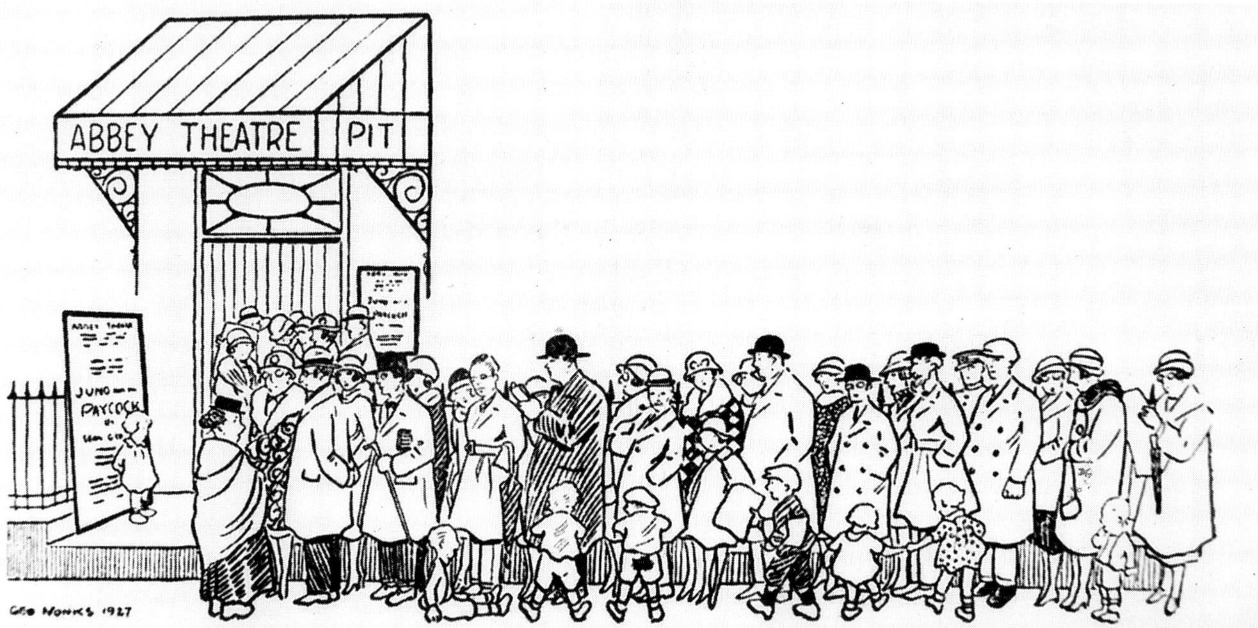

Below: *Controversial plays by Sean O'Casey drew record crowds to the Abbey Theatre, despite the protests of O'Flaherty and others.*

created a sensation in Ireland, though not the civil war that Liam had hoped for. His trenchant criticism of the priests, publicans, politicians and peasants of whom the Free State consisted was highly coloured but of a piece with his long-held views. This was brought out by Stephensen at the Mandrake Press. He sent a copy to Lawrence a little later – though Lawrence thought such pieces were a waste of time for writer and publisher.

During the summer John Huston wanted to buy the film rights to *The Assassin*. Though nothing came of that, the British version of *The Informer* was now under way. The producers had asked Sean O'Casey to write the caption dialogue for the film, but he had refused. The director was a noted German, Artur Robison, who gave the film a shadowy continental look.

Liam had already completed another novel, *The House of Gold*, which seems to draw on a Clare background connected, perhaps, with Francis Macnamara. He had a new book in mind, which he thought he could write in a month if he could find a secluded room somewhere in London. This was provided above the Mandrake Press in Museum Street, and there Liam completed the book as promised.

This autumn was a hectic one. At the end of September Cape published *The House of Gold*, some 3,000 copies of which were printed, an increase on earlier books. Later in the year another 2,500 were called for. There was also an American edition. Cape, apart from reissuing *Thy Neighbour's Wife* and *Spring Sowing*, now included *The Informer* in the Travellers' Library (in expectation of the film version, of course). In October the Mandrake Press brought out *The Return of the Brute*. After a period of silence the Great War had become a literary subject again, with the appearance of Blunden's *Undertones of War,* Sassoon's books, Graves's memoirs and Henry Williamson's *Patriot's Progress*. The work which may well have influenced Liam was Remarque's *All Quiet on the Western Front*, an international sensation, which had come out in January 1929 and a month later in England. In November Graves's *Goodbye to All That* appeared, and became a bestseller: some 30,000 copies were sold by Cape in a few weeks. Liam's *The Return of the Brute* was not a bestseller, though it deserved a better reception than it received – some found it nasty and brutish. It too was translated by Hauser into German, in 1930.

Early in October Liam was visited at his mountain cottage by Padraic Ó Conaire. Two days later the Gaelic writer died in a Dublin hospital. The neglect of this great writer, who had wandered the country in extreme poverty, was symptomatic of the Free State's indifference to art.

On 20 October the film version of *The Informer* opened in London. An attempt had been made to add sound to it, but this was technically flawed. The screenplay was by Ben W. Levey and Rolfe E. Vanio, and three of the chief players were German. Liam described the reception as a frost, though a review in *The Times* by Graham Greene thought favourably of it. In any case the silent era to which it belonged had come to a sudden end, and this would quite eclipse the film.

O'Flaherty's reputation as a womaniser, albeit a married one, was now established. In Dublin he was often to be found in Madame Cogley's celebrated establishment at 29 Harcourt Street, with Austin Clarke, Higgins, and even the young Beckett and Con Leventhal. In London his social life was even more hectic.

In November he was drinking in his favourite pub, the Plough in Museum Street, when he encountered the

Below: *Mass Man: citizens of the Soviet Union taking their rest from the task of building socialism in one country.*
Opposite: 'The Mechanised Toiler', *constructivist-symbolical drawing by Krinski, a contemporary Russian artist.*

Scottish poet Hugh MacDiarmid, with whom he staightaway had a battle royal on the floor of the pub. The Plough – then, as now, a literary pub – was the resort of Tom Driberg, the composer Peter Warlock (aka Philip Heseltine) and Catherine Carswell, another Scottish writer. Fighting was of interest to Liam: he reported on the fight featuring the Italian Carnera for the *Daily Express* in November. Though his reputation was now reaching its high point (signalled by an important article by K.C. Warren, with a portrait, in January's *Bookman*), Liam himself was more concerned with going to rugby matches with Roy Campbell. Campbell admitted that some of the best times he ever had were with Liam. In April they were in Dublin and got so drunk that they had to be rescued from the police by Senator Oliver Gogarty.

The film of *The Informer* was banned in Ireland in March 1930 – the film censor, James Montgomery, saw himself as a moral sieve 'preventing the Californication' of Ireland. The Censorship of Publications Act had been passed in July 1929, and came into force at the beginning of 1930. This was to shape the attitude of many Irish writers to their country in the decades to come. Yeats thought that one reason for the act was simply to prevent the circulation of novels like Liam's.

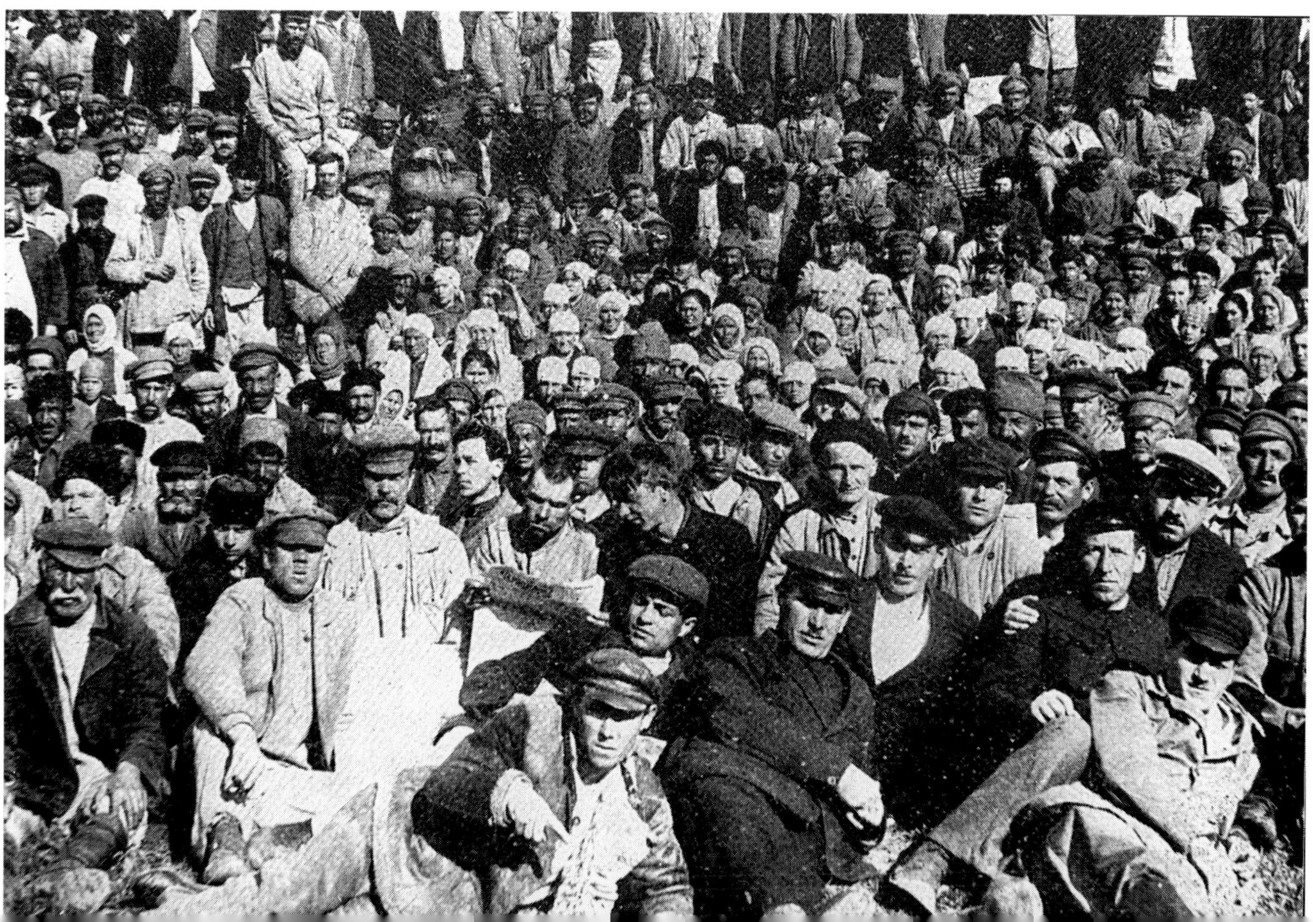

TO RUSSIA & BACK Though he never lacked material for his short stories, Liam had to forage for copy for his other books. During the autumn and winter of 1929-30 he had been writing *Two Years*, a picaresque account of his *wanderjahren* after the War. Though highly impressionistic, this book was nevertheless a valuable insight not only into his own particular experiences, but also into that general sense of post-war disillusionment which all across Europe and America was festering into political ferment. This book was due to appear in June, from both Cape and Harcourt Brace. It coincided with a reprint from Cape in the Travellers' Library of *The Black Soul.* Cape were confident enough of *Two Years* to increase the initial print run to 3,000 copies.

But by the time it appeared, Liam had set off on another adventure. In May he sailed from England to Leningrad on a visit to the Soviet Union. Passing the fortress of Kronstadt, with its memories of the rising in 1921, he landed at Leningrad. On 13 May his arrival in Moscow was duly reported by *Isvestia,* and repeated to the world by *The Times* of London – a useful piece of publicity. He planned to stay a month and to experience at first hand the wonders of this new political system. Russia was already into the Five Year Plan, Trotsky had been exiled and the Moscow show trials were on their way. There may well have been some distrust of Liam in communist circles, where it was known that his brother had left the American Communist Party as a supporter of Trotsky, whom Liam also admired at this date. His literary status was the subject of an admiring article by his official guide, Theodore Levit, in a literary journal. He claimed that he was interested in finding out about Dostoyevsky, whose works he had been introduced to by Edward Garnett, whose wife was a famous translator of Russian literature. He also got help

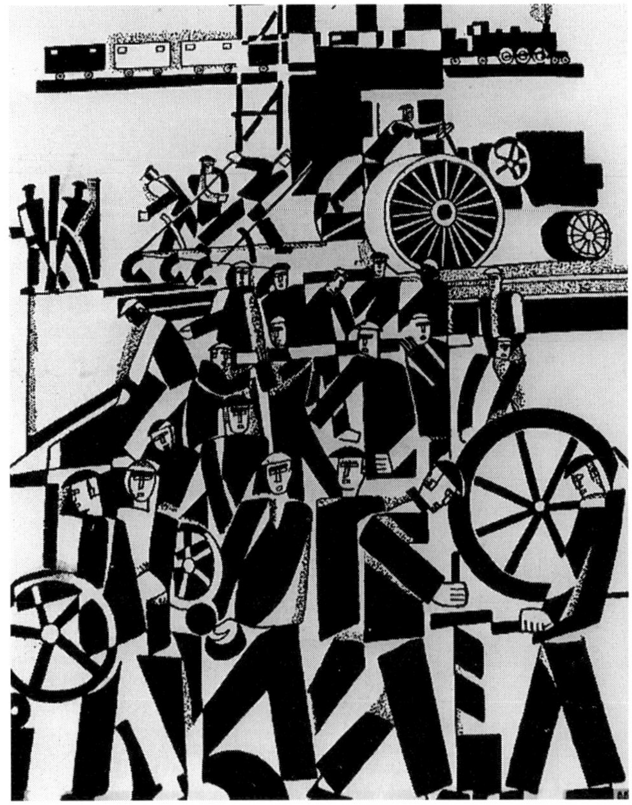

from Walter Duranty, the Moscow correspondent of the *New York Times* (later criticised for his Stalinist sympathies).

Unlike other visitors of the day, Liam was disillusioned by what he found in Russia. Though he carried the right political credentials, his individualism chafed at such an over-organised society. All of this would eventually find its way into his account of the trip, *I Went to Russia*.

He travelled back overland, through Poland, Germany, and France. In Berlin he met Heinrich Hauser, whose translation *Die Bestie erwacht* (*The Return of the Brute)* appeared at this time from the notable literary house of S. Fischer, publishers of Thomas Mann and other eminent writers. This book would be banned when the Nazis came to power in 1933. 'They thought the title referred to themselves,' Liam explained in 1979. 'It does – as it applies to all who make war.'

On his return to London Liam's views had hardened. He started out to write about Russia in a reasonable way, but the demon was in him, and as the book progressed

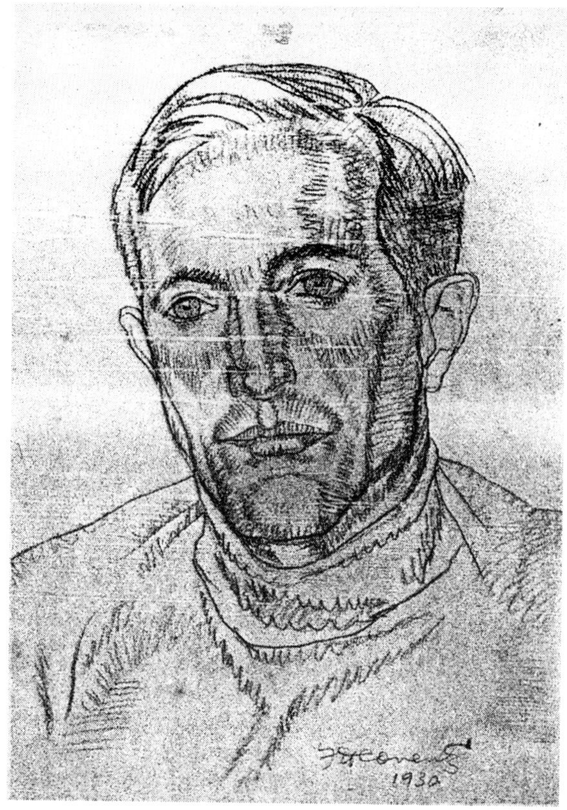

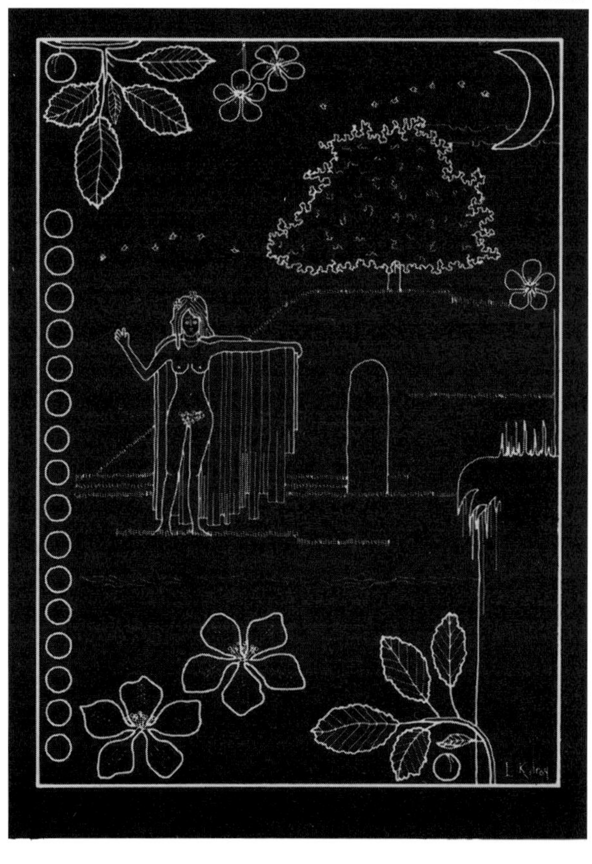

(through a variety of false starts) it dismayed his friends P.R. Stephensen and Albert Sachs. They were angry that he was playing the bourgeois game – or so it seemed to them. Liam was also angry that Cape had allowed the promotion of *Two Years* to drop, but he seems always to have had unreasonable expectations of his publishers in this respect. He compromised, however, with the Mandrake Press, allowing Stephensen to make cuts in his paean to paganism, *The Ecstasy of Angus*.

Robison's film was released in 1930 in the USA. At the same time Liam sold the dramatic rights in the USA to *Mr Gilhooley*, and with the money planned to make another trip. But he got only as far as St Malo and then Concarneau, where he worked on the Russian book. Stock were bringing out *Le reveil de la brute* at this time. After a brief, mysterious visit to Switzerland to help a friend, Liam returned to London. Finally, he sailed for New York on the *George Washington*. On board he dreamt up, literally, his story 'The Wild Swan'. On arrival he was met by his publisher's man and the press – the rites of the arriving celebrity. F.B. Elser's adaption of *Mr Gilhooley* opened at the Broadhurst theatre in a production by Jed Harris. However, it did not prove to be a great success and closed after four days.

Above right: *This sketch of Liam O'Flaherty* (top) *was drawn in London just before he left for Moscow. It reflects the sensitive side of O'Flaherty's nature, which was shocked by some things he saw in the Soviet Union.*

Below right: *The strong strain of pagan sexuality in O'Flaherty's life and work is epitomised in* The Ecstasy of Angus, *illustrated here by Lucy Kilroy.*

‘A Gypsy Girl in Moscow’ *from* I Went to Russia *by Liam O’Flaherty*

In Moscow there are hordes of beautiful little gypsy girls, the most exquisite little creatures I have ever seen. They dance in the public squares and sleep on the grass plots and beg everywhere. They are always accompanied by ruffianly fathers or mothers, who probably take all their money and beat them. But they are really very beautiful, with features as delicate as flowers and little hands that are enchanting. All as brown as berries, with extraordinary eyes that look so wicked.

One of these little women entered the restaurant, came to our table and begged for money or food; I could not tell which. I put my hand in my pocket at once to give her some money; not because I pity beggars, but because she was beautiful. But my friend tried to stop me in an excited manner. In spite of that, I gave the little girl a few roubles. My friend got really horrified.

‘It is a crime,’ he cried. ‘It is a counter-revolutionary act.’

‘Oh! Damn the revolution,’ I cried. ‘What harm will it do?’

He shook his head and said:

‘You are really hopeless. You are an anarchist. It is impossible to organise properly your psychology.’

The little person returned and began again to beg for something. Then she pointed to a mess of potatoes that lay on a plate. I was on the point of handing her the plate and asking her to sit down to table with us, when my friend jumped to his feet in a fury and threatened to call the police if the gypsy did not leave at once. As soon as she heard the word ‘Militia’ she fled, but at the door she turned back and said something. I'm certain it was an oath. Then she winked at me and blew me a kiss. I returned it with enthusiasm and I wanted to rush out after her; she was so perfect and tiny, like a little fairy animal. But my friend began to strike the table and then, seizing me by the shoulder, said furiously:

‘Comrade, I must warn you against such people. The situation is such. That girl is a gypsy. As in your countries, these gypsies have always lived by begging and robbery and such things. But here, since the revolution, they have been liquidated and settled on the land. Now the liquidated gypsies are a respectable fraction of the Soviet Union. Some of them are even doing good work for the Five Year Plan and the collectivisation of the land. But there are others that still remain unliquidated. This little girl is the child of such unliquidated people. By giving her money and food you only encourage her parents to remain unliquidated and therefore you are committing a counter-revolutionary act. For they take, of course, the money from her and drink it or speculate with it, being addicted to various illegal practices. Also, begging is condemned by Soviet law. So you see ...’

‘Oh! For Christ’s sake,’ I cried angrily, ‘do let a fellow have some fun. I can't go on all day thinking of liquidating gypsies and Esquimos. Why can't I give her money if she amuses me?’

‘But that also is false,’ he continued, ‘to do something wrong because it is amusing.’

‘But it's not wrong. It's human. I loved getting gifts when I was a child. It's really so sweet and gives great pleasure to children and softens their little cruel natures. Fact.’

‘You are hopeless,’ he said. ‘You are by nature a bourgeois.’

THE INJURED HEART Liam returned to Ireland and spent part of the autumn on Aran, where he was writing *The Puritan*, another novel of city life. He visited his mother's grave at Kileany, and brooded on past wrongs. On 30 October *The House of Gold* was banned in Ireland -- the first of Liam's books to be so distinguished. This rejection of his work by his own people was followed by further controversy at the end of the year. The government refused to accept from the estate of Harry Clarke a commissioned window for the League of Nations Building in Geneva which showed scenes from Irish literary classics, including Joyce and O'Flaherty. The semi-draped figure from *Mr Gilhooley* which Clarke had selected outraged ministerial sensibilities. Yet this novel, as its appearance in a German translation at the time showed, was one of Liam's most important works in the eyes of European readers. Though a collection of short stories appeared in Russia in 1931, it was as a novelist he was known. *The House of Gold* appeared in German in 1931, again translated by Hauser.

At the end of the year the Mandrake Press collapsed and Liam's agent had to find a new publisher for *The Ecstasy of Angus.* It was refused by the Cresset Press in London and by Random House in New York, and was eventually taken over by the small firm of Joiner and Steele.

The summer of 1931 was an exceptional one for Liam. *I Went to Russia* was published by Cape, selling three and a half thousand copies, and by Brace in New York. Cape also reprinted *Spring Sowing* and *The Informer* for the Travellers' Library, and at last the *Ecstasy of Angus* came out as a limited edition – with a careful note inside, to foil the censor, that it was 'For private circulation only'. Thus all levels of his readers

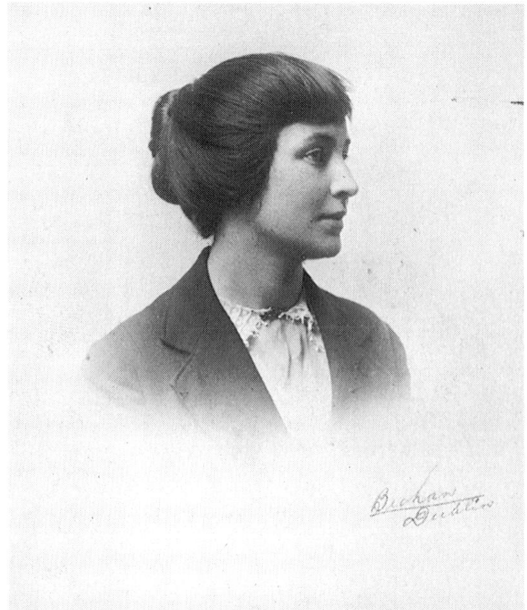

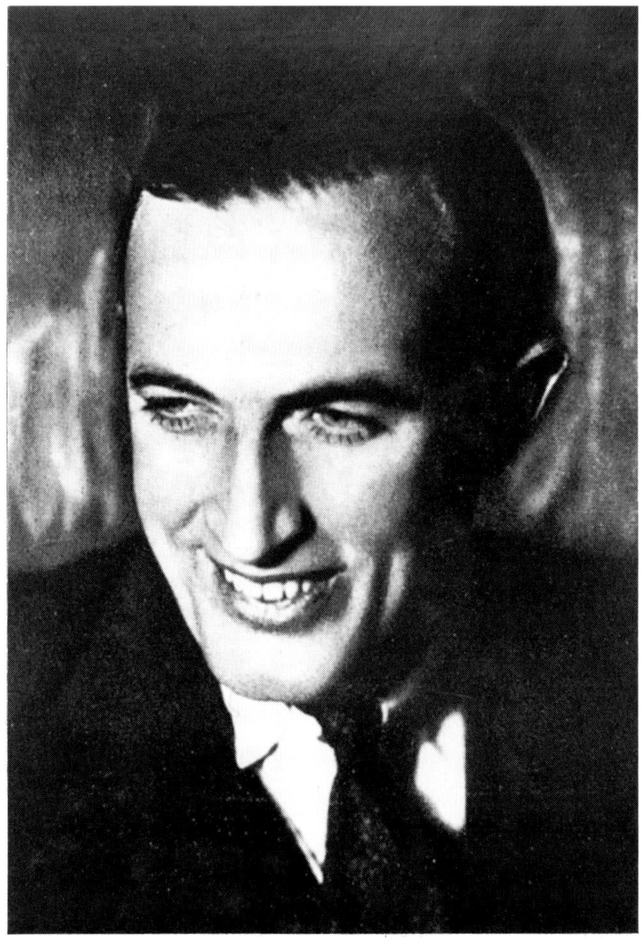

Top far left: *Margaret Barrington, O'Flaherty's beautiful and patient wife.*

Bottom far left: *Liam O'Flaherty, photographed in Moscow in May 1930, shortly before the break-up of his marriage.*

were supplied. Extracts from the Russian book were serialised in a London magazine with a headline which must have delighted him: 'The famous Irish novelist and most outspoken and fearless writer of today.' Liam published another pamphlet for Lahr, *A Cure for Unemployment*. He also had a story in the *Yale Review*, an early indication of the respect he would eventually achieve (though not for some years) in academic circles as one of the foremost writers of Ireland.

In keeping with this status, he was again seeing James Joyce, then living in London (where he and Nora Joyce were married in July). At the end of August Liam travelled with Joyce to Salisbury to visit Stonehenge, a site which Joyce had been longing to see for years and which he needed to experience for *Finnegans Wake*.

That summer David O'Callaghan, the schoolteacher, was said to have revisited Aran, to the surprise of the men who had been boys when he beat learning into them. He would die at the age of eighty-five at his native place in Limerick; his old rival Fr Farragher had already passed away to an unmarked grave in November 1928. The passing of the priest seems to have been the spur to Liam's notion of writing a novel about the events of his childhood. Having begun work at Gort na gCapall in the summer, he returned to Dublin to read the newspaper accounts of the Aran unrest in the National Library.

At this time his friendship with Francis Stuart – a poet who had also been involved in the Civil War and in the publication of *To-Morrow* – was at its most intimate, both feeling themselves isolated as artists in their own country. By December the Aran novel was finished. *The Puritan*, which Cape published over the New Year, was the last novel O'Flaherty did with them. It was duly banned in Ireland, a fact that was made the occasion of a

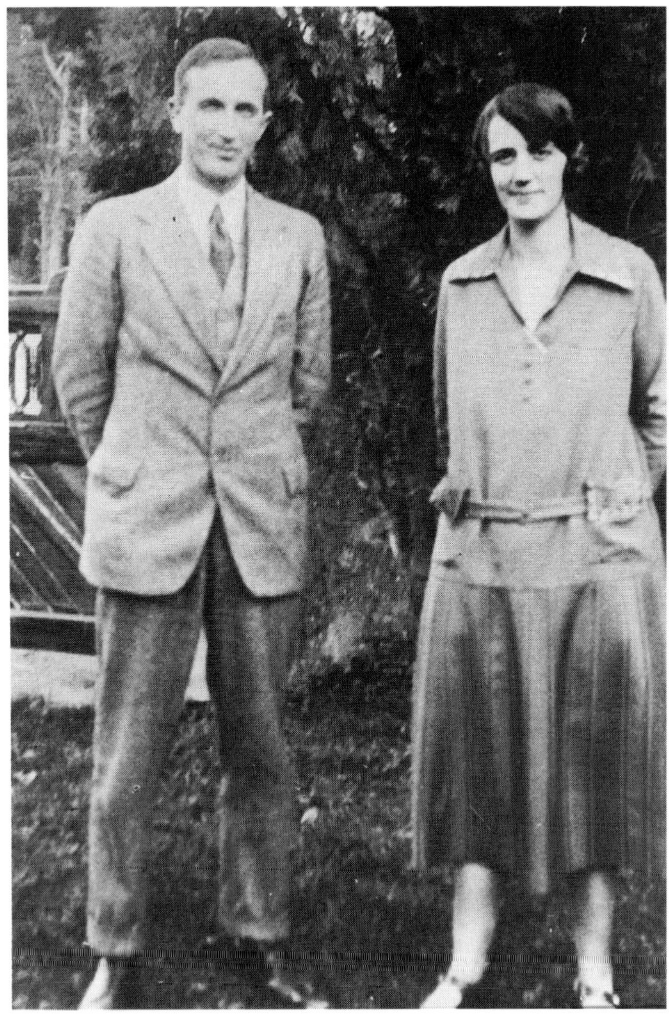

Liam and Margaret O'Flaherty, a contrasting couple.

furious attack on the censorship by W.B. Yeats. These novels of the early period, with their disturbed and outcast characters, have more in common with the literature of Weimar Germany – where *lustmord* was a dominant theme of art and literature – than they have with the writing of England or America.

The break with Cape and also with Edward Garnett, as well as the change of American publishers, were symptomatic. In March Liam and Margaret separated: his restless nature had proved in the end too much for her to cope with. After a few weeks of searching for somewhere to live, Liam settled for the summer in the small Kerry town of Caherciveen, where he observed with sour disdain the whole country's enthusiasm for the Eucharistic Congress and the advent of de Valera to government. De Valera promised great things, but the slums of Cahirciveen would remain when all the expense of the Congress was over and done with. *Skerrett*, the novel of Aran life which Liam published that summer (with his new regular publisher, the left-wing firm of Victor Gollancz), dealt explicitly with this anti-clerical theme, and made shocking reading for some in Ireland.

Yeats's reaction to the enveloping atmosphere of the new Ireland was to found the Irish Academy of Letters, into which he invited Liam and Francis Stuart. But Liam did not attend the first meeting of the Academy, as he had moved to London. There, aside from a regular morning routine of work, he was mixing in a frivolous society group, based in the Plough Tavern in Museum Street and at the Café Royal. Liam had taken a flat off the Strand.

But he was passing through a nervous crisis, which was to form the background to his fevered confessional work *Shame the Devil.* Something of his state of mind was also apparent in the strange novel of the Civil War, *The Martyr* (published in January 1933), which drew on the Kerry scenes of the previous summer. Almost inevitably, the Irish Censor banned it in March. By the end of the summer Liam had reached the end of his tether and was feeling suicidal. He had begun a new novel about the great Irish Famine, but it was a slow creation. His friend Rupert Grayson (a former Irish Guards officer) agreed to finance a book, and provided paper and a typewriter; and Liam took off on wanderings which became the framework for his backward glances at what had made him. These would become *Shame the Devil* (eventually published in April 1934).

By this time Liam was moving beyond the mental stress of these years into a calmer, though still restless, period, in which he was more involved in film-making than in writing.

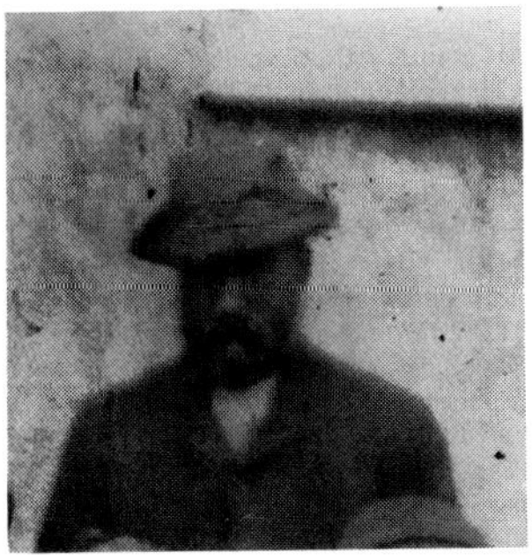

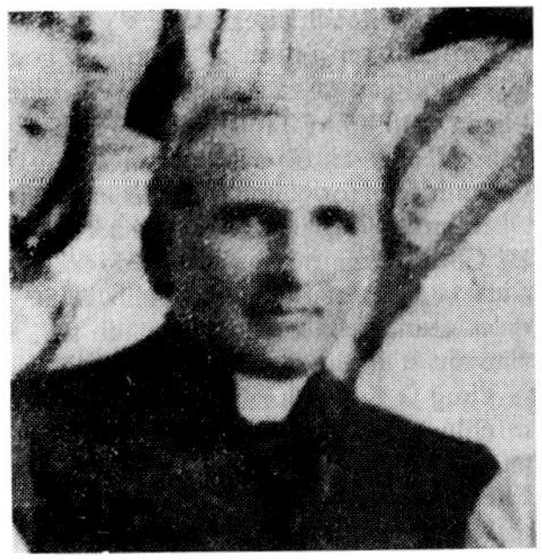

Left: *David O'Callaghan, the Oatquarter schoolmaster, who inspired the writing of* Skerrett. Right: *Fr Murtagh Farragher, the model for Moclair in* Skerrett, *parish priest on Inishmore, who organised the boycott of the Dirranes and O'Flahertys.*

Below: *The priest's house (with the flat roof to right) in Kilronan early in the century, which Roger Dirrane bombed, one of the background events to O'Flaherty's novel* Skerrett.

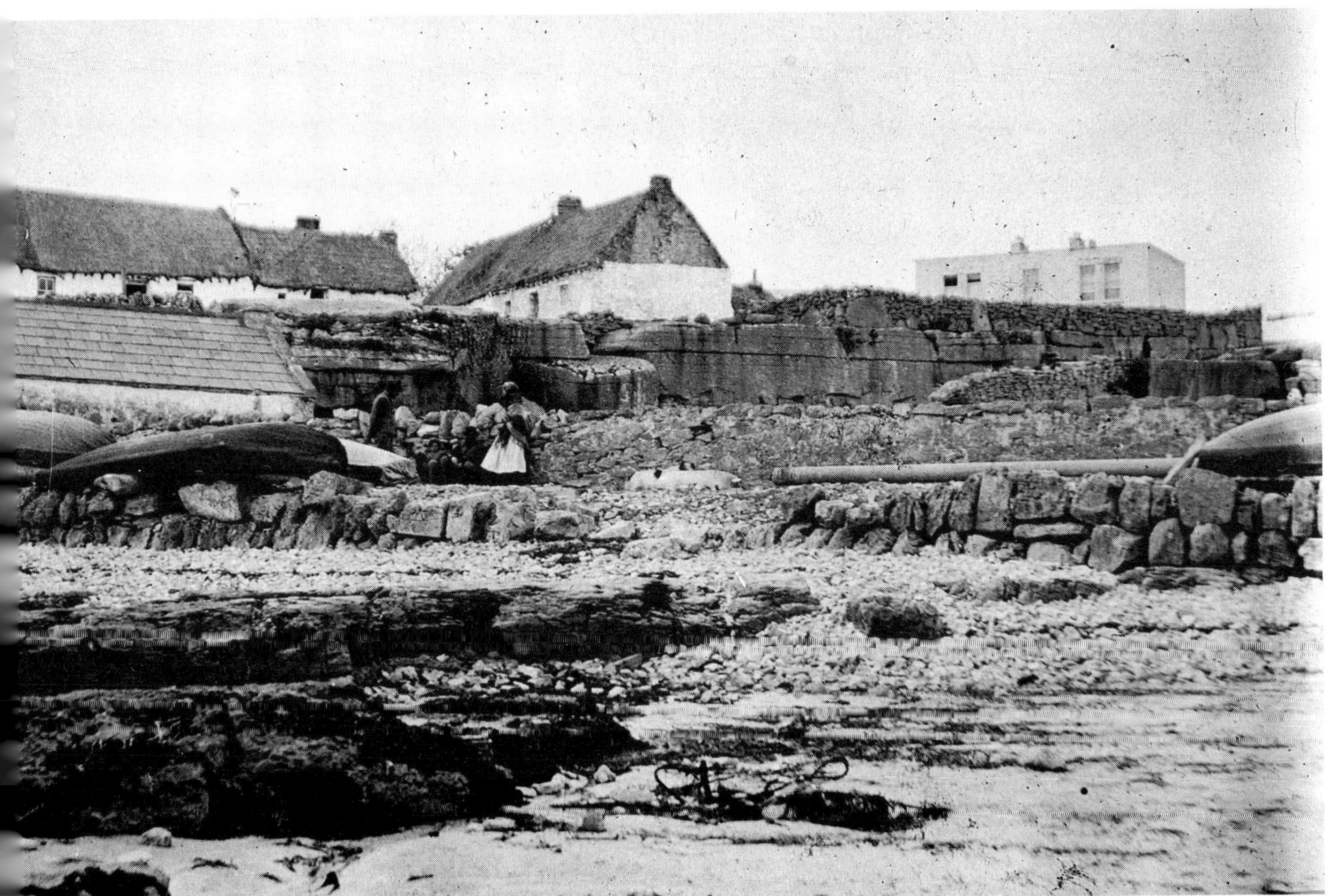

Below: *Scene from Jeff Musso's film* Le Puritain, *with Jean-Louis Barrault as Ferriter the murderous journalist.*

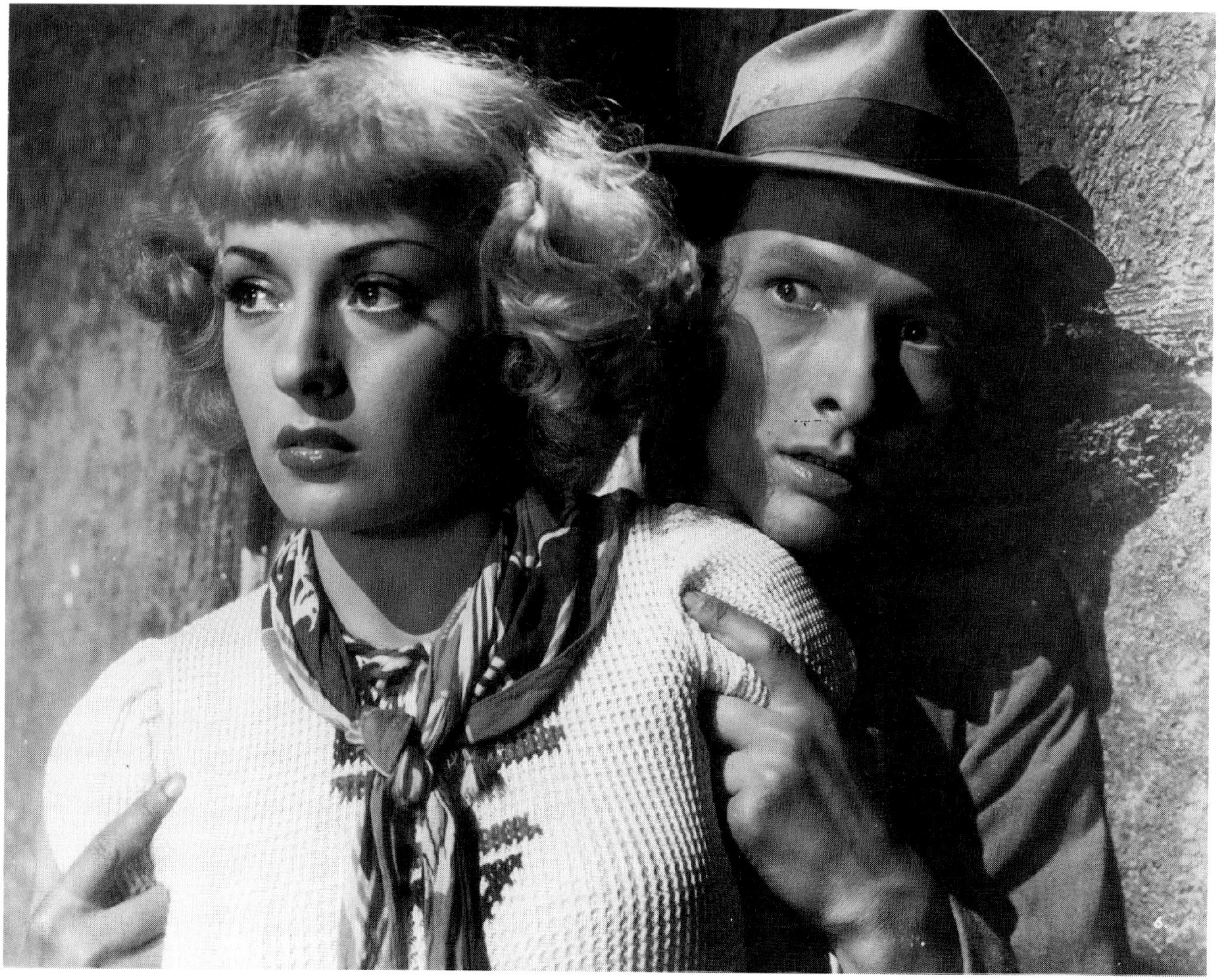

‘A Gratuitous Act’ *from* The Puritan *by Liam O’Flaherty*

He returned to his room and locked the door. Then he drank a cup of tea. Now he was beginning to get nervous. The two faint patches on his cheeks had become bright red and the root of his tongue was getting in the way of his breath. He went over to his desk, sat down, unlocked a drawer and took out some sheets of manuscript that were pinned together. On the title page was written in red ink: ‘THE SACRIFICE OF BLOOD by FRANCIS FERRITER’. He toyed with the pages for a little while. Then he lit a reading lamp that stood on the table and pulled the blind over the window. He turned over the title-page and began to read, but ceased after the first sentence and got to his feet, trembling with excitement.

‘No, no,’ he said aloud. ‘It would tire me and make me quite unable to do what I’m going to do. In any case, it’s absolutely correct and there’s no necessity to revise it. I shall leave it here under this weight.’

He put a paper-weight over the manuscript on the desk.

‘If for any reason I fail to execute my purpose or lose my senses afterwards, as is quite possible in my weak condition, I shall be able to prove through this confession the motives that inspired me.’

His agitation had now increased so much that he felt giddy. He sat down in the chair, covered his face with his hands and began to pray. However, he was unable to form the customary image of God in his mind and he merely repeated words without any fervour. This made him angry and he recovered his self-possession. His jaws set firmly and he remained entirely without thought for a long time, staring at the table. It seemed as if his mind passed slowly downwards into a state of complete oblivion, like death. Then it returned, with the same slowness, in a state of complete unity, being possessed of one idea, which attained such power that it passed down from his mind into his whole body, so that his limbs acted directly in obedience to it, without any guidance from his will. Yet it had no form, either in words or in substance, being symbolized merely by a small cloud of vague colour.

Like a man moving in a dream, he rose from the chair and walked to the wardrobe, where he took a pair of kid gloves from the pocket of his raincoat. He pulled them on slowly and went to the door. As he was unlocking it, the idea suddenly took shape for a few moments and visions of extraordinary vividness flashed through his mind. His body tingled and he had to make a great effort of will in order to prevent himself from shouting and rushing headlong from the room. Then the visions disappeared as suddenly as they had come, and he moved steathily out of the room, pausing on the landing in order to listen for sounds from his neighbour’s room. He heard nothing at first, but after a little while he heard the creaking of a bed, as caused by a man turning in his sleep. He looked at his watch and not being able to read the time, he went back into his room, in order to examine it in the lamplight. He hurried back to his writing desk, found that it was half-past one and then put out the light. Again he left the room and leaving the door open, moved carefully down the stairs in his stockinged feet, carrying his slippers in his hand.

On the second landing he stumbled against the banister as he was rounding the corner. The banister creaked, making a slight noise that seemed thunderous to his excited ears. He stopped dead and his agitation returned. Again the bright red patches came to his cheeks and his tongue lurched against the mouth of his throat. A heaviness spread from his shoulders to his wrists, and his hands became so light that he had to keep rotating them on his wrists. Fearing that he was going to lose control of himself, he hurried down the stairs to the bathroom, careless of what noise he made, hardly drawing breath until he found himself standing within the white door. Now the heaviness in his arms spread to his whole body and he grew panic-stricken, lest he might at the last moment fail to achieve his purpose through physical weakness. In a rage, he set his jaws and made a supreme effort to recover his strength, closing his eyes and throwing back his head until his neck became rigid. This movement made him hold his breath. His face became suffused with bright colour and his nervous tension increased until he was on the point of shouting; but when he reached a point where he thought he could endure the strain no longer, the panic ceased and his mind grew clear. Then he relaxed and began to rehearse what he had to do.

At one point he raised his hand, pointed his finger and said:

'If the knife is not there what am I to do?'

He thought for a few moments and then looked around him wildly.

'Not that way,' he said. 'She might scream. And in any case there would be no blood.'

He shuddered and continued:

'The knife must be there. Otherwise I am wrong and that is obviously impossible. If the knife is not there is means that I have been inspired by the devil acting on my vanity, that I am mad, and that belief in the divine destiny of man is an illusion. This act must be a final solution of the problem – Does God exist?'

Now he began to breathe heavily and to sway backwards and forwards slightly like an intoxicated person. His mind became confused and a sombre enthusiasm, that was almost sensual, made him forget completely where he was and what he was going to do, until he was roused from this ecstasy after twenty minutes by the turning of a door knob down below. In spite of the ecstasy, his senses had remained marvellously acute, for the sound was hardly audible at the distance to the average human ear, yet it reached him loudly and distinctly. He at once became intent, with his head turned sideways, listening.

After a few moments he heard steps in the hallway, followed by a voice whispering 's-s-sh.' Then he heard more footsteps. He counted ten. Then he quickly pulled open the bathroom door and crept out on the stairs. He put on his slippers. The sounds of footsteps were now at the bottom of the stairs leading to the basement. He moved quickly down the stairs, turned to the left and entered by the second door, which was standing ajar. He found himself in a large bedroom. The air was thick with cigarette smoke. There was also a smell of stale beer. From the centre of the ceiling, a large gas chandelier was hanging, surrounded with glass pendants. One of its five lamps was lit. There was a table beneath the chandelier. Several empty Guinness bottles and a half-empty whisky bottle lay on the table, together with two ashtrays laden with cigarette butts. A double bed stretched across the room on the far side of the table. The bedclothes were in disorder, and there were various parts of a woman's underclothing scattered here and there on the floor and on chairs.

After glancing quickly around the room, he moved to a door that led into the front room. This door was protected by a heavy curtain, hung from a brass rod. He passed behind the curtain, opened the door leading into the front room and walked straight towards the fireplace. On the wall over the mantelpiece an Eastern dagger was hung in a sheath. He steadied the sheath with his left hand and then pulled forth the knife with his right. He ran across the room on tiptoe, pulled the door wide open into the sitting room and hid behind the curtain. Now his face bore an expression of pain, like a man straining to lift a heavy weight. He stood with his shoulders drawn together and his right hand, holding the dagger, raised to the level of his ear. A noise like the ticking of a watch resounded in his head.

He had not been many moments standing behind the curtain when he heard light footsteps in the hall outside and then he moved his head close to a slight opening in the curtain. A woman entered the bedroom, closed the door behind her and turned the key in the lock. Immediately he shuddered and a violent hatred of the woman mounted to his eyes. Then he felt a savage exaltation, which made him clutch the dagger so fiercely that he burst the fastening of his glove. He got ready to spring from behind the curtain, by gripping the folds with his left hand and putting his right foot a little forward.

After locking the door the woman paused for a few seconds, looking at the floor. Then she yawned and stretched her arms above her head. She laced her fingers and then brought down her hands to the back of her neck. Holding her neck between her joined hands, with her elbows close together, she walked swaying towards the table, yawning and frowning. She was a beautiful woman, young, with golden hair and a very fair complexion. She wore a blue silk kimono with white stars, fastened at the waist with a belt, and sandals with green heels. When she reached the table she picked up the whisky bottle as if to pour out a drink, but she put it down again, muttering something. Then she came over to the bed and began to arrange the disordered clothing. The foot of the bed was within two feet of where Ferriter was hiding. When she came to the foot in order to tuck the end of the sheet under the mattress, he decided that the moment had arrived.

Suddenly he swept aside the curtain with his left hand, took deliberate aim at her bended back above the waist and struck with all his might. As he did so, he experienced such a violent exaltation that he grew quite limp as soon as he had struck the blow, loosing the dagger and letting his arm drop to his side. The knife had sunk to the very hilt, finding by chance a clear passage between two ribs straight to the heart. The handle quivered after the blade had become buried and the woman, uttering no sound, fell forward, until she lay straddled across the low rail at the foot of the bed. Then she made a low, rough sound in her throat like a hiccough and her body began to quiver.

Ferriter stood while her body continued to quiver, entirely devoid of any feeling. Then he heard the squelching sound the dagger had made, and he put his hand to his forehead to allay an acute pain caused by something sharp that seemed to be running around inside his skull. As this pain became more acute, he stepped to one side, leaned forward, took the corpse by the hair and pulled it off the bed on to the floor, where he dropped it face downwards. Then he rubbed his gloved hands together, stared at the corpse and tried to remember what he was to do next. He felt utterly exhausted and could not think. Until this point he had acted instinctively according to the plan which he had repeatedly rehearsed in his mind, but now his instincts also had become confused, failing to remind him that he should leave the room at once, go upstairs and get into bed. Several times he started slightly, feeling urged by a childish curiosity to turn the corpse over on its back so that he could see its face, but even this suggestion was so vague that he only became actively aware of it when his groping consciousness realized that the plunged dagger, protruding from the back, was in the way of such an act.

Immediately he uttered an exclamation of disgust and held out his two hands towards the hilt of the dagger. Blood had began to ooze through the kimono all around the hilt. The blue silk had become a heavy, dark colour and one of the white stars had almost entirely disappeared.

'It will get ruined,' he said in a whisper.

He looked around the room furtively and then stood over the corpse. He seized the dagger with both hands and tugged. The weapon had a curved blade and it had become firmly set in position by the stiffening of the body, so that it resisted all his efforts. That made him very excited and terrified, especially as blood now began to ooze freely from the wound and the corpse shifted to and fro as he pulled. He wanted terribly to let go his hold, to scream and run away and yet he kept pulling, until at last, he began to gibber hysterically. Then he became savage. He put his right foot on the corpse, bent down and made a final effort. The dagger rushed out, followed by a great spurt of frothing blood. With his foot still on the corpse, he gaped, uncomprehending, at this blood. Then he became horrified when he saw that it was staining his slipper. He dropped the dagger to the floor, drew back his foot and picked up the skirt of the kimono, to wipe the blood from his slipper. When he had done so, he dropped the skirt and then flushed with shame, seeing that the dead woman's naked thigh was exposed. With his face turned away, lest he might look again upon her nakedness, he drew the skirt gently down as far as it would reach. Then he stepped back, folded his arms on his bosom and said aloud:

'I must go upstairs now. It's getting late.'

He nodded assent to this statement several times, yet he could not persuade himself to move towards the door. Something which he could not understand held him in the room near the corpse. He felt vaguely that he had lost something precious, that he must find it and take it with him from the room.

At last he remembered that he had seen a photograph on the dressing table two months previously, on the night he had found the dead woman drunk in the bathroom and had put her to bed. He had also on that night been unwilling to leave the room, for some reason he could not understand. He had walked about after the woman had fallen into a stupor and gazed at the photograph; whereupon the woman had opened her eyes and said to him that the likeness had been made while she was 'still a silly young bitch.' For two months, while he contemplated the crime, the difference between the two faces, that of the woman and that of the girl in the photograph, had been an important factor in helping him to come to a decision.

Now he looked towards the dressing table, saw the photograph and decided to take it with him. He walked over slowly and looked at it. It was the size of a post card, set in a square, black, pasteboard frame. The picture was of the head and bust of a young girl, with long, golden hair and a countenance of great beauty and innocence. The medal worn by a Child of Mary hung around her neck.

HOLLYWOOD The film rights to *The Informer* had been bought by John Ford, and Liam contributed to the treatment which was written by Dudley Nichols. The final script when it came was, however, all Nichols's work. It was through Ford (who was a remote cousin of his) that Liam was introduced to Hollywood. The possibilities of the motion picture business were immense for many writers of the period.

He went to America in April 1934, and by the summer he was living on Sunset Boulevard, working for Paramount (a rival to RKO, who were producing *The Informer*), though what the film was remains unknown. They were delighted with his original treatment, and he with his dialogue-writing contract. He moved north to Santa Barbara, where he met a charming young divorcée at a fancy dress party: Kitty Harding Tailer would remain his companion for the rest of his life. In October 1934 the final go-ahead was given for the John Ford film, which went into production and was filmed in February and March 1935. Though there had been many difficulties put in its way, even in the final days of shooting, the film opened in America in May, and in London in October. The initial public reception was not overwhelming, though the critics, ravished by its shadowy European art-house look, loved it. In due course it won Oscars for Best Director, Actor, Music and Screenplay. None of these was for Liam directly, but it does no harm to have one's creation become one of RKO's best earning films. Actually, Liam made little money from the film, as much of his potential was taken up in a legal row over the rights; and though the film grossed well, it did not go into profit for ten years.

Liam's Hollywood experiences prompted him to the writing of *Hollywood Cemetery*, eventually published in November 1935. This satirical novel was very different from his other work, and some publishers and most critics have hated it; but it is actually an amusing and entertaining satire on the motion picture business which draws its scenes from real life, very closely in some cases. The makers of *The Informer* appear, very lightly disguised. Fears of libel haunted Gollancz, and no American firm would bring the book out. Today it reminds one a little of both Evelyn Waugh and Gore Vidal. For Liam, Tinseltown was a necropolis haunted by lost souls.

During June 1936 he wrote for Columbia, with Dalton Trumbo (a well-known Hollywood communist of the day), the script for *The Devil's Playground,* a remake of an earlier film, which was produced in the early autumn. By now, however, he had completed the novel about the Great Hunger which he called *Famine.* This was to be published in England by Gollancz in January 1937, but there was some difficulty, given the grim theme of the book, in finding an American firm to take it. Eventually, however, Random House agreed to. *Famine*, on which he had worked for over five years, was seen at once as O'Flaherty's finest book – the one in which his themes of man's struggle against nature and the injustice of all human society were given their most finished treatment.

Though O'Flaherty tried to sell *Famine* in Hollywood (to be directed, of course, by Ford), it never came off. The publication of a collected volume of stories, drawn from an earlier collection then out of print, provided a culmination to the hectic decade in which he had written some of his most important work. He had been essentially a writer of the 20s. For the 30s he would have to find a new direction.

The Spanish Civil War had broken out in July 1936, and very quickly proved to be the test of political commitment all across Europe and America. As a

'Two Sides of Hollywood' *from* Hollywood Cemetery *by Liam O'Flaherty*

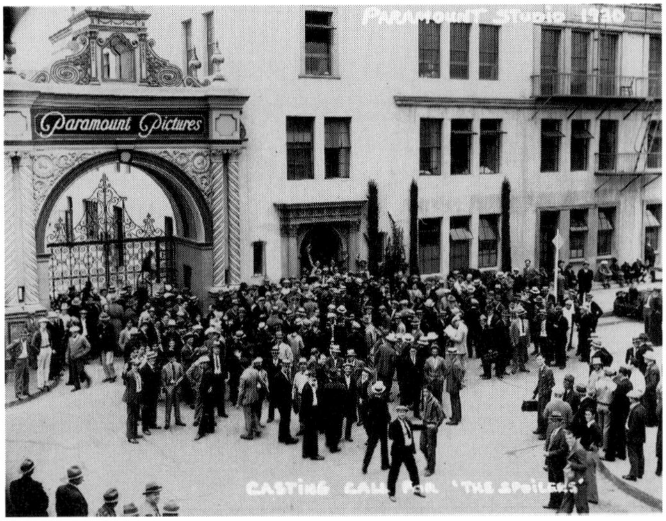

communist, though no longer a party member, Liam's sympathies lay with the Republican government. In February 1937 he was one of those (Clifford Odets and Paul Muni were others) who were banned from Spain by Franco because of their signatures to a message of support for the government. This led to all Liam's works being banned in Spain for political reasons – at the same time as the Irish government was banning *Hollywood Cemetery* for reasons of indecency. In November he was one of the many contemporary writers who contributed to the symposium *Authors Take Sides on the Spanish Civil War.* He was trenchant in his support for the Reds:

I am for the legal government and the people of Republican Spain against Franco and Fascism.

As an Irishman I realise that the toiling masses of Spain are waging the same struggle which we have waged for centuries in Ireland against landlordism and foreign Imperialism.

Long live the Republic in Spain and all over the earth.

Carey felt completely bewildered. He gaped like a rustic being in a city for the first time. But was it a city? They had already gone ten miles, passing through streets that were identical, with identical houses in each street, through a maze of automobiles, which even at that early hour covered the ground like a horde of scurrying ants, screeching, rumbling, Irritated by Gunn's neurotic conversation, he felt that he was caught in a labyrinth from which he could never extricate himself and he thought the place was the most frightful place he had ever seen. It gave him the impression of having been devastated by an evil genius, who, with a gigantic comb of uneven teeth, had torn away the upper layers of the city, leaving only the jagged base, with the interiors of the houses exposed and the furniture scattered about in disgusting confusion.

'Hollywood,' cried Donlin a few minutes later.

'Where?' said Carey, leaning forward excitedly and looking in all directions.

'Right here,' said Donlin. 'We're right in it.'

'I agree with you,' said Gunn. Then he laughed and added: 'That's excellent. Where, indeed? It's merely a illusion. It's a point of view, not a place. A mirage. Later. Later. The thing is to relax.'

Then Carey saw written on the side of a mountain to the right, in enormous letters, the word:

'HOLLYWOODLAND.'

'By Jove!' he said. '*Imagine that!* So this is really Hollywood!'

After a Turkish bath and a shave, Tracy and Gunn set forth to keep their four o'clock appointment with Mortimer. Smartly dressed in a white jacket and tie, a blue shirt, grey trousers and black and white shoes, Tracy looked quite a different person. Gunn was more normal. They were both in a serious mood and drove in

Opposite: *The famous gate to Paramount Studios on Sunset Boulevard, where Liam worked and which is described in his satirical novel* Hollywood Cemetery *(1935) – the mill of extras he saw as Tinseltown's lost souls.*

silence. Indeed, it was a very serious matter for them, this business of fixing *The Emigrant*; and the ballyhoo about Angela Devlin.

They had both been connected with Mortimer for some time. Mortimer, Tracy and Gunn formed one of those 'teams' that were fashionable at the moment in Hollywood, a combination of the same producer, director and screen writer for successive pictures. Together they had now made four pictures that had earned a profit. They were shoddy pictures, efficiently directed and with a serviceable, well-written script. But Tracy and Gunn knew that they could not go on turning out shoddy pictures and retain the attention of the public. The public always demanded something new. It had no mercy on directors and screen writers that failed to give them something new. So they had picked on *The Emigrant* as something new and different, to startle the public appetite. Furthermore, they were ambitious to attract the attention of the highbrow critics in New York and London, by turning out something that would be called 'artistic'; especially as a director had been given a gold cup by a European dictator during the previous winter (there was even a rumour that the director in question was going to receive some mark of recognition from His Majesty the King, and that of course made their mouths water, as only the mouths of republicans can water).

And now Mortimer had returned from Europe with Angela Devlin, obviously with the intention of fixing *The Emigrant* to make it a suitable medium for a new star, reeking with slush, sugar and nonsense. Tracy and Gunn were very grave indeed. As they drove down the Boulevard, it was the hour when that thoroughfare is crowded by an endless procession of the most beautiful creatures imaginable, women gathered into Hollywood from all the corners of the earth by the lure of a screen career, all dressed with a view to giving the onlooker an exact idea of their form. Many an eye tried to catch the attention of the two men, greedy female eyes that were willing to pay any price for the favour of recognition by two of the most famous and important triumvirate in the celluloid city. But the two men never smiled nor looked. The owners of the lovely eyes said to themselves as they looked: 'God! Wouldn't it be wonderful to be either Tracy or Gunn. Even to spend an evening with them.'

And even then, Gunn was saying to Tracy:

'If I had enough will power left to get really angry, Bud, I'd blow up this town with a monstrous bomb.'

'Good idea,' said Tracy savagely, 'if you blew me up with it. If it weren't for the wife an' kids, I'd do the job myself.'

They swung out of the Boulevard down a side street, and after going a mile or so they parked their car on a lot opposite a large mass of buildings that were done in a dull yellow colour. These buildings were World Studios Incorporated. Outside the studio gates there was a crowd of people waiting, all dressed in costume, some as cowboys, others as Western 'bad men,' others as peasant women from Europe, others as harlots of the 'nineties, others as Cossacks, others as monks. They were all middle-aged and wan, with expressions of despair on their faces, rather like the expressions of old gamblers that hang around casinos, where they have no longer the ability to play, owing to their penury. When they caught sight of Tracy and Gunn, their bodies became rigid, like dogs that have sighted prey. Their lips moved in silence. Their eyes appealed. They made slight forward movements like beggars. And then, when the two men had been admitted through the gates by a uniformed gunman, they sank back once more into listless attitudes. Outcasts.

Opposite: *Liam O'Flaherty photographed on his arrival in New York on 8 February 1940.*

Below: *Ward Bond and Delores del Rio in a scene from* The Devil's Playground, *a film scripted by O'Flaherty with Dalton Trumbo in 1936.*

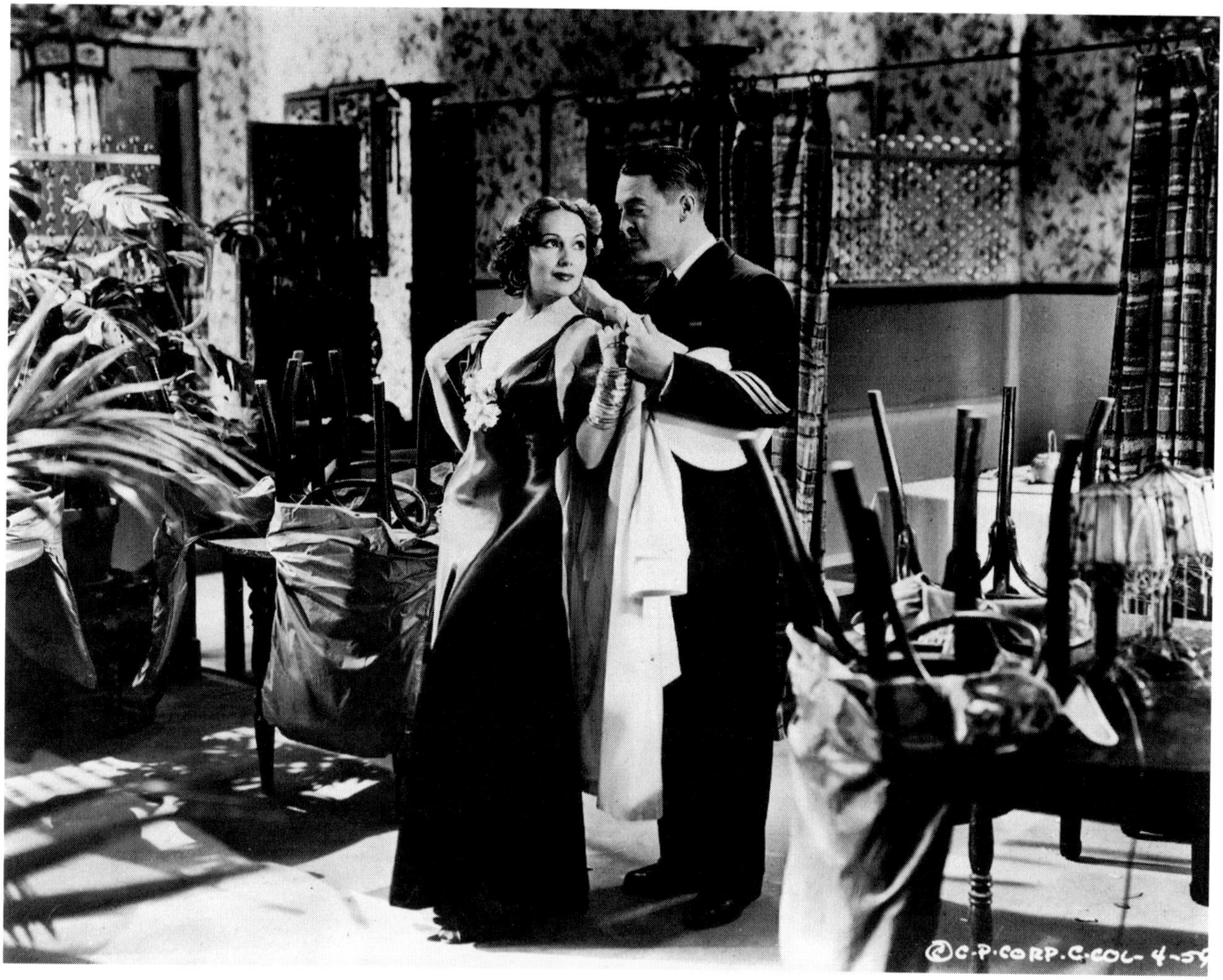

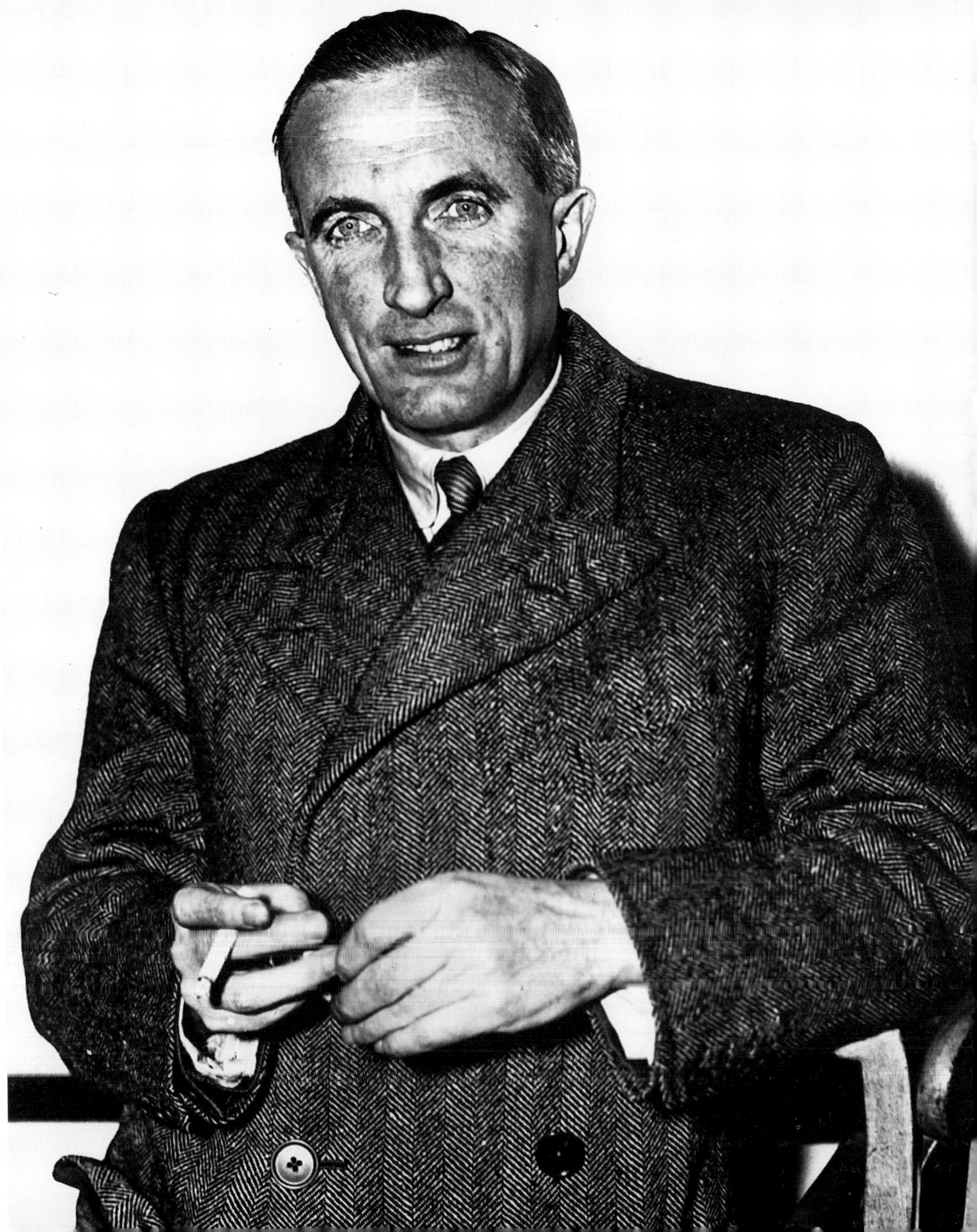

WANDERINGS After a hectic decade of creation, the 1930s were Liam's peak period. It was not only that he was the subject of long critical articles in literary journals in Ireland, England, France and Italy, and that his novels and stories were translated into most major languages, but also that his creativity was in full flow. The publications of *Skerrett* and *Famine* were landmarks in his literary life.

He gave a copy of the latter novel to Kitty Tailer with a handwritten inscription: '*This is Kitty's book. In Memory of Jamaica, Marlow, Martinique, Greenwich Village, Guéthary, Paris, where we wrote, from Reilly.*' This was a touching summary of the restless wanderings of the lovers that lay behind the great book.

The publication of *Famine* was followed by a falling-off in O'Flaherty's literary powers. He went to France to work with the young musician-turned-director, Jeff Musso, on a version of *The Puritan* which was released in December 1937, and a month or so later won the Prix Deluc, the new prestigious French form of the Oscars. It starred a young Jean-Louis Barrault as Ferriter the murderous journalist, and though the sets gave a curious idea of Dublin, it had unusual psychological power. Liam stayed with Musso, who directed in April 1939 another film, *Dernière Jeunesse*, based on *Mr Gilhooley* (also released in an Italian version called *Ultima Giovinezza).* Though the story of the older man's infatuation with a young woman was retained, the action was transferred to Le Havre. Again there was critical approval, but no popular success. This was not quite Musso's last film, but his career soon evaporated in production difficulties – one of his cheques to O'Flaherty bounced – which was unlucky for O'Flaherty.

O'Flaherty resumed his wandering lifestyle. He was in Ireland when war came to Europe. He had hoped he might get a divorce from Margaret, but this was not to be. Margaret Barrington had been living in London, writing for the left-wing *Tribune,* and helping the Spanish Republican cause. She was also working on a novel in which her husband appears as Egan O'Docherty. In 1939 she moved back to the south of Ireland. Though Liam was supporting his daughter Pegeen and her mother as well as he could, he could not often see the child given his wandering life.

His future with Kitty would have to be in America. When Italy finally entered the war after a period of havering, he sailed for the USA on an American liner. He arrived in New York in February 1940 and in an interview with the *New York Times* spoke of Ireland's need to stay neutral. He claimed he was on his way to Mexico – that scene of anti-clerical turmoil and revolution – but St Patrick's Day was spent with John Ford and others in Hollywood. There he was given the job of adapting the best-seller *How Green Was My Valley*, for Zanuck. Unhappy with Liam's initial treatment, Zanuck fired him. Liam, with typical style, stormed into Zanuck's office to demand his pay at the point of a pistol! When John Ford finally made the film, O'Flaherty had no hand in it.

Mexico was visited in due course, and O'Flaherty also spent time in Arizona. For the duration of the war Liam and Kitty Tailer stayed not only in California (where they mixed with the Hollywood literary set) but also in Florida, the West Indies and South America. Editions of his novels still appeared in Spanish and Italian, even in war-ravaged Europe. *The Informer* also appeared in special military editions. For a general readership Liam O'Flaherty – for all his magnitude as an artist of the short story – was the author of only that one book. Much of their time was spent, however, among the commuting stockbrokers of New Canaan in Connecticut. There he worked well, having the luxury of a secretary for the first time, and (as he later told Patrick Campbell) 'I didn't speak to anyone for six years.' In so far as he was ever happy, Liam O'Flaherty was happy then.

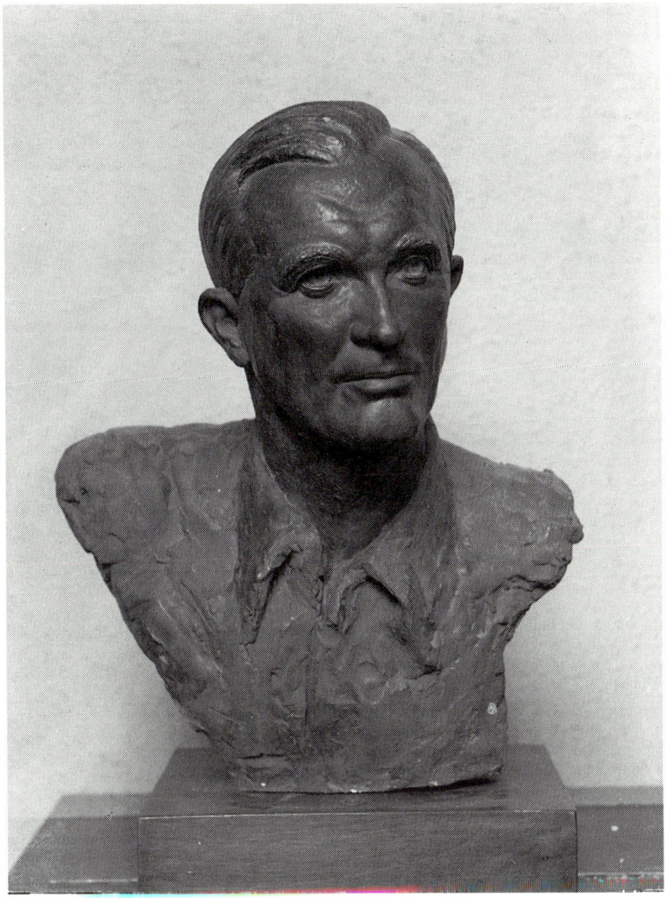

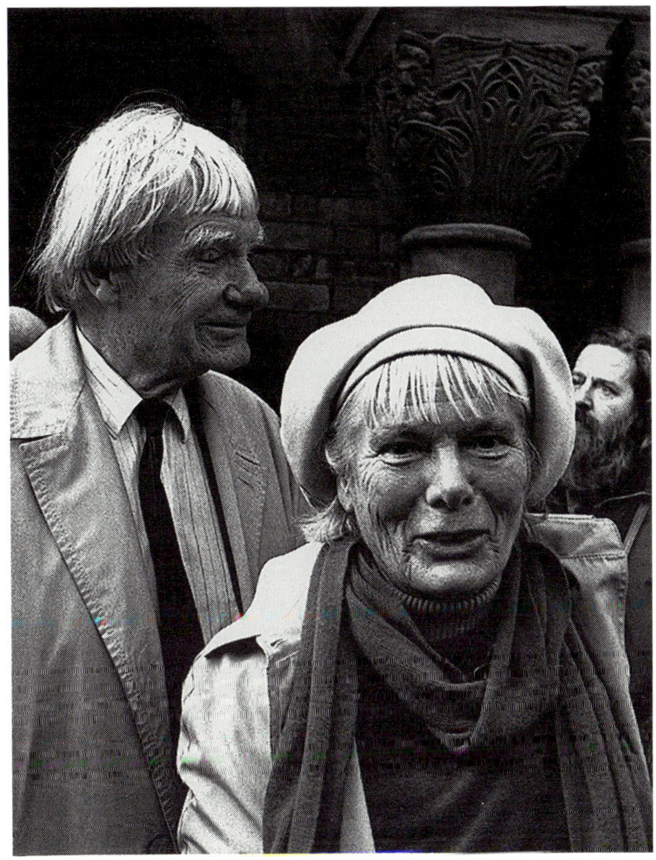

Above: *Bust of Liam O'Flaherty by Hilda O'Malley, done from life in the late 1930s.*

Left: *Francis and Madeline Stuart, close friends of Liam O'Flaherty. Francis Stuart and Liam shared a mutual interest in horse racing and writing.*

'The Blight Comes'
from Famine *by Liam O'Flaherty*

In spite of the previous year's blight and the scarcity of food, the quantity of potatoes planted that spring was even greater than usual. Now the crop showed signs of being a bumper one. The spring had been severe. There had been frost and snow even in the first part of April. But June brought a heat that was almost tropical. Under the urge of this heat, the potato plants grew to an enormous size and their luxuriant foliage, dotted with beautiful white and pink blossoms, made Black Valley look like a flower garden. The people began to hope that their hardships were nearly over and that God would again bless their labour.

On St. John's Eve, they made bonfires in accordance with the ancient custom. Then they took coals from the fires and carried them around the boundaries of their gardens, to ward off evil from the earth's fruit. Next morning, they went out and plucked a few stalks in each garden. Lo! the seed had increased abundantly. There was wild rejoicing everywhere. Old Kilmartin was exalted.

'What did I say?' he shouted, as he spilt a small kish of the new potatoes on the kitchen floor. 'God doesn't send hunger for long. He sends it to remind us of our sins. But when we repent he sends riches. The earth is rich. God has blessed our earth.'

At noon, on the feast of St. John, they sat down to a meal that was for them a real feast. Mary had got a few young onions from the plot at the back of the house. She chopped them up and mixed them with the new potatoes. There was a piece of salt fish which Sally O'Hanlon had given her, the result of another bit of thieving on the part of that generous neighbour. Although there was no milk to complete this favourite meal, hunger supplied its place as a savoury. They all gorged themselves. Even Maggie had left her bed and taken her place at table, excited by the wonderful news of the new crop. The dog had his dish by the back door and the poor animal ate so much that his stomach swelled out to a point on either side. Of late he had got thin.

It was at this moment, while they were happily eating their meal, that the destructive attitude of Divine Providence again manifested itself. All morning, the sky had been spotless and the sun shone in all the glory of its summer heat. And then, suddenly, the sky darkened. Lightning flashed. A torrent of rain began to fall. Thunder rolled across the firmament. It grew as cold as in the midst of winter. It was horrifying. It all happened within the space of a few minutes. They were struck with awe. They dropped their knives into the kish and stared at one another. They crossed themselves.

Thomsy was the first to speak.

'Has it come again?' he whispered. 'That's how it started last year.'

'Silence,' said the old man, rising from his stool. 'Do you know what you're saying?'

'Let's go on our knees,' Mary said, 'and ask God to have pity on us.'

They all went on their knees and recited the rosary, begging God not to send the blight on their crop. When they had finished, it seemed that the Lord heard their prayer, for the storm ended as suddenly as it had begun. The sky did not clear, but the thunder and lightning ceased. A drizzling rain continued to fall and it became very hot. The old man then suggested that they should sprinkle holy water on the gardens. Mary took a bottle of holy water they had in the house and went with him. They visited all the gardens and sprinkled the water on the plants here and there, in the name of the Father, Son and Holy Ghost. A number of other families, seeing them so engaged, came forth and did likewise.

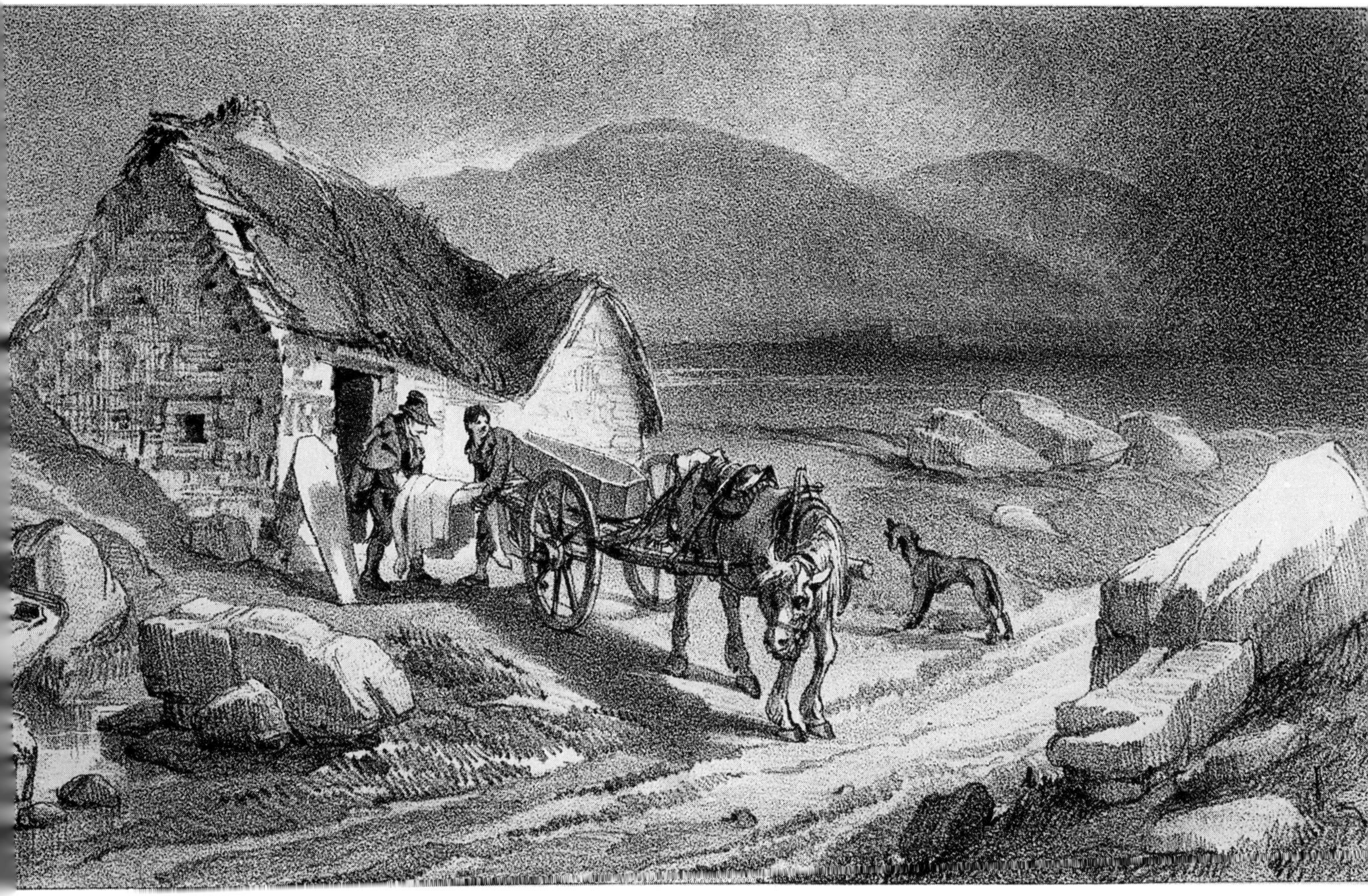

Carrying out the dead during the Great Hunger – a scene which might have been from O'Flaherty's masterpiece Famine.

It was a strange sight, truly, in the drizzling rain, under a dark sky, to see all those simple people going around their gardens with holy water, asking pity of the Lord.

Next day, the sky cleared and the sun came forth. It had rained heavily during the night and the blossoms had been washed from the stalks by the downpour, but when the old man went out with his spade once more and dug, he found that the crop was still wholesome.

'Praised be God!' he said.

Mary and Thomsy had come out with him and when they saw that the potatoes he threw out with his spade were whole, they burst into tears with joy.

'Oh! Aren't they big?' Mary said, as she went on her knees to pick them carefully. 'I never saw them so big at this time of year.'

'True for you,' said the old man, digging eagerly. 'That proves to you how it pays people to stint themselves. There are fools over there in Glenaree that ate some of their seeds and now they'll only have half a crop in spite of the great harvest that's coming. Two extra gardens I sowed. We'll have seventy bushels this year instead of the usual forty, or my name isn't Brian. Don't be talking, woman, we'll soon be on our feet again. Never say die. If our stock is taken, we'll begin again little by little. While we have the land we have riches. Now that the tyrant is dead, we're safe from persecution. The new agent that will come to be over us might be a Christian man. He'll give us time over the rent and maybe the government might step in with a loan. It happened before in the time of the great hunger. Ah! If only Martin was here with us, to see this great crop. Poor man! Many a drop of his noble sweat he gave sowing them.'

At the mention of Martin's name, Mary stopped picking. She felt a sharp pain in her bosom and then a terrible emptiness spread all over her body, as if she had been suddenly disembowelled by a monstrous hand that carried off at one scoop, her heart, her lungs, all her vital being. With a rush, the agony passed into her brain and a feeling of shame made her go weak, so that the colour left her cheeks and she rose to her feet trembling. The thought flashed through her head.

'For days I haven't thought of him.'

Thomsy looked at her anxiously and said:

'What ails you, Mary?'

'Nothing,' she said, laughing foolishly. 'Only I got so excited and ...'

'Go on into the house,' said the old man, too intent on his own joy to notice that it was Martin's name which had disturbed her. 'You've been doing too much lately. Rest yourself. Pick those potatoes, Thomsy.'

Mary went towards the house. What heavy heat it was! The smell of the growing plants was still in her nostrils even after she had left the garden. It was sickening. Tears were now streaming down her cheeks.

'Oh! darling,' she muttered, 'it wasn't for want of love of you that I didn't think of you this while. I was afraid to think of you. Oh! I'm afraid of the hunger, and the little milk I have for our Michael.'

Indeed, such was the case. Every moment of the day and during most of the night, her mind was tortured by the terrible thought that soon there would be nothing for the little child and that she would have to go out on the highways with him, begging. And this torture dulled all else, dulled even the torture of Martin's absence. Only once had she heard of him since Chadwick's death. A man brought news that he was with a band of men on an island off the coast, away to the west, and that he was safe there, at least for the present. But that was a poor consolation. What of the future? What prospect was there of ever being with him again, or of escaping from the country? It was this awful thought which made her afraid to think of him.

Another violent storm came on the last day of the month. They did not trouble greatly about this one, since the first had done no damage. Even so, a rumour got abroad that the blight had struck in the County Cork. Would it come this far? Every day, they anxiously inspected the crop. But the days passed without any sign of the evil. The potatoes that were dug for food still remained wholesome. It promised to be a miraculous crop. Even Mary began to take courage. And then, on the fifteenth of July, the bolt fell from the heavens.

When old Kilmartin came into his yard shortly after dawn on that day, he looked up the Valley and saw a white cloud standing above the Black Lake. It was like a great mound of snow, hanging by an invisible chain, above the mountain peaks. It was dazzling white in the glare of the rising sun.

'Merciful God!' he said. 'What can that be?'

The rest of the sky was as clear as crystal. The old man stared at it in awe for some time. Then he ran into the house and called out the family to look at it. Mary and Thomsy came out. They were as startled as the old man.

'Did you ever see anything like that?' the old man said.

'Never in my natural,' said Thomsy. 'It's like a ...'

'Snow,' Mary said. 'It's like a big heap of snow.'

'How could it be snow?' said the old man. 'And this the middle of summer? It's a miracle.'

'Or would it be a bad sign, God between us and harm?' said Thomsy.

Other people came from their cabins and stared at the cloud. There was a peculiar silence in the Valley. The air was as heavy as a drug. There was not a breath of wind. The birds did not sing. And then, as the people watched, the cloud began to move lazily down upon the Valley. It spread out on either side, lost its form and polluted the atmosphere, which became full of a whitish vapour, through which the sun's rays glistened; so that it seemed that a fine rain of tiny whitish particles of dust was gently falling from the sky. Gradually a sulphurous stench affected the senses of those who watched. It was like the smell of foul water in a sewer. Yet, there was no moisture and the stench left an arid feeling in the nostrils. Even the animals were affected by it. Dogs sat up on their haunches and howled. Not a bird was to be seen, although there had been flocks of crows and of starlings about on the previous day. Then, indeed, terror seized the people and a loud wailing broke out from the cabins, as the cloud overspread the whole Valley, shutting out the sun completely.

All this time, the whole Kilmartin family had remained in the yard. Mary clutched the baby in her arms. Nobody thought of preparing breakfast, although the morning was now well advanced. It was only when the wailing began and Maggie joined in it, that Mary came to her senses and said:

'Don't frighten the child with your whining. There's no harm done yet. Hold the baby, mother, while I get breakfast ready.'

'True for you,' said the old man. 'There's no harm done yet. Into the house, all of you. Pooh! Afraid of a fog, is it?'

Maggie stopped crying, but she went back to bed and closed the door of her room. The others made an attempt to be cheerful. Like people who feel the oncoming panic of despair, they gave voice to expressions of optimism, which they knew to be false.

'I often saw fogs heavier than that,' Ellen Gleeson said, as she rocked the baby in the hearth corner.

'As heavy as that?' said Thomsy. 'Sure that's not a heavy fog. I saw a fog once that was as thick as night. You can see to the end of the yard in this one.'

'You can see farther,' said the old man. 'On the south side there, you can see as far as Patsy O'Hanlon's house. It's not a thick fog. It's funny the smell that comes from fogs.'

'I never smelt a fog before like that,' said Mary. 'It must be a new kind of fog. But a fog can do no harm in any case. If it was rain now, that would be a different story. Rain might rot the potatoes and they ...'

'Nothing will rot the potatoes,' said the old man. 'God forgive you for saying such a thing.'

Mary cooked some Indian meal and turnips, of which a few still remained. While they were eating, a further astonishing thing happened. The sky cleared almost instantaneously. The sun shone brillantly. Yet this change, which should have cheered the watchers, only increased their awe, for the stench still remained. They all stopped eating. The old man got to his feet. He reached for his hat and fumbled with it, looking about him at the others with the expression of a small boy who has committed some offence of which he is ashamed.

'Blood an ouns!' Thomsy said, jumping to his feet.

With his mouth wide open, he stared at the old man. Then they both clapped their hats on their heads and rushed from the house. Mary ran to the cradle, picked up the child and pressed it to her bosom.

'What ails ye?' her mother said.

Maggie began to wail in the bedroom. All the colour had gone from Mary's cheeks and her eyes seemed to have enlarged. She handed the baby to her mother and whispered:

'I'm going out to look at the gardens.'

Thomsy and the old man, one after the other and with their hands behind their backs, were walking slowly down towards the potato gardens. Mary ran until she reached them. Ahead she could see the gardens, still shining in all the glory of their dark-green foliage, under the radiant sun. But the stench was now terrible. In single file, they came to the first garden and leaned over the stone fence close together, staring at the plants.

'They're alright,' said the old man. 'There's nothing on them.'

'Whist!' said Thomsy. 'What's that I hear?'

Towards the north, in the direction towards which Thomsy pointed, Mary and the old man saw people looking over fences, just as they themselves were doing. These people had begun to wail. In this wailing there was a note of utter despair. There was no anger in it, no power, not even an appeal for mercy. It was just like the death groan of a mortally wounded person, groaning in horror of inevitable death.

'It's the blight,' Mary whispered. 'Oh! God in Heaven!'

'Look,' gasped the old man through his teeth. 'Look at it. It's the devil. It's the devil himself.'

With outstretched hand, that trembled as if palsied, he pointed to a little hollow about ten yards within the fence. Here the growth was particularly luxuriant and the branches of the potato stalks were matted as thickly as a carpet. Mary and Thomsy followed the direction of his hand and while he babbled foolishly they saw the evil appear on the leaves. A group of little brown spots had appeared and they spread, as if by magic, while they watched. It was just like the movement of an incoming tide over a flat, sandy shore. It was a rain of spots, spreading rapidly in all directions.

'Oh! God Almighty!' Thomsy cried. 'Save us, oh, Lord! Jesus! Mary and Joseph!'

Rubbing his short, fat arms against his sides as if he itched, with his round, bearded face turned towards the sky, he prayed for mercy. Mary felt the same emptiness within her as on that other day when the old man mentioned Martin's name. Now, however, she did not think of Martin. The whole world seemed to have become emptied. The hand had scooped out everything. There seemed to be weights at the back of her eyes and her forehead became deeply ridged by the labour of keeping them open. Then a violent sobbing shook her. She closed her pained eyes and covered them with her hands. She leaned against the fence and gave way to a fit of sobbing. Yet no tears came from her eyes.

'The devil,' shouted the old man, 'he's on us. He's on us.'

Uttering shriek after shriek, he climbed over the fence, fumbling so much that he dislodged several stones. He strode through the stalks, that came up to his waist, across the ridges, until he came to the affected spot. The stench was now that of active corruption. The old man seized the stalks that were marked with spots and began to pull them. The leaves withered when he touched them and the stalks snapped like rotten wood. But the potatoes clinging to the uprooted stalks were whole. The old man dug into several of them with his nails.

'They're not rotten,' he cried, laughing hysterically. 'Come on, Thomsy. Pull the stalks that are rotten. We must stop it spreading. Mary, you come as well. Pull the stalks. Pull. Stop it spreading.'

Excited by the old man's frenzy, Thomsy also climbed over the fence and waddled through the stalks, but he halted when he was a few yards from the old man, who was pulling feverishly and shouting. The old man was now surrounded by a widening lake of spots.

'Sure, it's flying all over the garden,' said Thomsy. 'Look, man. It's all round you. You can't stop it.'

'What's that?' said the old man, raising his head.

He looked all round him pathetically. Then his mouth fell open and he stood up straight. His hands dropped to his sides.

'You're right,' he said faintly. 'It's the hand of God. God's will be done.'

Thereupon he crossed himself and bowed his head. Not troubling even to collect the potatoes he had pulled up with the stalks, he marched slowly back to the fence, carelessly trampling over the stalks that were still untouched. Mary turned away from the fence as he approached. She began to walk back to the house.

The wailing was now general all over the Valley.

LANDSCAPES OF THE PAST In 1945, almost as soon as the war was over, Liam stepped again into the literary scene – or rather, his agent learnt that his business affairs were now to be ordered by his friend Kitty Tailer and that the return of peace meant a return to active work. He had a novel in progress which was soon completed: *Land*, published by Random House in America in May 1946. He had begun this in 1938, and it was a continuation of his recreation of significant moments in Irish history, following his novel of the Famine of the 1840s with a story of the start of the Land War in 1879 – his chief character actually invents the device of the boycott. As a novel, however, it did not rank with the epic simplicity of *Famine.*

O'Flaherty came back to Ireland for the publication of the London edition in June. He was in high good humour about a holiday in Aran with Pegeen and the ultimate demise of civilisation in a nuclear disaster. 'Europe and this thing [the Irish Republic] are finished.' He told Patrick Campbell he should get out to California. 'Aldous Huxley is creating a nice little colony there, with Isherwood, and other interesting people.' This was in contrast to a series of interviews and articles he published in the *Irish Press,* the official paper of the Fianna Fáil party. To this audience he spoke not of Huxley and Isherwood, but in favour of compulsory Irish – indeed, of actually beating the language into children. This rash of activity was brought up short, however, when soon after publication the Censorship Board banned *Land.* From then on Liam's stories appeared in *The Bell* and in *Irish Writing.*

The flirtation with Fianna Fáil was over, though he paid his own kind of tribute to the Republic in his novel about 1916, *Insurrection,* eventually published in 1950. One of the significant passages in that book is where Madden, his Connemara-born character, listens with rapture to the poet Patrick Pearse reading out the Proclamation, thoughts of his childhood scenes racing through his mind.

These were productive years for O'Flaherty, not only in English but also in Gaelic. As his novels suggested, he was happier now with the landscapes of the past, with that 'backward look' which Frank O'Connor would later characterise as typical of Irish literature. Though O'Flaherty claimed that he wrote even his English stories in Gaelic first drafts, the evidence about this is not consistent, and the Gaelic stories are, it seems, his own translations of his work. Nevertheless, he brought into the language of his childhood many of the virtues which had been so admired in his storytelling from the 1920s. This was a new note in Gaelic writing, cloyed as it was by a great deal of miserable journeyman work done for a government pension. The real writers, of whom Liam was an outstanding example, were few; but those few (among them Máirtín Ó Cadhain, then at his creative stage) were of true eminence.

The publication in 1953 of *Dúil* (by the adventurous new firm of Sáirséal agus Dill) was important for the Gaelic literature movement of the day. It was reviewed with appreciation, for instance, by Richard Power, himself the author of a powerful novel set on Aran. Stories in English still appeared from time to time in *The Bell*, and in America Devin-Adair, the conservative Irish-American publishing house, brought out in 1956 *The Stories of Liam O'Flaherty* with an introduction by Vivien Mercier, an Irish-born literary critic of the new generation. This book was in reality the last significant publication of O'Flaherty's career. Though there would be many reprints, some with introductions, there would be no more really new work.

Though primarily seen as an Aran Islander, O'Flaherty lived in many parts of Ireland, and wrote about them in his novels and stories: Wicklow, Kerry, Donegal, Sligo. But the Irish landscape, wherever it was, for him was suffused with a sense of magic and wonder – never still, never calm, always alive.

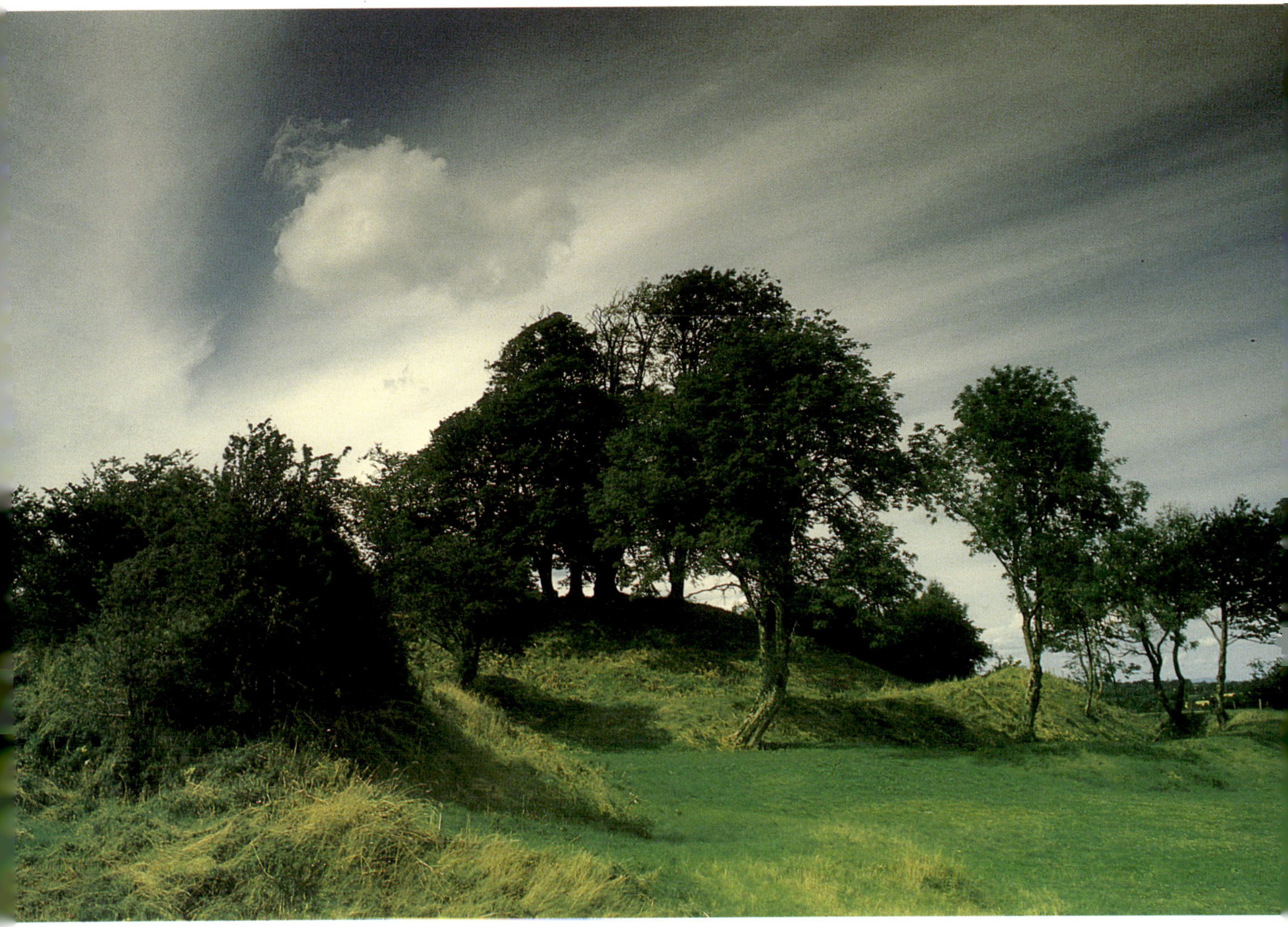

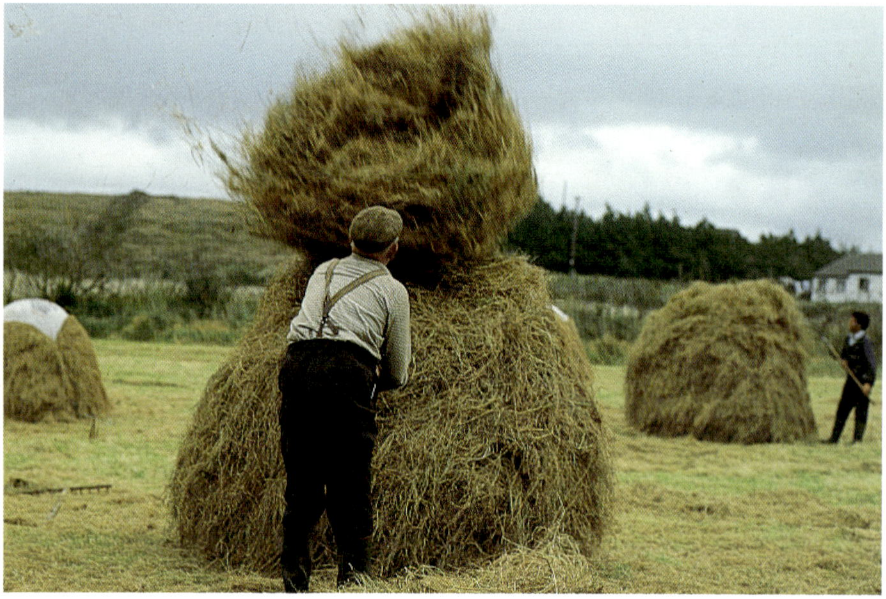
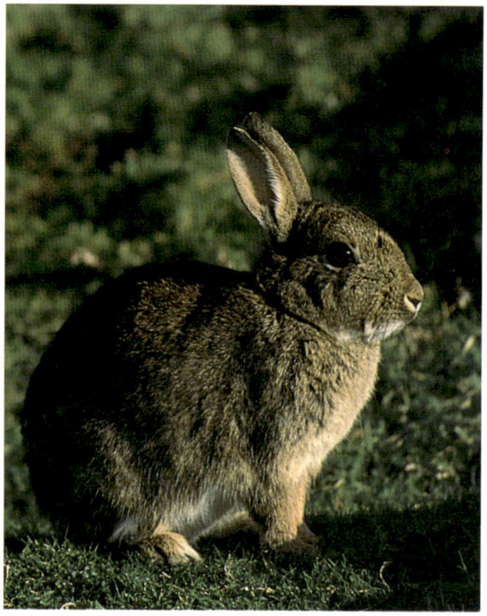
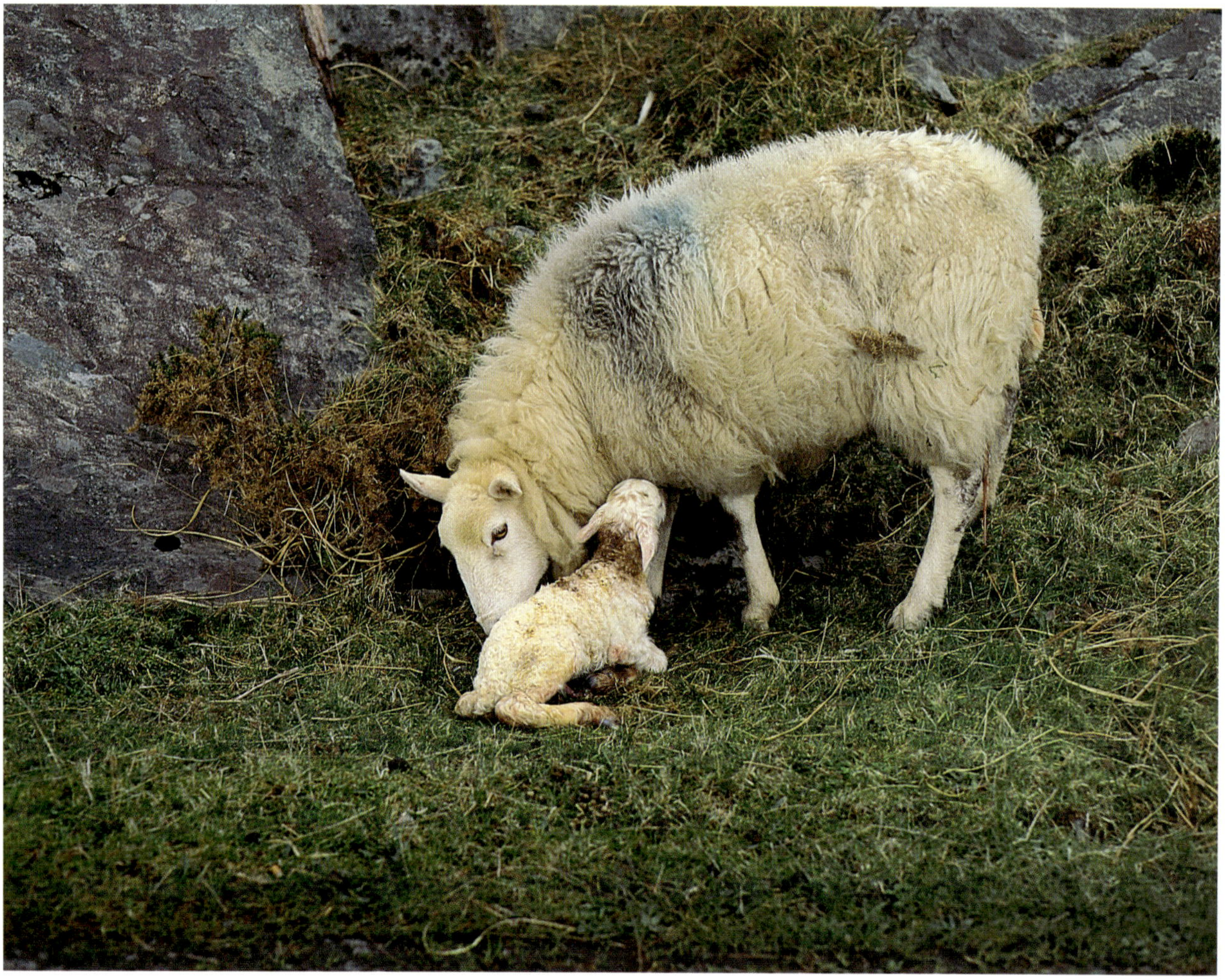

In this landscape, man and his work (however important to him) were only a small part of a greater whole. Life, wild and semi-wild, reflected something more primeval, something far more ancient than man.

The cycle of birth, growth, maturity and death – whether natural, or violent as in a dying wild fox weltering in its own blood – which he celebrates in so many of his stories, was for O'Flaherty a fact of nature, the proper order of things, a given that man must live with, because he cannot change it.

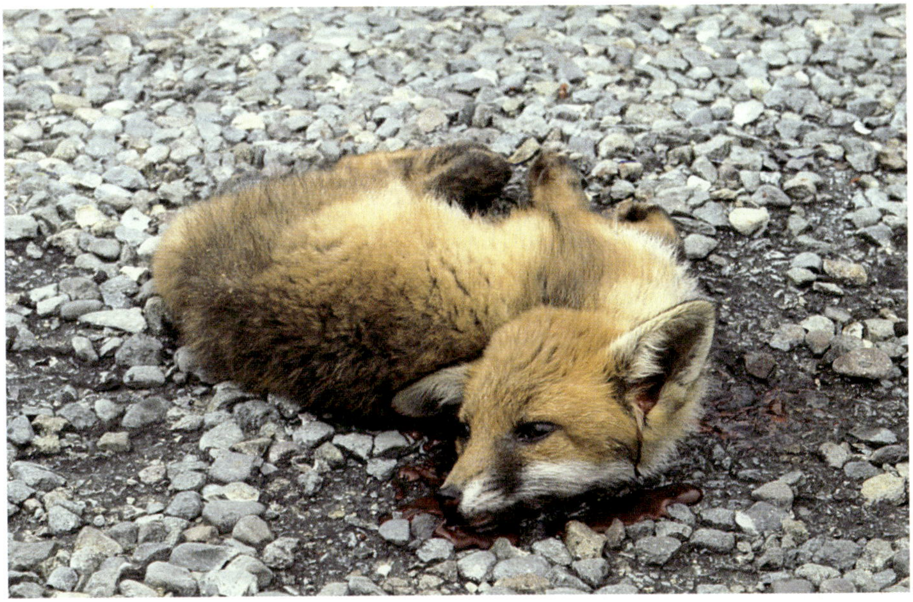

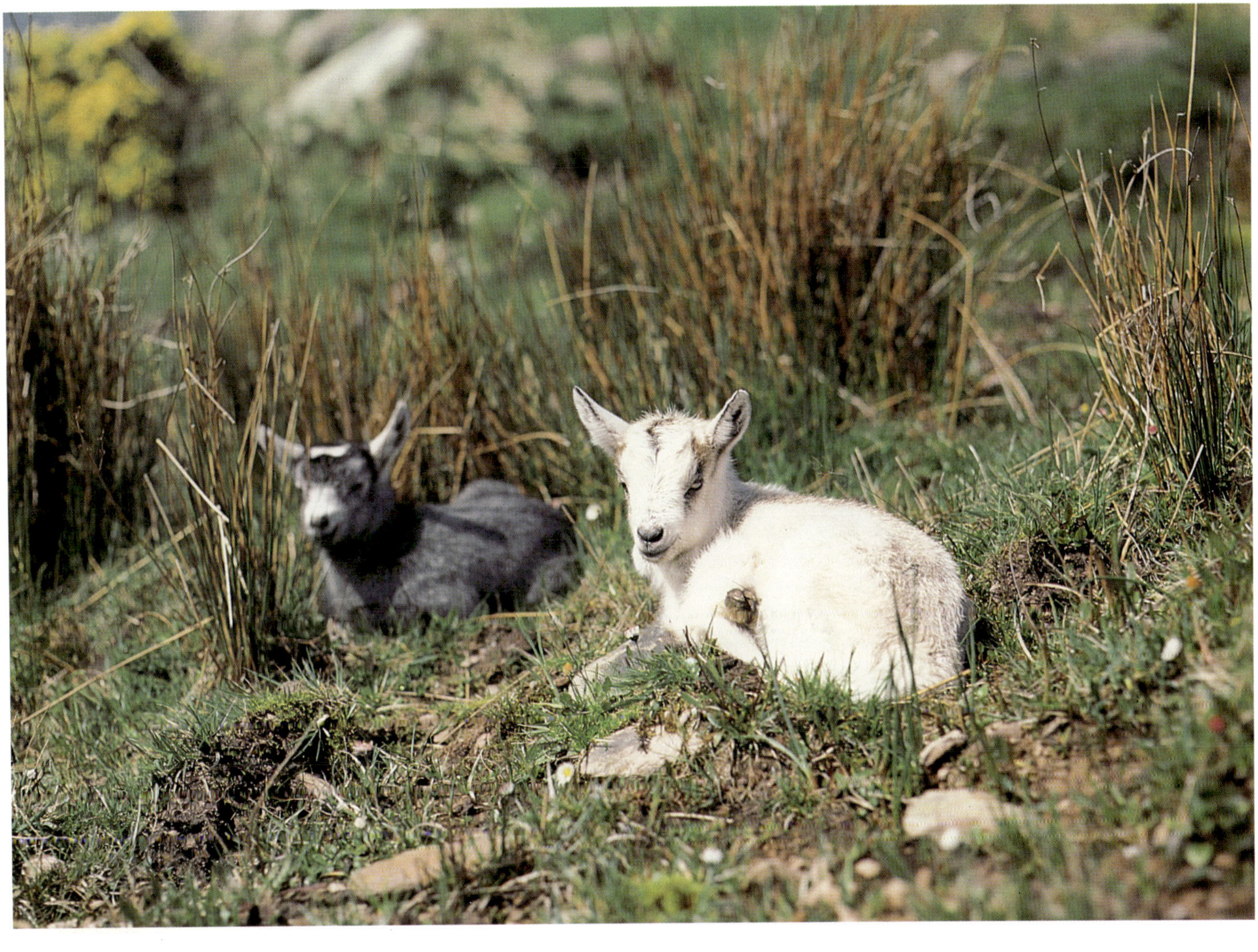

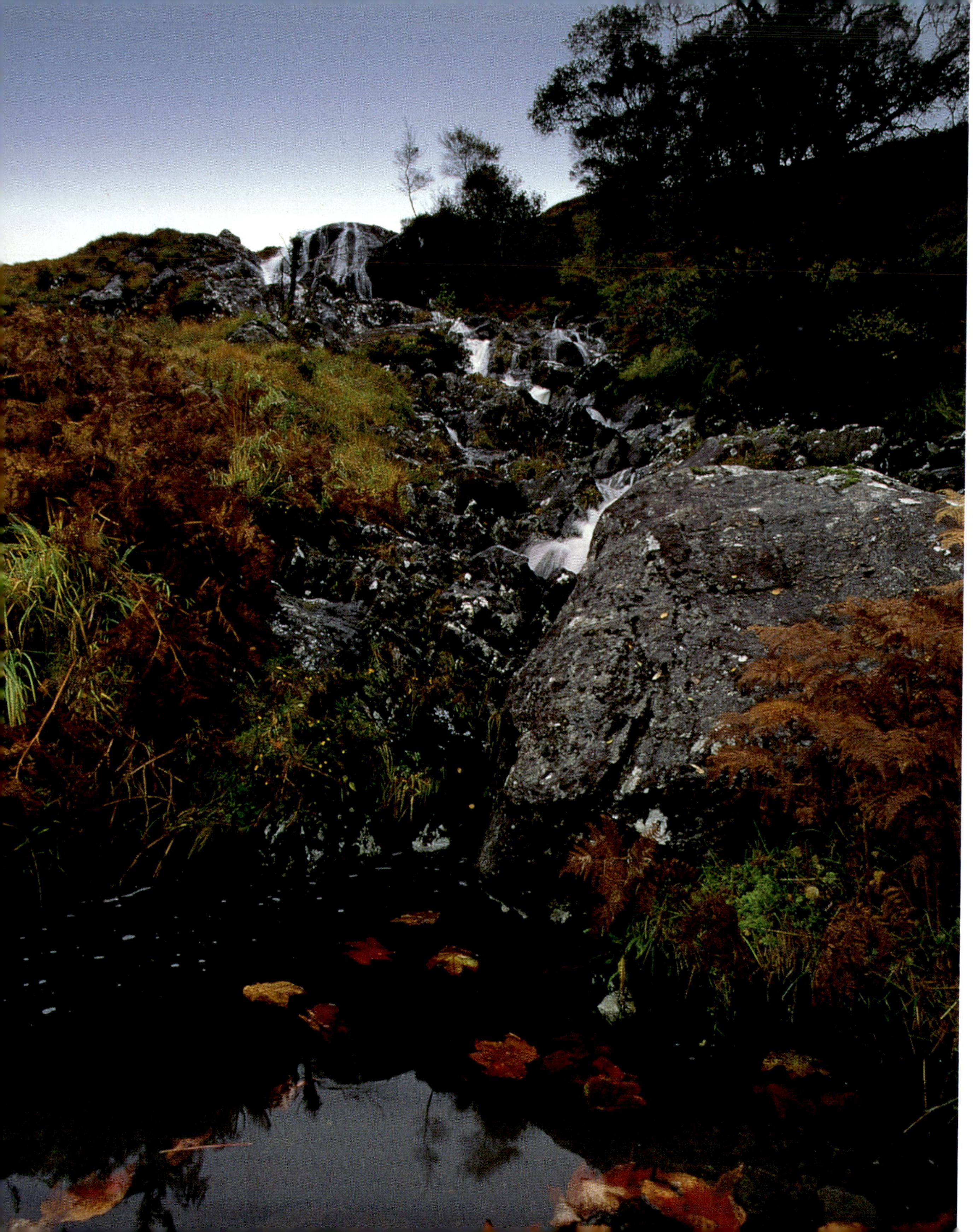

The natural order of things was not only bloody and violent, it could also be hauntingly beautiful, especially in the Irish autumn when the livid colours of the fading foliage make a brave show.

Even in the harshest Irish landscape, traditional life merged with the landscape around it, as with this Connaught cottage, similar to those in which O'Flaherty and so many of his people lived.

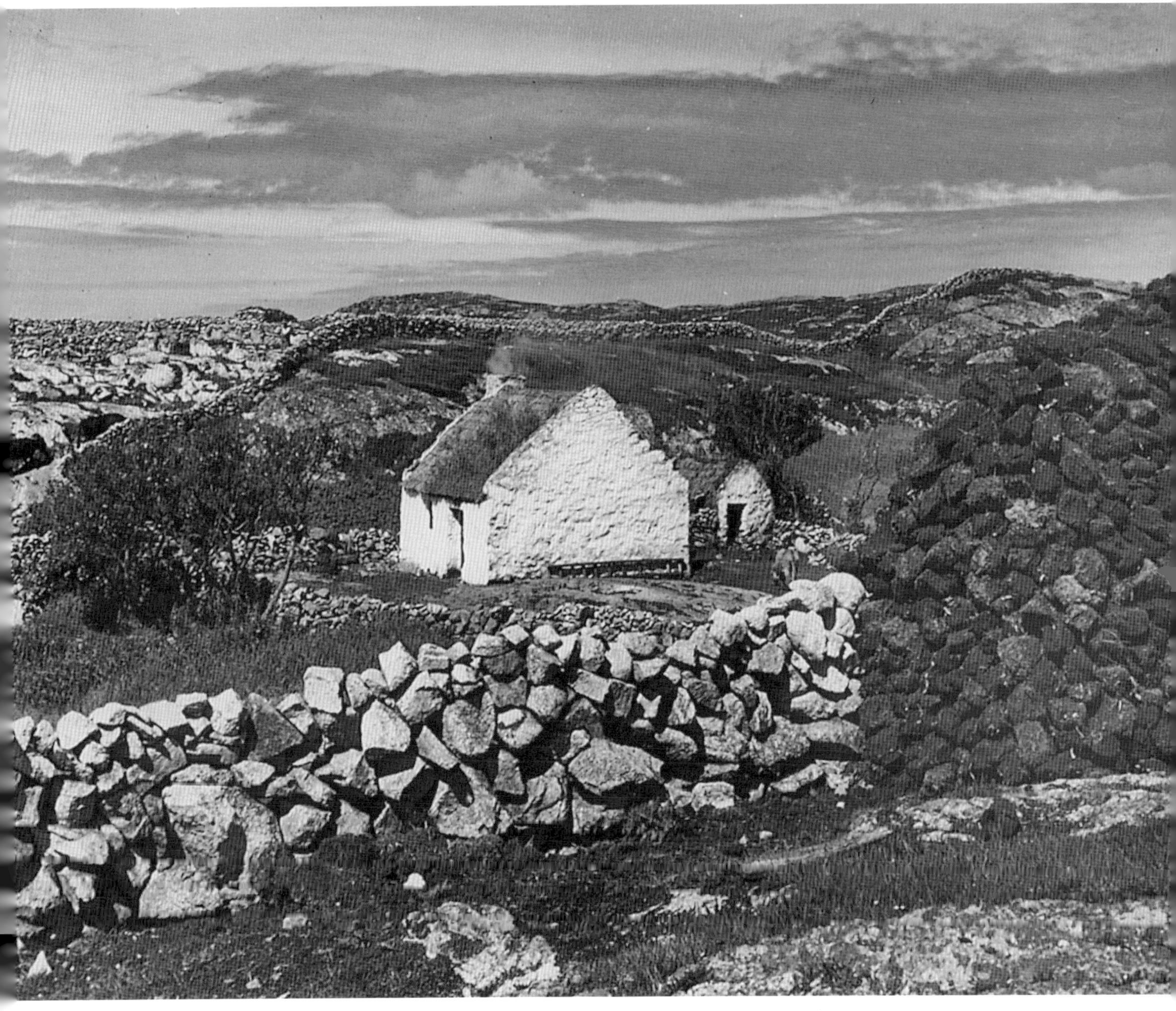

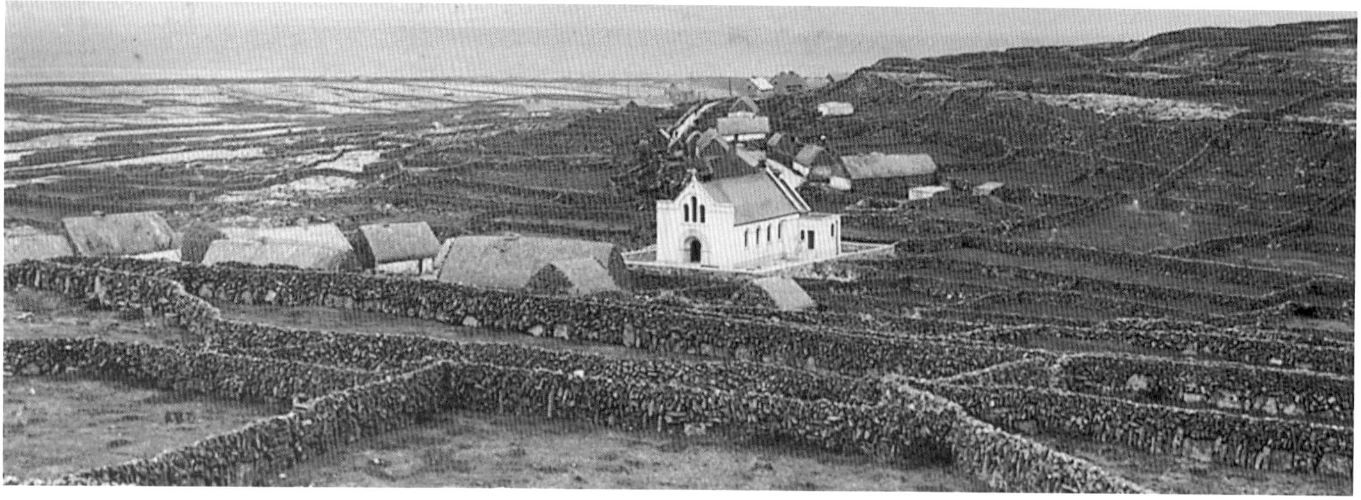

For Irish people the hardship of their life in this world often found consolation in religion, but O'Flaherty, at heart a pagan, would have seen the church (unlike the cottages) as an intrusion into the scene. Yet the feelings and hopes of the people in their lives of hardship and deprivation would have been admirable to him.

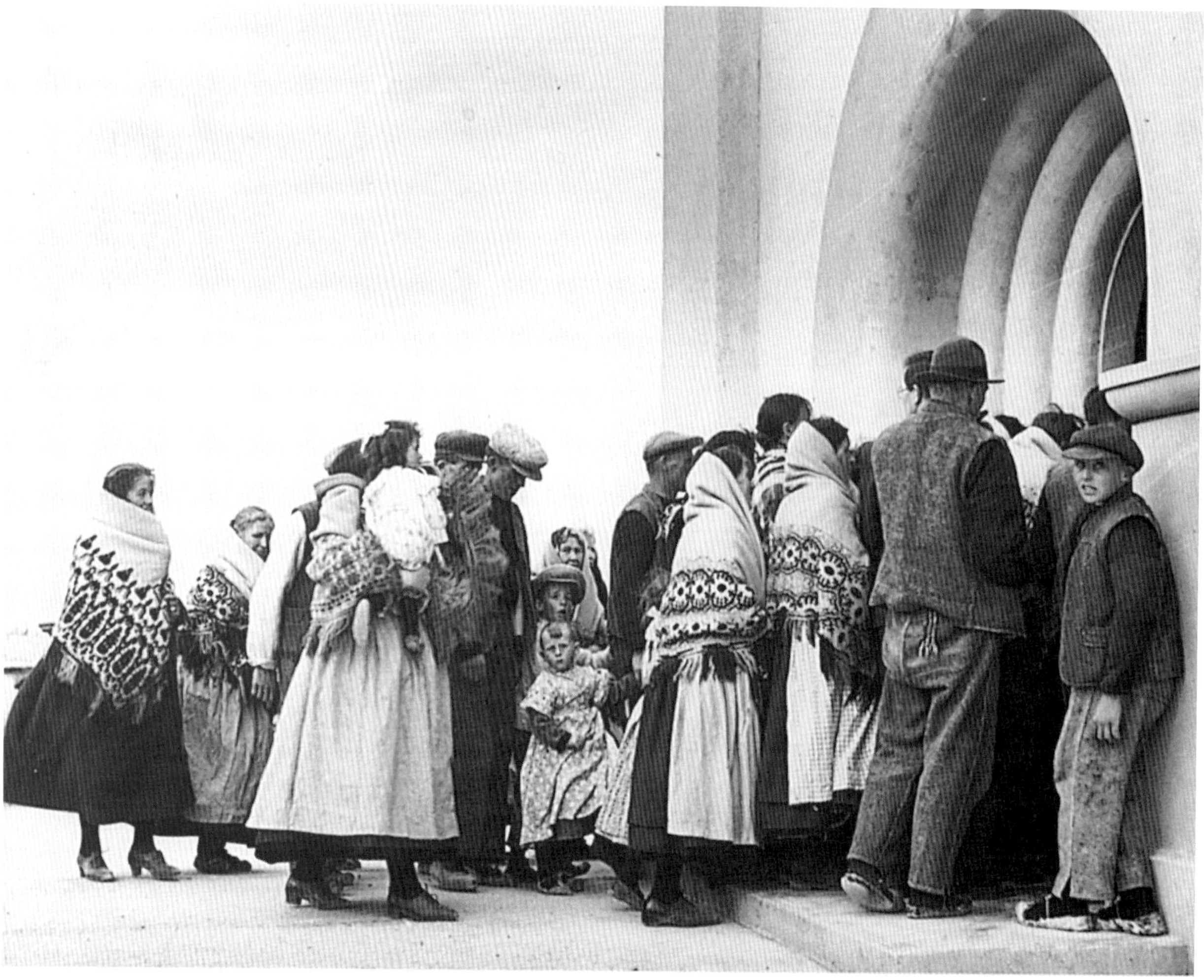

Right: *Transient moments of beauty, whether of a swan gracefully dividing the waters of a lake, or the fading of the last light of day along the western seaboard* (overleaf), *are the essential background to the life and the work of Liam O'Flaherty.*

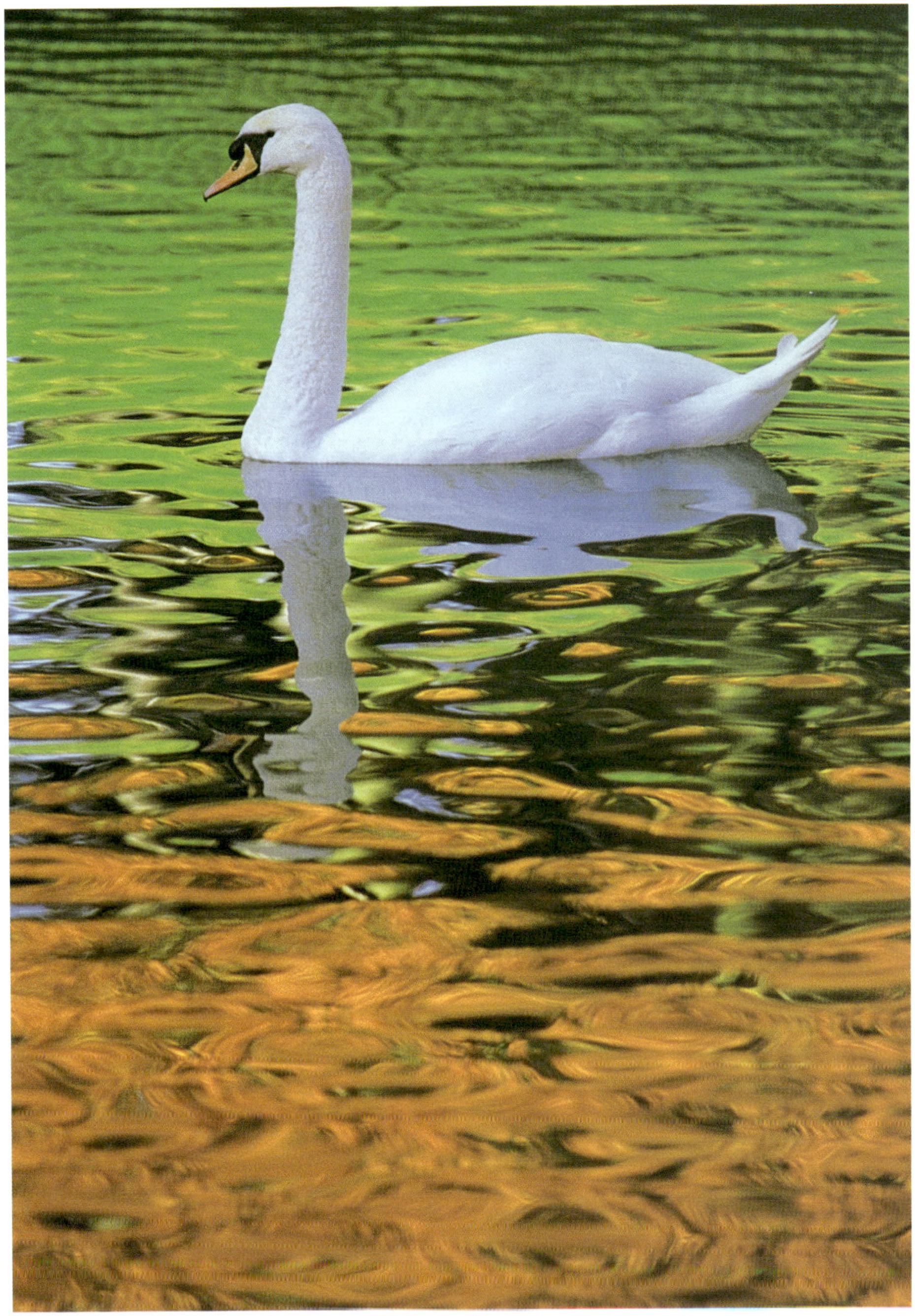

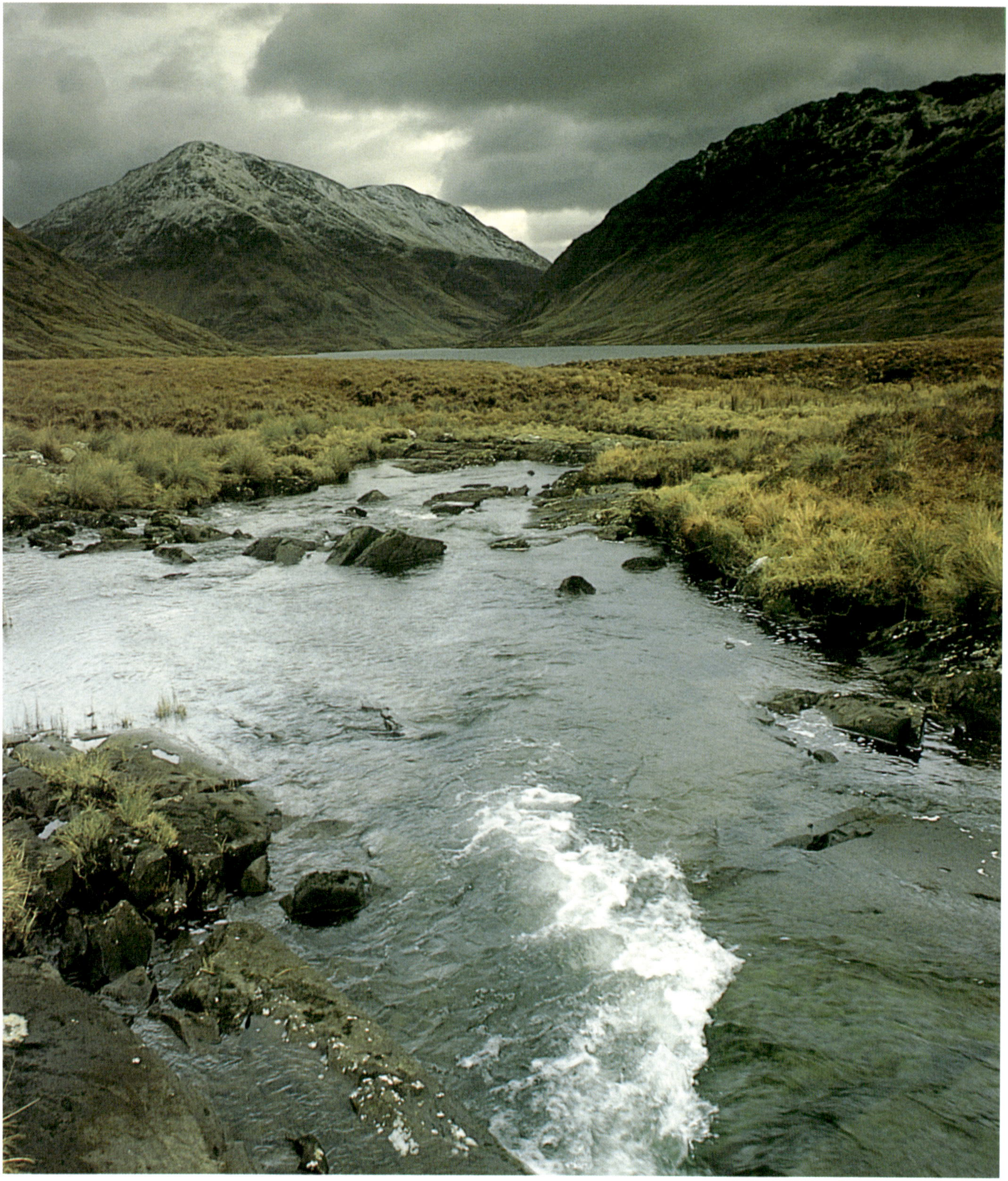

In 1952 he moved into a newly-built flat, no. 9 Wilton Court, beside the Grand Canal at Baggot Street Bridge. This was one of the first apartment blocks in Dublin and would be his base for the rest of his life. The flat was lovingly decorated with care by Liam and Kitty. Though Baggot Street – with Parson's Bookshop and the poet Patrick Kavanagh, the dramatist Brendan Behan and other literati in the neighbourhood – was Dublin's nearest thing to a literary quarter, Liam was little seen and did not mix much. Frank O'Connor would take a flat in the same block, but while his apartment was alive with comings and goings, O'Flaherty gained the reputation of a solitary.

He was, however, still tentatively involved with film work. Along with his old friends Patrick Kirwan and Patrick Campbell, he wrote the screenplay for *Jacqueline*, an adaptation of a Catherine Cookson novel which for some reason the producers transferred to working-class Belfast, of which Campbell and O'Flaherty had no experience. The film was not a success, and was indeed an embarrassment to Miss Cookson. In 1962 Liam's friend the actor Kieron Moore bought an option on *The Assassin*, but the film was never made, though a television version by Hugh Leonard was broadcast by BBC2 in 1968. In the same year the Greek director Jules Dassin remade *The Informer*, with an all-black cast, as *Up Tight.* Though *The Infomer* was dramatised (once by O'Flaherty himself with Walter Macken), efforts to turn it into a musical dragged on for well over a decade and came to nothing. It was in fact television, rather than his old hope, film, that made the most of Liam's work, with several adaptations in the last decades of his life.

The Rank screenplay was not quite Liam's last literary work – that was a story which appeared in *Lilliput* in 1958. *Insurrection*, which completed his trilogy of historical novels, turned out to be his last. He had begun a new novel, set in the decades before World War II, about (among other things) horse racing; it was called *The Gamblers* (with a nod to his old hero Dostoyevksy). He would talk of this from time to time until the early 1980s – 'I'm on a new novel now' – but the drive to complete it petered out.

An eviction during the Land War in Ireland, a period described in O'Flaherty's novel Land *(1946).*

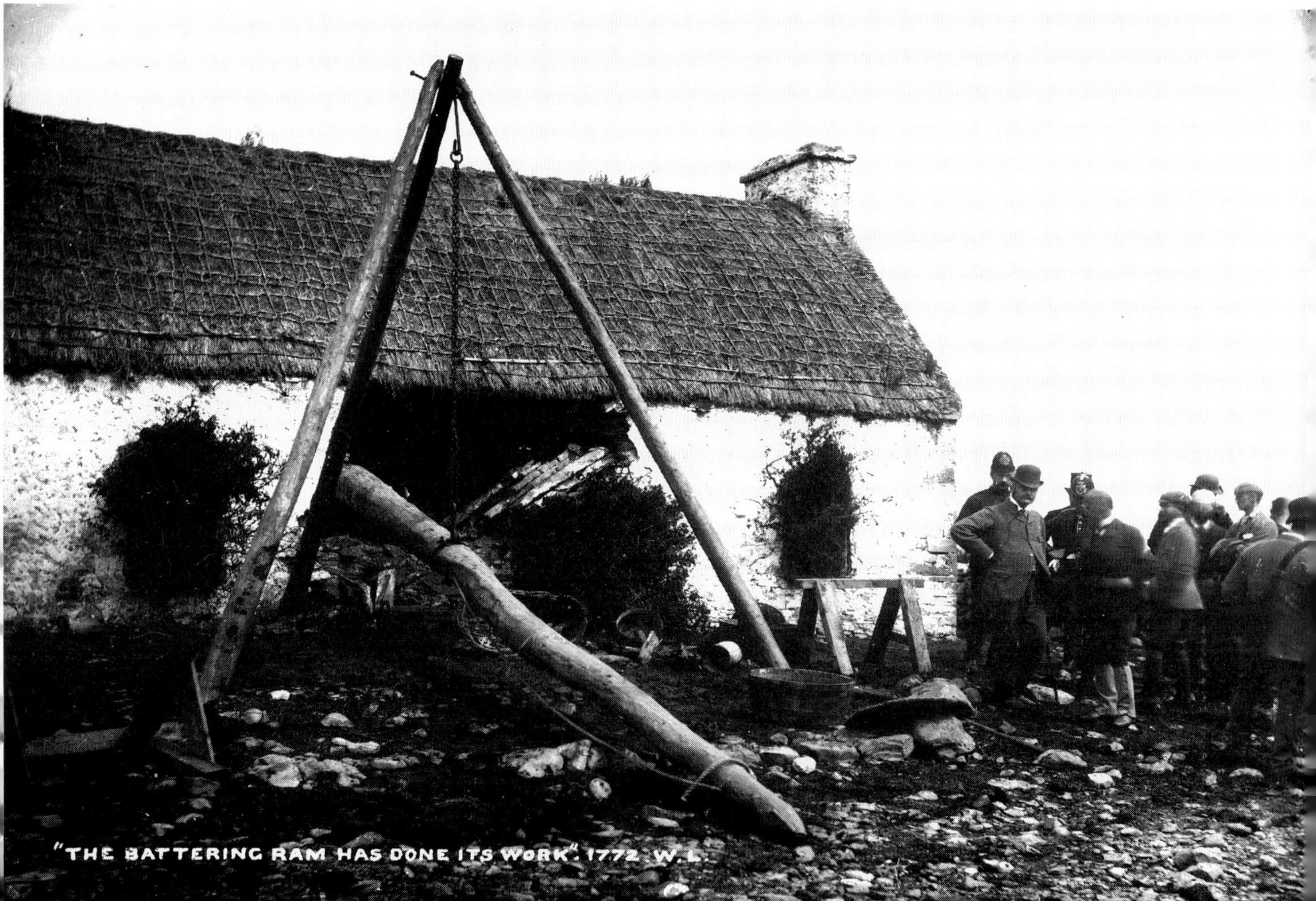

‘The Way to Act’
from Land *by Liam O’Flaherty*

‘O’Dwyer said you invited him to visit you,’ the priest continued.

‘Where is the young man?’ Raoul said.

‘He’s outside there,’ said Father Francis, nodding towards the window, ‘waiting for a signal from me.’

‘Really?’ said Raoul. ‘Why didn’t he come with you?’

‘I wanted to see if the coast were clear,’ the priest said. ‘Your sister doesn’t sympathise with us and you yourself might have changed your mind. Then again, O’Dwyer is in a bad state of mind. The Government people are playing with him, the way a cat plays with a mouse. Having no evidence that could convict him before a jury, they are pretending to look the other way. Yet they watch him the whole time, ready to pounce when it suits them. That sort of thing is hard on a young man like O’Dwyer. He’s in a bad state. I thought I’d tell you that first, so you wouldn’t be offended by his strange manners. By your leave, I’ll call him now.’

‘By all means,’ Raoul said.

The priest went to the window, opened it wide, leaned out and whistled softly. There was an answering whistle almost at once. Then the priest went out to open the hall door.

‘This is all very fortunate,’ Raoul said, caressing his beard. ‘I feel that I’m on the verge of finally becoming involved in something decisive.’

O’Dwyer seemed to be in great spirits when he came into the room, contrary to what Father Francis had said about his temper. He was wearing a well-fitting suit of blue serge that made him look very smart. With his face lighted by a gay smile, he came over to Raoul, shook his hands and began to apologise for the trouble he had caused on the previous meeting.

‘How is the cut?’ Raoul interrupted. ‘Upon my soul! I see no trace of it.’

‘It was only a scratch,’ O’Dwyer said with a shrug of his shoulders. ‘It has been healed for weeks.’

‘Do sit down,’ Raoul said. ‘I envy your strength. One moment you were lying unconscious on the kitchen table, dead to the world, as Annie Fitzpatrick would say. The next moment you were gone. I was very impressed by your vitality. I wanted terribly to know why a man of your great energy and courage could behave in such a stupid fashion.’

O’Dwyer had sat down in front of the fire between Raoul and Father Francis. His gaiety of expression changed suddenly as Raoul uttered the word ‘stupid.’ His face became frightening. Now it was apparent that Father Francis had not exaggerated when he said that the young man was in a bad state of mind.

‘What do you mean by that remark?’ O’Dwyer said slowly, clasping his laced fingers so tightly that the blood went out of them.

His cruel blue eyes were staring fixedly at Raoul, who was unable to prevent himself from feeling a little nervous.

‘You are the living image of your father,’ Raoul said. ‘I recognised you that day in my kitchen. Your father was the bosom friend of my youth. He was some years older than I, but similarity of ideas brought us together. Had he lived, he might have done great things. He had a brilliant intellect, together with indomitable courage and a natural capacity for leadership. His death was a great blow, not only to his friends, but to his country.’

‘Thank you, sir,’ O’Dwyer said in an angry tone, as he bowed jerkily.

‘I had an idea,’ Raoul continued, putting the tips of his fingers to his beard, ‘that you were trying to revenge your father’s death.’

O'Dwyer remained silent. He continued to stare fixedly at Raoul.

'Next to love,' said Raoul, 'revenge is possibly the most exalted emotion. However, it must be subtle in order to be completely satisfying.'

He paused for a moment, smiled and then added in a lower tone:

'If Butcher had not been wearing a metal vest, where would he be now?'

'In hell,' O'Dwyer said curtly.

Raoul shrugged his shoulders.

'If such a place really exists, which I doubt,' he said, 'we have no guarantee that Butcher would now be there. He is a clever fellow, and a famous man has said that God is always on the side of the big battalions. One simply does not know. All one knows is that he would be dead and out of mortal pain. Death by gunfire must be a pleasant sort of death, sudden and rather exciting. If I wanted to revenge myself on an enemy, I'd choose a much more subtle and lingering method.'

He paused, smiled once more and added:

'I'd torture him.'

Father Francis took his clay pipe out of his mouth, stared at Raoul in horror and then got to his feet.

'That's a terrible thing you have said,' he cried angrily. 'Let me tell you that the Irish people would never tolerate such methods. They are gentle and good people. What you are advocating is paganism.'

O'Dwyer put his hand on the priest's arm and said curtly, like a man speaking to a subordinate:

'Sit down.'

The priest winced on feeling the rough touch of O'Dwyer's arm. He looked at the young man reproachfully, as he resumed his seat.

'What kind of torture do you mean?' O'Dwyer said to Raoul.

'The torture of isolation,' Raoul said.

'Isolation?' said O'Dwyer.

'To isolate an enemy in the military sense,' Raoul said, 'means cutting him off from all means of supply, reinforcement and escape. In this instance, I give a different meaning to the word. The isolation of Captain Butcher would not need to be physically complete, in order to be effective and bring about his destruction. He would merely require to be deprived of his power little by little, until he was alone and utterly helpless.'

'Horrible!' Father Francis said.

Raoul looked at the priest haughtily and said:

'To isolate a priest, for instance, one denies him access to the performance of certain rites, by means of which he renews his belief in God and the immortality of the soul.'

Father Francis jumped to his feet once more.

'All that is paganism,' he cried. 'It's inspired by the Devil.'

'How many times more do I have to tell you to keep quiet?' O'Dwyer said in the same curt tone. 'Sit down at once.'

'Michael,' said the priest in a humiliated voice, 'I didn't think your father's son would say a thing like that to me.'

O'Dwyer flushed a little and glanced towards Raoul.

'All right,' he said gruffly, looking once more at the priest. 'Forget about it.'

'I went out with the Fenians in '67,' Father Francis cried, with a note of arrogant defiance in his voice. 'For that act of rebellion against my vow of obedience, I have since been deprived of the right to administer the sacraments. For twelve years I have followed my fate, the most miserable of God's creatures, an anointed priest that is denied the right to perform the miracle of all miracles.'

'That's enough now,' O'Dwyer said.

'I thought so,' Raoul said to himself. 'An isolated priest. The torture of the Vatican.'

He got to his feet and bowed to Father Francis with great ceremony.

'I apologise,' he said, 'for failing to realise that you are a great poet, until you spoke just now. Won't you shake hands and forgive me for my discourtesy?'

The priest hesitated for a moment, while he looked at Raoul critically. Then he suddenly grasped Raoul's extended hand.

'Forgive me, too,' he said with deep emotion, 'for failing to realise that you are a good man. Even though you say queer things, that no good man should say, you are still a good man. We all have our foolish vanities. I see that giving voice to queer ideas is your pet vanity. God will forgive you for that. God forgives everything to the good. I want to be friends with you.'

'Splendid!' said Raoul. 'I know that I'm going to value your friendship highly. The soldier, the poet and the monk represent what is finest in man. They represent man's will to power, to beauty and to immortality. They alone among men are capable of complete love, because they love the unattainable. Their love is never tarnished by possession. Before all three of them, I always bow low. When I bowed to you, I bowed to all three.'

Father Francis sat down, took out a large red handkerchief and blew his nose violently to conceal his emotion. Raoul also sat down.

'How would you go about destroying an enemy by means of isolation?' said O'Dwyer, who had been staring intently at the fire during this interlude.

'For that,' said Raoul, 'the efforts of a single man, or even a group of picked men like the Fenian Society, would be useless. The help of the whole people would be necessary.'

'The whole people?' O'Dwyer said excitedly, now fixing his gaze on Raoul.

'The whole people,' Raoul said, 'disciplined and acting in obedience to a single will.'

There was silence for a few moments. Then O'Dwyer's face suddenly lit with enthusiasm.

'I see that you now understand me,' Raoul said, touching his beard with his finger-tips.

'Maybe I do,' O'Dwyer said. 'I want to hear your plan.'

'So do I,' Father Francis said.

'Then you are no longer opposed to the idea of torture?' Raoul said to the priest.

'Who am I to condemn the methods of such a wise man as you?' Father Francis said. 'Great ideas are more powerful than an army with banners.'

'Thank you,' Raoul said, getting to his feet. 'I'll tell you about my plan, as soon as I have notified my daughter that she has two guests for supper. You can both stay, I trust.'

The two men accepted the invitation.

'Good,' said Raoul. 'I hope that we have laid plans for setting the wheel of Irish destiny spinning by supper-time. I'm not a mystic, but I believe in destiny. A vice of some sort is necessary to maintain sanity.'

The last days of the Easter Rising – an imaginative reconstruction by artist Walter Paget, with Pearse and Connolly (wounded on stretcher) contemplating defeat.

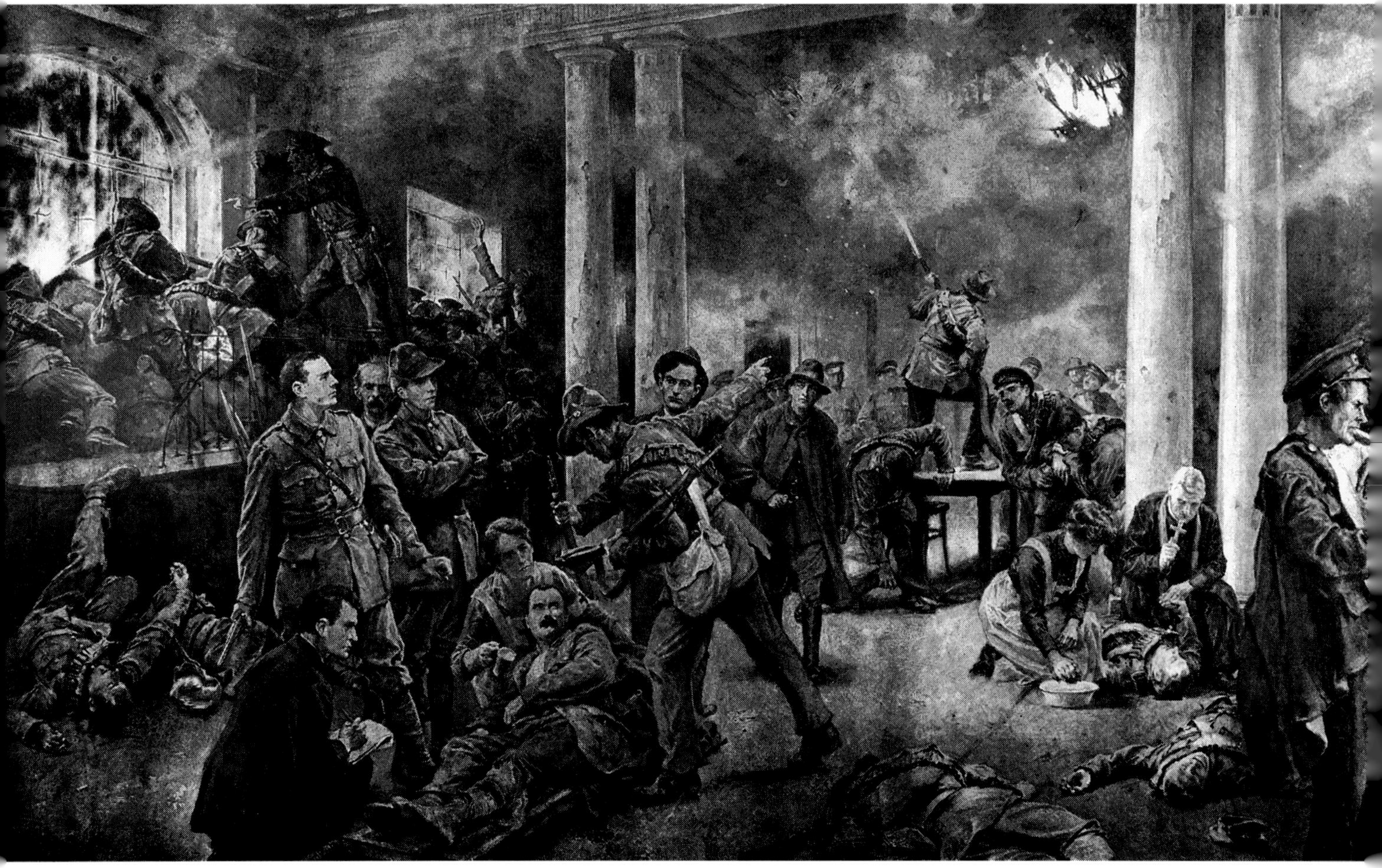

'Patriotism'
from Insurrection *by Liam O'Flaherty*

The great crowd was now silent. All eyes were turned towards the Grecian columns of the portico, where Patrick Pearse stood ready to proclaim the purpose of the insurrection. The people were now like an audience at a theatre, tensely waiting for the climax of a play's first act. Even the windows and the roofs of the houses on either side of the street were thronged with spectators. The hoarse rattle of machine-gun fire came from beyond the river.

'Irishmen and Irishwomen!' Patrick Pearse cried out in a voice of great beauty. 'In the name of God and of the dead generations from which she receives her traditions of nationhood, Ireland, through us, summons her children to her flag and strikes for her freedom. Having organised and trained her manhood through her secret revolutionary organisation, the Irish Republican Brotherhood, and through her open military organisations, the Irish Volunteers and the Irish Citizen Army ...'

At that moment, Madden threw his head forward and stared in rapture at the poet's face. He trembled and his face shone like that of the smiling woman that stood close to him. For the first time in his life, his mind had conceived an abstract idea that lit the fire of passion in his soul. Although the words that he heard were beyond his comprehension, their sound evoked the memory of all that had exalted him since childhood. Like music, they carried him away into enchantment.

He heard his mother's crooning voice and he felt the cool touch of her hand on his sick forehead, while the roar of the distant sea came through the moonlit window of his room. He heard the twitter of birds in the eaves of the village houses, as the lovely summer days faded into night. He heard the creaking of ropes through their blocks and the great rustle of unfurling canvas as the hookers hoisted sail going down Kilkerrin Bay. He heard the larks sing in April above the smoking fields, where the shining spades were opening the black earth.

'We declare the right of the people of Ireland,' Patrick Pearse continued, 'to the ownership of Ireland and to the unfettered control of Irish destinies to be sovereign and indefeasible. The long usurpation of that right by a foreign people and government has not extinguished the right, nor can it be extinguished except by the destruction of the Irish people. In every generation the Irish people have asserted their right to national freedom and sovereignty. Six times during the last three hundred years they have asserted it in arms. Standing on that fundamental right and again asserting it in arms, in the face of the world, we hereby proclaim the Irish Republic as a sovereign independent state and we pledge our lives and the lives of our comrades in arms to the cause of its freedom, of its welfare and of its exaltation among the nations.'

Madden now recalled a flock of wild geese that he had seen fly across the starry sky one winter's night, above the bleak mountainside on which he lived. The soft whirring of their wings in the silence of the vast firmament had then rent his soul with longing for a beauty that he could not comprehend; just as he now longed for the beauty that the poet proclaimed.

The men with rifles fired a volley into the air when Patrick Pearse had finished reading the document. As the group returned to the Post Office the whole garrison began to sing the battle anthem of the insurrection. Some of the crowd began to cheer. Others joined in the singing. The great majority, however, gave voice to hatred of what the poet had said. Sticks and fists were again raised, like waves bursting into foam on the surface of a turbulent sea that has been calmed for a little while by the pouring of oil.

Madden stood in a trance amid the renewed tumult, staring at the door through which the poet had disappeared. The images still coursed in sombre rapture through his mind. Then suddenly they vanished and he felt unbearably lonely, as if he had lost somebody very dear to him. Elbowing the people fiercely from his path, he rushed towards the General Post Office, in order to re-establish contact with the man that had given him such extraordinary pleasure.

When he was within ten yards of the portico, he was halted by a great mass of people that pressed slowly towards the south. Even though he tried with all his strength to break through this mass, he was thrown back inch by inch towards the south-east. Then he managed to halt by putting his arm round one of the standards that supported the electric power line of the tram-way. There he looked northwards over the heads of the people and saw that they had been set in motion by a great number of priests, who formed a line that stretched across the whole width of the thoroughfare.

The black line of priests advanced in silence, with their arms locked, calm and inscrutable, being obeyed without question by the multitude. Their silence went before them, like a subtle element, gradually infecting layer after layer of the crowd in an advancing tide, till the vulgar turbulence was drowned by their mysterious order and there was no sound in the thoroughfare other than the dull shuffle of southward-moving feet and the singing of the insurgents within the General Post Office.

When the line reached him, Madden abandoned his hold, turned his back and marched southwards with the people. He had not gone far when he heard a heavy burst of gun-fire from beyond the river. Almost at the same moment, the insurgents broke into the chorus of their song.

He listened intently to the words:

'Soldiers are we whose lives are pledged to Ireland.
Some have come from a land beyond the sea;
Sworn to be free, no more our ancient sireland
Shall shelter the despot or the slave ...'

He again heard the whirring wings of the wild geese, calling him to the pursuit of a beauty that he could not comprehend. He recalled the beautiful voice of the poet and he became unbearably lonely.

Wilton Place, with the Wilton Court flats, where O'Flaherty leased an apartment in 1952. In the foreground is the Baggot St. lock of the Grand Canal.

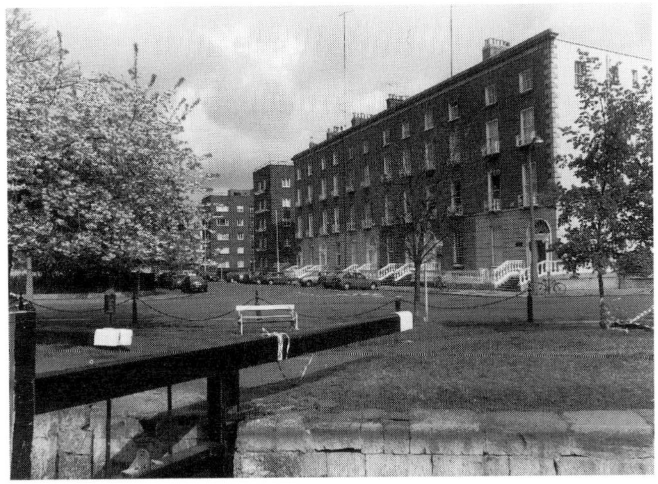

RETURN TO ARAN In Dublin Liam was seen from time to time at public events, such as the annual dinners given then by An Club Leabhar. At one of these in the Shelbourne Hotel in the early 1950s Harry Boylan recalls being at the same table with O'Flaherty, a large impressive man. All went well until the allotment of wine ran out. Liam took the initiative, rose to his feet and banged the table with his sword-stick, crying out in Gaelic 'More wine'. The sword-stick, which had just the right kind of romantic panache for O'Flaherty, went everywhere with him (according to Dublin legend), as a protection in the tight corners he was thought to get himself into in the wild regions of the world. No one ever saw it drawn in Dublin. The wine was brought.

Though friendly enough, Liam could not be drawn too far into the Gaelic language movement. In the late 1960s Eoghan Ó hAnluain approached him to write for *Comhar*, the influential liberal-minded Gaelic monthly, but though they met under the Cusack Stand at Croke Park, Liam only wanted to discuss the famous three-in-a-row win by Galway.

In Wilton Court he had become a kind of pagan hermit, escaping from time to time for holidays in Europe, sustained by the love, visits and material aid of Kitty Tailer. Though there were still stormy passages in their relationship, it had been sustained through the decline of his literary powers and the advent of physical frailty. His letters of these years are heart-rending in both their courage and their loneliness. Even so, something of his old fire remained in acid comments on the world and a sustained interest in reading left-wing literature.

Though Sean O'Faolain and Frank O'Connor still involved themselves in political and literary controversies, Liam did not. O'Connor, always an enemy of censorship, gave as an example the odd situation in 1962 of a continental university looking for the works of Mr O'Flaherty and discovering that in the whole of Ireland there was no such thing.

On 28 August 1970 there was a celebration of Liam's seventy-fifth birthday. This ended with a drinking session in Fitzharris's in Ringsend. The poet Anthony Cronin recalls that people there, though they knew little or nothing about Liam, sensed that he was a hero and treated him as such, walking back with him as far as Baggot Street Bridge. Liam might occasionally invite people back to the flat, even when Kitty was not there; but generally he kept himself to himself. By the early 1960s friends such as Francis Stuart realised that the novel would never be finished; that Liam was suffering from writer's block. It is significant that in April 1973 he made out the will which was still in force when he died over a decade later.

It was at this time that he got to know his second daughter, Joyce Rathbone, a pianist and author of *Martin Bosey* (London 1979), a children's book, who had been born in New York in 1930, but grew up in England.

Below: *Liam O'Flaherty on his final visit to Aran, with his nieces Alice Powell (right) and Maureen Concannon (left)*
Opposite: *The bleak, rockfast landscape of Aran, the essential scenery of so much of O'Flaherty's work.*

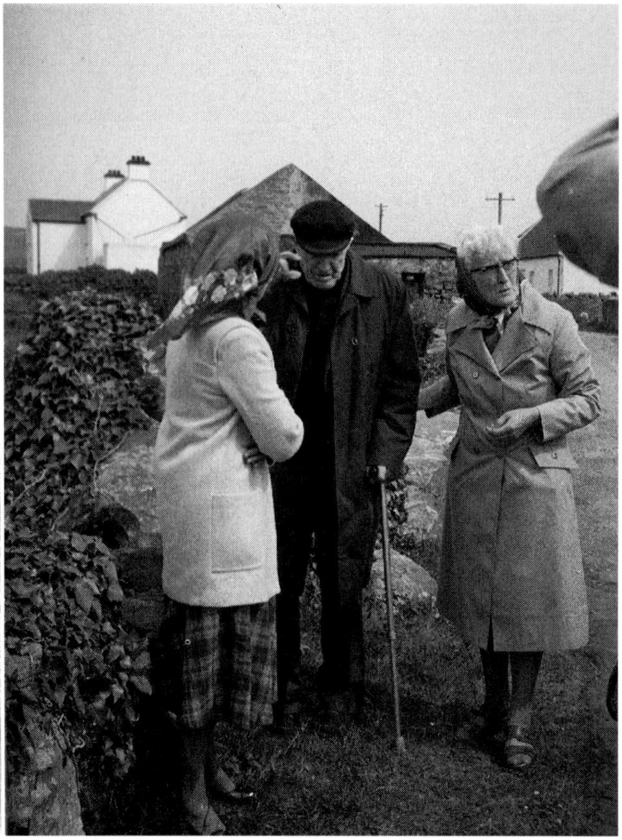

Though new work might not be written with the ease it once was, the 1970s found his old work again in demand. In Dublin Wolfhound Press began a programme of reissuing such work as it could get the rights to, and though this would not include *The Informer,* it did include *Skerrett, Famine* and the early novels, as well as lesser books. Liam had now reached the age at which to have survived at all brought honours in its wake: an honorary degree from University College Galway in 1974 (an eventful day during which he managed to upstage Siobhan McKenna), literary prizes, television adaptations. He was surprised and pleased when his eightieth birthday was marked by a telegram of congratulations from the President of Ireland, Cearbhall Ó Dálaigh, perhaps the most cultured occupant of that office; and by an official reception at the Arts Council. He also had the admiration of younger writers, and not only those who wrote in Gaelic: in a collection of stories by Ronan Sheehan there is a vignette of how as a student the writer was introduced to O'Flaherty through the medium of university lectures by Professor Martin, who had included several of Liam's stories in the new-style English schoolbooks introduced in the 1960s. *Dúil* had a fixed and popular place in the school curriculum as well – Liam's daughter Pegeen recalls that children would approach him in the street to tell of their pleasure in reading it. Critical works on O'Flaherty by American academics began to appear. The *enfant terrible* had become an accepted classic.

Together he and Kitty – accompanied by his writer nephew, Breandán Ó hEithir, and Wolfhound Press publisher Seamus Cashman – made a two-day journey to Aran on 16 June 1980 (Liam's first visit in seventeen years) and visited Gort na gCapall. There they saw his childhood home, and he evoked the past for his companion and the friends who came with them, apostrophising the rock that stood nearby: 'Bail Dhia ort, a chloch mhór; tá aithne agam ortsa.'

After talking to his nieces and seeing their children ('Show me the boys! I'm not interested in the girls'), and seeing a dramatic performance from his work by local schoolchildren, a sense of bemusement came over him. Tired of the manoeuvres of a television crew, he decided he had had enough. 'Come on, Kitty,' he finally growled. 'Let's get the hell out of here.' They escaped a day early by plane to Galway.

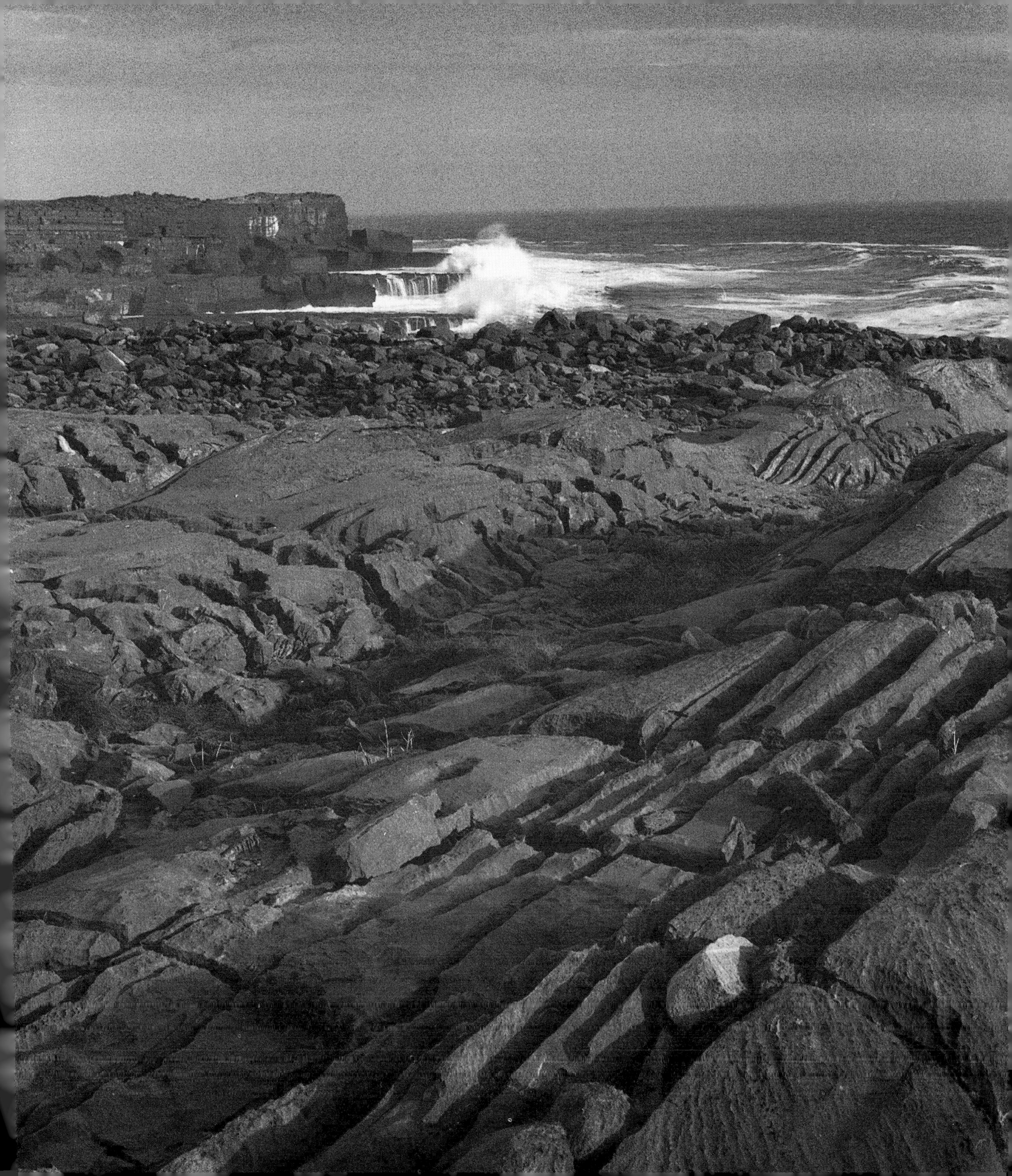

Below: *Liam O'Flaherty and Kitty Tailer on his last visit to Aran, with his nieces Maureen Concannon (far left) and Alice Powell (second from left).*

An Aran horse at Gort na gCapall – seeming to take its life from the very earth it moves on.

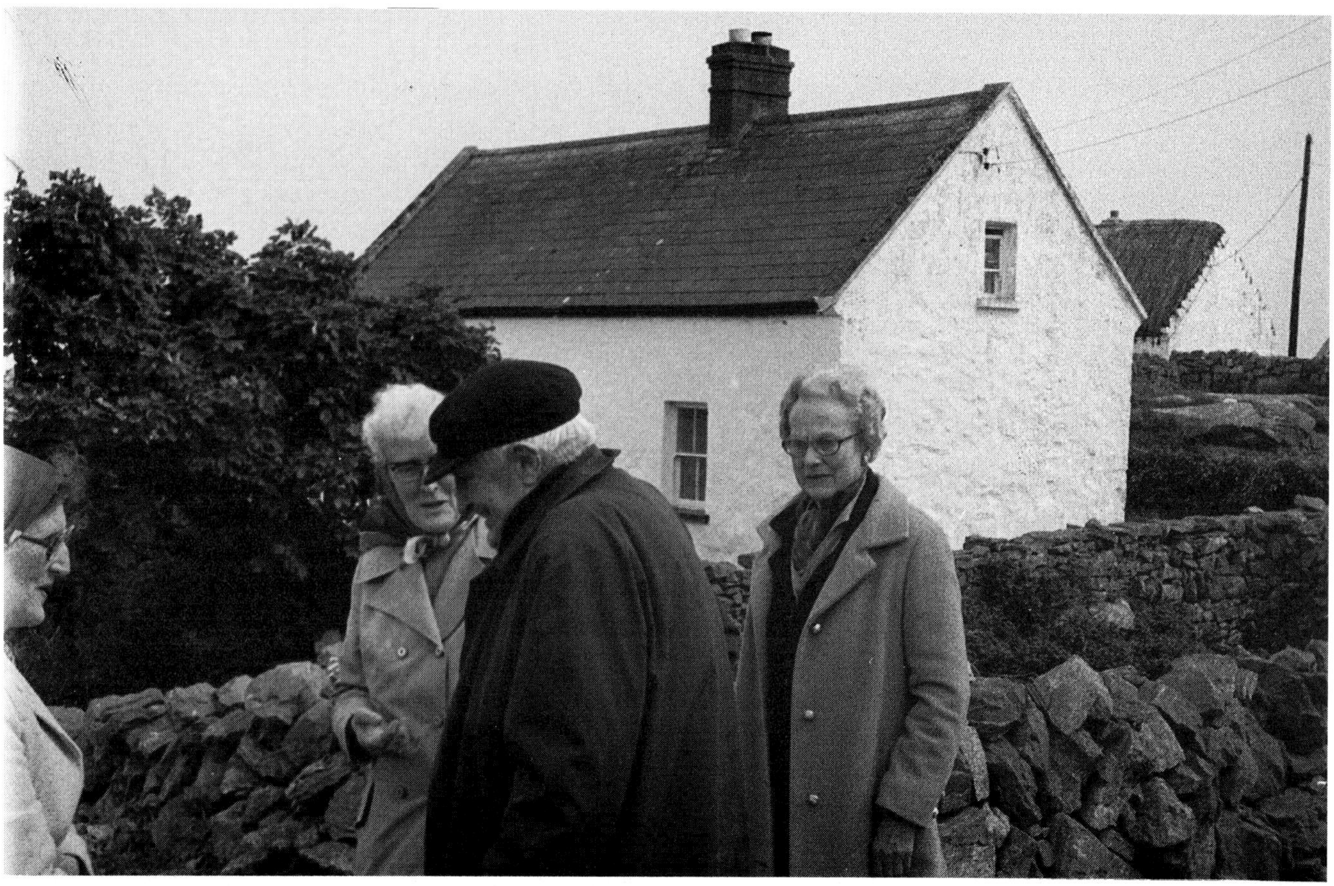

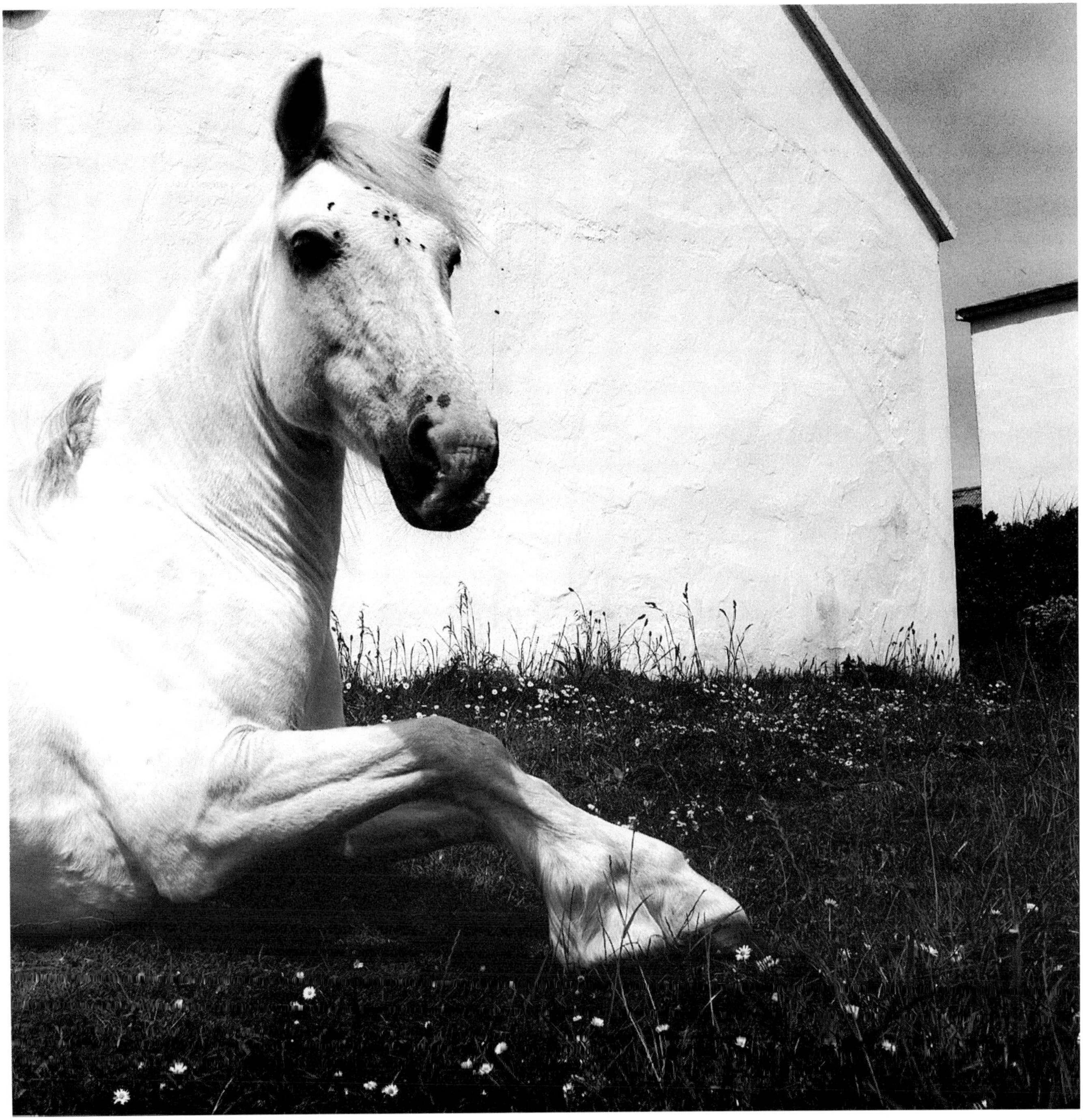

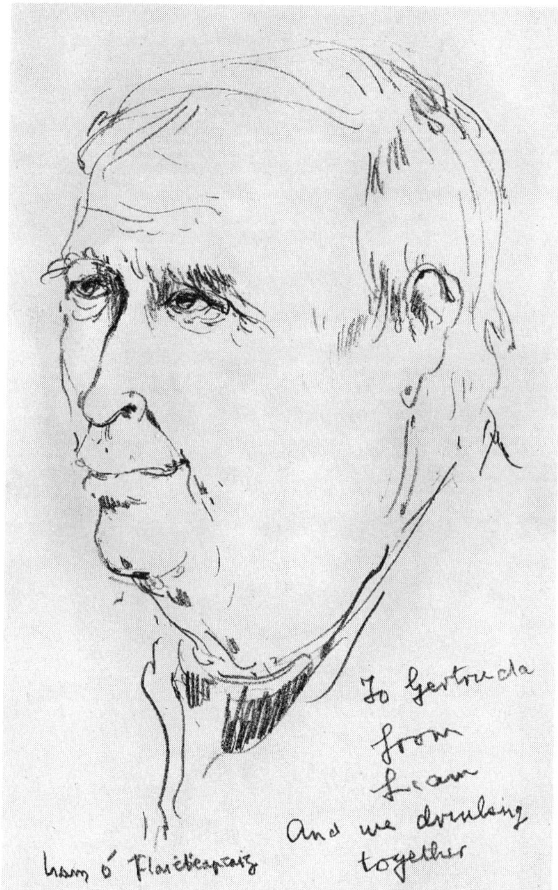

The private man: drawing of Liam O'Flaherty by his admirer, the German artist Gertrude Degenhardt, 1975.

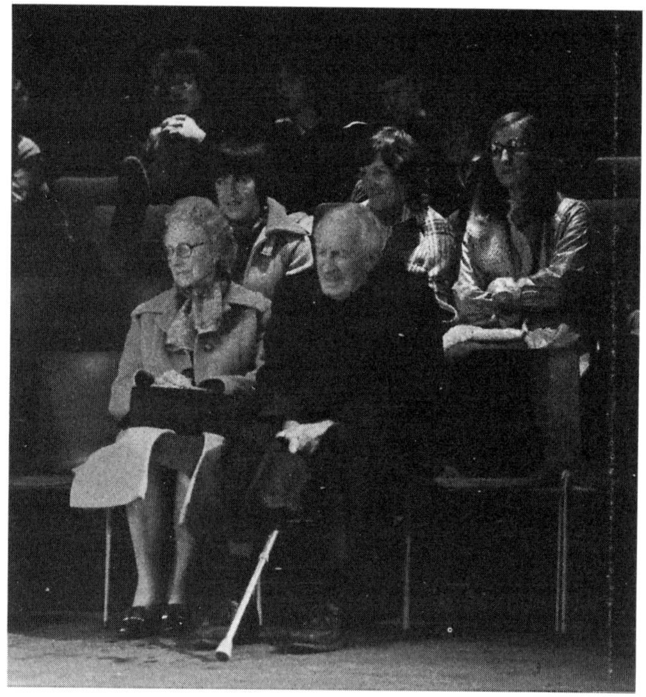

The public figure: Liam and Kitty at a public reading of his work, organised by his publishers.

‘An tAonach’ *le Liam Ó Flaithearta as* Dúil

Bhí Liam Ó Flaithearta chomh cumasach céanna ag scríobh i ngaeilge agus a bhí sé in mbéarla. Sa ghearrscéal seo as **Dúil**, *an t-aon cnuasach gearrscéalta in ngaeilge atá foillsithe aige, léirtear a oilteacht agus a liriceacht in úsáid na teanga chun fuaimeanna agus sainchomhartaí an haonach tuaithe a chur ós ár gcomhar.*

Bhí cnagadh bodhar ag crúba móra na mbeithíoch ag bualadh na sráide, ag siúl, ag rith, ag brú, ag sciorradh anuas; meall mór dearg daingean ag gluaiseacht go bosach agus ag búiriúch; fuaim análach na mbúir ar nós toirní, measctha le glór garbh na bhfear a bhí ag tiomáint le maidí.

Súile móra boga gan meabhair; adhairt chuileog greamaithe sna sramacha fliucha a bhí ag sileadh le gach súil. Craicne dearga báite le allas, ag lonradh faoi sholas na gréine; craicne móra dearga ag cur deataí uathu, deatach allais; deatach fhionn measctha le smúdar geal an bhóthair.

Másaí leathana feolmhara na mart á lascadh. Ioscadaí lúbtha ag gíoscadh faoi mheáchan na gcorp. Adharca bánbhuí á gcasadh os cionn droim na droinge; adharca ardaithe; fir arda ag lascadh.

Shroicheadar ceann an aonaigh ag deireadh na sráide ar aghaidh geata dubh an teampaill. Chuireadar a gcinn le talamh, ag smúrthacht go tromanálach, a dtaobhа ag bualadh, ag ceilt a súl faoi bholg a chéile ar na cuileoga. Ó gheata an teampaill bhíodar ina scuaine ag sileadh suas go teach an dochtúra ar cheann eile an bhaile; an bóthar ar fad brataithe leo, agus le botháin bheaga chanbháis lucht díolta milseán.

Ól. Ní ólfad. Ól. Bhí gach uile dhuine ag ól. Ní bhlaisim de. Ól fíon. Níl aon dochar i bhfíon. Ólann sagairt é. Ní ólfad, thug mé geall. Níl aon dochar i bhfíon. Ólann sagairt é. Ní olfad, thug mé geall. Sea. Sú na dtor. Sú fuar ag blubarnaigh as an mbuidéal, seacht míle bolgán ag fiuchadh ina chúr. Is fearr liomsa leann. Leann dubh. Cúr buí. Corcán de. Fuisce. Fuisce gan uisce. Gáir. Craitheadh lámh. Go mbeire muid beo ar an am seo arís.

Gach uile dhuine lofa le airgead, bailithe ó Cháisc, le n-ól lá an aonaigh. Mná péacaithe agus fuinneamh ina gcruth, ag ceannach ribíní agus earraí, greamaithe gléasta. Páistí beaga santacha ag cnagadh milseán idir fiacla beaga boga.

Tá na beithígh bhainne á mbleán agus na ceannaitheoirí ag faire go glic ar an steall gheal, te, ag teacht as na siní suaite, barrchaola. Torann úr an bhainne ag titim sa soitheach, síos tríd an gcúr. Boladh úr na mbó. Úthanna cruinne, suaite, á bhfolmhú go mear. Sine i ndiaidh sine folamh. Climirt i gcanna beag. Ólann na páistí é.

Ceannaitheoirí ag imeacht thart, cruashiúl, bolg orthu, maidí fada, drad oscailte, buille anseo, lasc ansiúd, greim ar lag droma. Féach ar na másaí sin. Cé mhéid? An as do mheabhair atá tú? Tá an margadh déanta. Cuir ansin í. Buachaill! Níl inti sin ach crupach. Budóg, an ea! Sea. Go deimhin ní hea. Bulán leathadhairce agus tairbhín beag na bliana seo. Tairbhín crosach Phaitch Taimín. Níl putóg gabhair aici. Cróilí, chomh cróilí le cat. Múchadh agus deargbháitheadh air mar scéal. Gamhain. Taise ar cheithre cosa. Ná leag lámh air. Titfidh sé. Cé mhéid? Ní miste liom, bíodh sé agat.

Tá gach uile bheithíoch díolta. Ceannach mór agus goile mór ag faire thar lear; ag faire ar na másaí leathana feolmhara, goile Sasanach. Díbirt agus seoladh agus tiomáint, ag imeacht suas bóthar an teampaill ghallda, thar ard an chaisil, thar mhóinín an rince, go dtí páirc na gcaorach. Isteach leo ar fad ar féarach go maidin. Gach uile bheithíoch ceannaithe, díolta; gach uile phus fliuch ag cromadh go santach ar an bhféar glas, gach uile theanga gharbh ag casadh go stróiceach. Plaic! Smailc! Tá siad ar fad díolta. Buailfear go gairid le urchar sa gclár éadain iad, agus déantar giotaí sumhara dá gcuid feola, leis an mbolg Sasanach a líonadh; ach níl fhios sin acusan. Smailc! Plaic!

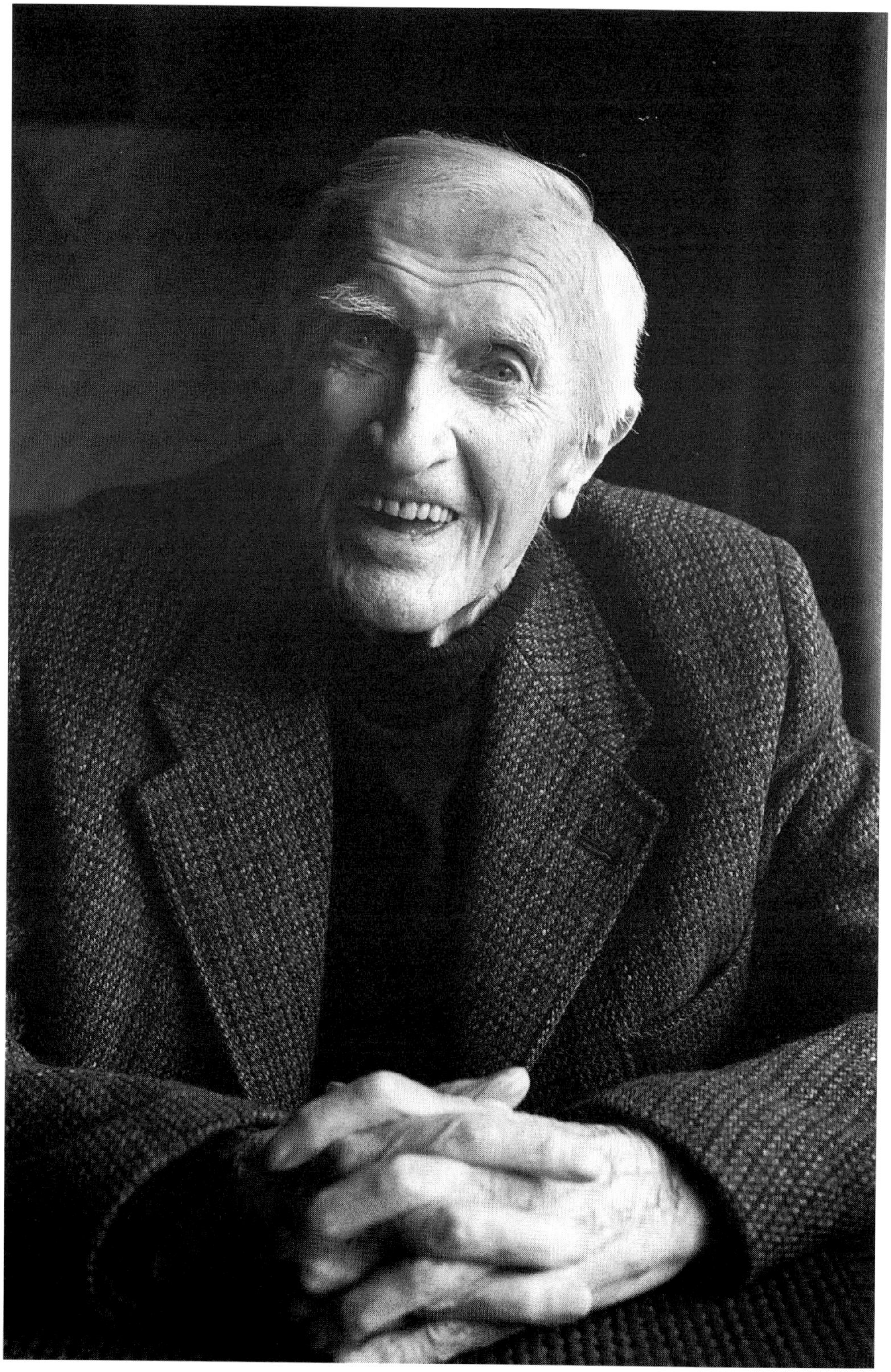

Opposite: *Despite the hardships of old age, Liam O'Flaherty retained much of his youthful spirit.*

Below: *Liam O'Flaherty's remains arriving at University Church, Dublin.*
Pegeen O'Sullivan (right) and Joyce Rathbone, O'Flaherty's daughters, after his funeral.

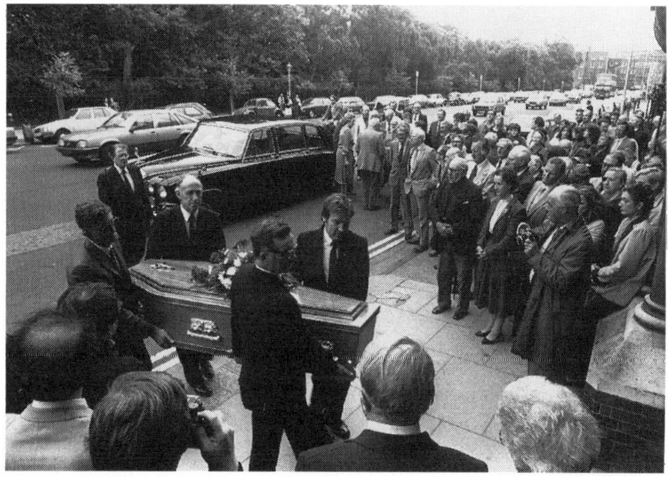

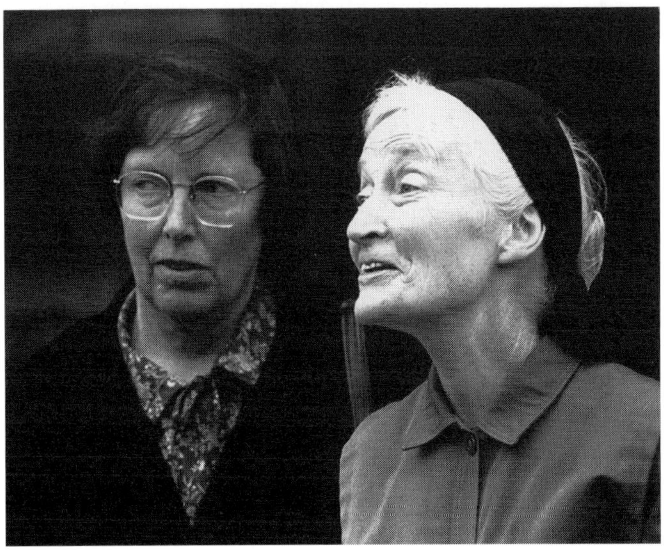

LATE HARVEST In March 1982 Margaret Barrington, who had been living for some years at Kinsale, died in Cork. She had never ceased to love O'Flaherty, and had refused to divorce him. Though Liam's stature was further recognised by a handsome new edition of *Famine* in America, and the following year he was granted honorary membership of the Royal Dublin Society, Liam himself was now moving beyond any interest in the wider world. Paris, a city which had been a joy to him and Kitty since the war, was no longer visited, though he spoke with nostalgia to friends about evenings in the Luxembourg Gardens, and the atmosphere of the Place des Vosges. Though he still carried himself well, and was often seen shopping in Baggot Street (though he would not demean himself to enter the supermarket) or lunching in the Burlington Hotel nearby, his health was not good. His sight had failed. Senile dementia was setting in. When Madelaine Stuart visited him she sang *Lili Marlene* for him, but found his mind clouded. At this time he was also visited from time to time by Fr Dermod McCarthy of the Pro-Cathedral, who thought he had reconciled Liam with the Catholic Church. But in all honesty Liam was well beyond giving any informed consent to such a profession.

28 August 1984 was Liam's birthday. He was now ill with diverticulitis. A week later his condition took a more ominous turn, with the appearance of rectal bleeding. There was little that could be done for him at St Vincent's Hospital in Elm Park, to which he was taken, and three days later, on 7 September, he died. On his death certificate, with the cold realism of official forms, the occupation of the eighty-eight-year-old widower was recorded as 'Writer (Retired).' That might well have been true, but in his time Liam O'Flaherty had

made a permanent place for himself in Irish literature.

On 10 September, his remains were removed to University Church, and were later cremated at Glasnevin. (By one of those small ironies of Irish life, one of the priests who concelebrated the funeral mass, Sean Farragher, a Holy Ghost Father of Blackrock College, was a relative of Fr Farragher of Aran.) At this time Kitty Tailer was also in hospital; the news of his death was brought to her by Seamus Cashman, Liam's publisher at Wolfhound. She would not long survive Liam, dying with great courage in August 1990. His two daughters and some of his friends gathered in his memory at the Shelbourne Hotel, that long-favoured haunt of O'Flaherty and Francis Stuart. Madelaine Stuart, though herself a Catholic, was moved to protest about the claim made at the funeral of Liam's reconciliation with the Church: Liam would have revolted against such an annexation of his spirit.

But perhaps by now it did not matter. The writer was beyond that. In Auden's felicitous words about the death of Yeats: Liam O'Flaherty had become his admirers.

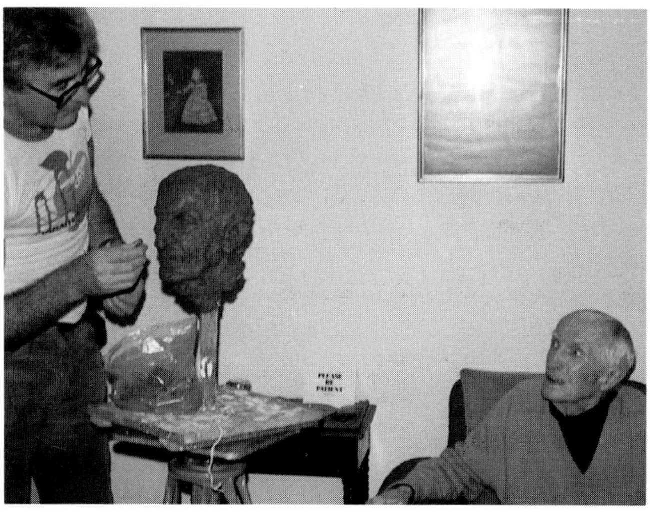

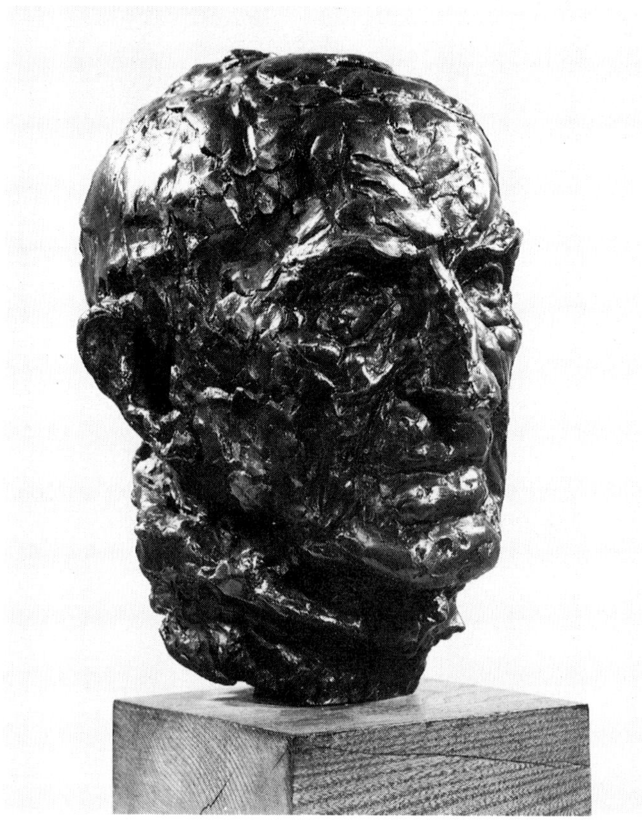

Left and above: *Anthony Stones, portrait sculptor modelling O'Flaherty's head in clay, 1983. And (above) the bronze cast*

'Spring Sowing' *by Liam O'Flaherty*

It was still dark when Martin Delaney and his wife Mary got up. Martin stood in his shirt by the window a long time looking out, rubbing his eyes and yawning, while Mary raked out the live coals that had lain hidden in the ashes on the hearth all night. Outside, cocks were crowing and a white streak was rising from the ground, as it were, and beginning to scatter the darkness. It was a February morning, dry, cold and starry.

The couple sat down to their breakfast of tea, bread and butter, in silence. They had only been married the previous autumn and it was hateful leaving a warm bed at such an early hour. They both felt in a bad humour and ate, wrapped in their thoughts. Martin with his brown hair and eyes, his freckled face and his little fair moustache, looked too young to be married, and his wife looked hardly more than a girl, red-cheeked and blue-eyed, her black hair piled at the rear of her head with a large comb gleaming in the middle of the pile, Spanish fashion. They were both dressed in rough homespuns, and both wore the loose white frieze shirt that Inverara peasants use for work in the fields.

They ate in silence, sleepy and bad humoured and yet on fire with excitement, for it was the first day of their first spring sowing as man and wife. And each felt the glamour of that day on which they were to open up the earth together and plant seeds in it. So they sat in silence and bad humour, for somehow the imminence of an event that had been long expected, loved, feared and prepared for, made them dejected. Mary, with her shrewd woman's mind, munched her bread and butter and thought of ... Oh, what didn't she think of? Of as many things as there are in life does a women think in the first joy and anxiety of her mating. But Martin's mind was fixed on one thought. Would he be able to prove himself a man worthy of being the head of a family by doing his spring sowing well?

In the barn after breakfast, when they were getting the potato seeds and the line for measuring the ground and the spade, a cross word or two passed between them, and when Martin fell over a basket in the half-darkness of the barn, he swore and said that a man would be better off dead than ... But before he could finish whatever he was going to say, Mary had her arms around his waist and her face to his. 'Martin,' she said, 'let us not begin this day cross with one another.' And there was a tremor in her voice. And somehow, as they embraced and Martin kept mumbling in his awkward peasant's voice, 'pulse of my heart, treasure of my life,' and such traditional phrases, all their irritation and sleepiness left them. And they stood there embracing until at last Martin pushed her from him with pretended roughness and said: 'Come, come, girl, it will be sunset before we begin at this rate.'

Still, as they walked silently in their raw-hide shoes, through the little hamlet, there was not a soul about. Lights were glimmering in the windows of a few cabins. The sky had a big grey crack in it in the east, as if it were going to burst in order to give birth to the sun. Birds were singing somewhere at a distance. Martin and Mary rested their baskets of seeds on a fence outside the village and Martin whispered to Mary proudly: 'We are first, Mary.' And they both looked back at the little cluster of cabins, that was the centre of their world, with throbbing hearts. For the joy of spring had now taken complete hold of them.

They reached the little field where they were to sow. It was a little triangular patch of ground under an ivy-coloured limestone hill. The little field had been manured with seaweed some weeks before, and the weeds had rotted and whitened on the grass. And there was a big red heap of fresh seaweed lying in a corner by the fence to be spread under the seeds as they were laid. Martin, in spite of the cold, threw off everything above his waist except his striped woollen shirt. Then he spat on his hands, seized his spade and cried: 'Now you are going to see what kind of a man you have, Mary.'

'There now,' said Mary, tying a little shawl closer under her chin. 'Aren't we boastful this early hour of the morning? Maybe I'll wait till sunset to see what kind of a man have I got.'

The work began. Martin measured the ground by the southern fence for the first ridge, a strip of ground four feet wide, and he placed the line along the edge and pegged it at each end. Then he spread fresh seaweed over the strip. Mary filled her apron with seeds and began to lay them in rows, four, three, four. When she was a little distance down the ridge Martin advanced with his spade to the head eager to commence.

'Now in the name of God,' he cried, spitting on his palms, 'let us raise the first sod!'

'Oh, Martin, wait till I'm with you!' cried Mary, dropping her seeds on the ridge and running up to him. Her fingers outside her woollen mittens were numb with the cold, and she couldn't wipe them in her apron. Her cheeks seemed to be on fire. She put an arm round Martin's waist and stood looking at the green sod his spade was going to cut, with the excitement of a little child.

'Now for God's sake, girl, keep back!' said Martin gruffly. 'Suppose anybody saw us trapesing about like this in the field of our spring sowing, what would they take us for but a pair of useless, soft, empty-headed people that would be sure to die of the hunger. Huh!' He spoke very rapidly and his eyes were fixed on the ground before him. His eyes had a wild, eager light in them as if some primeval impulse were burning within his brain and driving out every other desire but that of asserting his manhood and of subjugating the earth.

'Oh, what do we care who is looking?' said Mary; but she drew back at the same time and gazed distantly at the ground. Then Martin cut the sod, and pressing the spade deep into the earth with his foot, he turned up the first sod with a crunching sound as the grass roots were dragged out of the earth. Mary sighed and walked back hurriedly to her seeds and began to spread them rapidly to drive out the sudden terror that had seized her at that moment when the first sod was turned up and she saw the fierce, hard look in her husband's eyes, that were unconscious of her presence. She became suddenly afraid of that pitiless, cruel earth, the peasant's slave master, that would keep her chained to hard work and poverty all her life until she would sink again into its bosom. Her short-lived love was gone. Henceforth she was only her husband's helper to till the earth. And Martin, absolutely without thought, worked furiously, covering the ridge with black earth, his sharp spade gleaming white as he whirled it sideways to beat the sods.

Then as the sun rose the little valley beneath the ivy-covered hills became dotted with white frieze shirts, and everywhere men worked madly without speaking and women spread seeds. There was no heat in the light of the sun, and there was a sharpness in the still thin air that made the men jump on their spade hafts ferociously and beat the sods as if they were living enemies. Birds hopped silently before the spades, with their heads cocked sideways, watching for worms. Made brave by hunger they often dashed under the spades to secure their food.

Then when the sun reached a certain point all the

women went back to the village to get dinner for their men, and the men worked on without stopping. Then the women returned, almost running, each carrying a tin can with a flannel tied around it and a little bundle tied with a white cloth. Martin threw down his spade when Mary arrived back in the field. Smiling at one another they sat under the hill for their meal. It was the same as their breakfast, tea and bread and butter.

'Ah,' said Martin, when he had taken a long draught of tea from his mug, 'is there anything in this world as fine as eating dinner out in the open like this after doing a good morning's work? There, I have done two ridges and a half. That's more than any man in the village could do. Ha!' And he looked at his wife proudly.

'Yes, isn't it lovely,' said Mary, looking at the black ridges wistfully. She was just munching her bread and butter. The hurried trip to the village and the trouble of getting the tea ready had robbed her of her appetite. She had to keep blowing at the turf fire with the rim of her skirt, and the smoke nearly blinded her. But now sitting on that grassy knoll, with the valley all round glistening with fresh seaweed and a light smoke rising from the freshly turned earth, a strange joy swept over her. It overpowered that other feeling of dread that had been with her during the morning.

Martin ate heartily, revelling in his great thirst and his great hunger, with every pore of his body open to the pure air. And he looked around at his neighbours' fields boastfully, comparing them with his own. Then he looked at his wife's little round black head and felt very proud of having her as his own. He leaned back on his elbow and took her hand in his. Shyly and in silence, not knowing what to say and ashamed of their gentle feelings, for peasants are always ashamed of feeling refined, they finished eating and still sat hand in hand looking away into the distance. Everywhere the sowers were resting on little knolls, men, women and children sitting in silence. And the great calm of nature in spring filled the atmosphere around them. Everything seemed to sit still and wait until midday had passed. Only the gleaming sun chased westwards at a mighty pace, in and out through white clouds.

Then in a distant field an old man got up, took his spade and began to clean the earth from it with a piece of stone. The rasping noise carried a long way in the silence. That was the signal for a general rising all along the little valley. Young men stretched themselves and yawned. They walked slowly back to their ridges.

Martin's back and his wrists were getting a little sore, and Mary felt that if she stooped again over her seeds that her neck would break, but neither said anything and soon they had forgotten their tiredness in the mechanical movement of their bodies. The strong smell of the upturned earth acted like a drug on their nerves.

In the afternoon, when the sun was strongest, the old men of the village came out to look at their people sowing. Martin's grandfather, almost bent double over his thick stick, stopped in the lane outside the field and, groaning loudly, he leaned over the fence.

'God bless the work,' he called wheezily.

'And you, grandfather,' replied the couple together, but they did not stop working.

'Ha!' muttered the old man to himself. 'Ha! He sows well and that woman is good, too. They are beginning well.'

It was fifty years since he had begun with his Mary, full of hope and pride, and the merciless soil had hugged them to its bosom ever since each spring without rest. But he did not think of that. The soil gives forgetfulness. Only the present is remembered in the spring, even by the aged who have spent their lives tilling the earth; so the old man, with his huge red nose and the spotted handkerchief tied around his skull under his black soft felt hat, watched his grandson work and gave him advice.

'Don't cut your sods so long,' he would wheeze, 'you are putting too much soil on your ridge.'

'Ah, woman! Don't plant a seed so near the edge. The stalk will come out sideways.'

And they paid no heed to him.

'Ah,' grumbled the old man, 'in my young days, when men worked from morning till night without tasting food, better work was done. But of course it can't be expected to be the same as it was. The breed is getting weaker. So it is.'

Then he began to cough in his chest and hobbled away to another field where his son Michael was working.

By sundown Martin had five ridges finished. He threw down his spade and stretched himself. All his bones ached and he wanted to lie down and rest. 'It's time to be going home, Mary,' he said.

Mary straightened herself, but she was too tired to reply. She looked at Martin wearily and it seemed to her that it was a great many years since they had set out that morning. Then she thought of the journey home and the trouble of feeding the pigs, putting the fowls into their coops and getting the supper ready and a momentary flash of rebellion against the slavery of being a peasant's wife crossed her mind. It passed in a moment. Martin was saying, as he dressed himself:

'Ha! My soul from the devil, it has been a good day's work. Five ridges done, and each one of them as straight as a steel rod. Begod, Mary, it's no boasting to say that ye might well be proud of being the wife of Martin Delaney. And that's not saying the whole of it, my girl. You did your share better than any woman in Inverara could do it this blessed day.'

They stood for a few moments in silence looking at the work they had done. All her dissatisfaction and weariness vanished from Mary's mind with the delicious feeling of comfort that overcame her at having done this work with her husband. They had done it together. They had planted seeds in the earth. The next day and the next and all their lives, when spring came they would have to bend their backs and do it until their hands and bones got twisted with rheumatism. But night would always bring sleep and forgetfulness.

As they walked home slowly Martin walked in front with another peasant talking about the sowing, and Mary walked behind, with her eyes on the ground, thinking.

Cows were lowing at a distance.

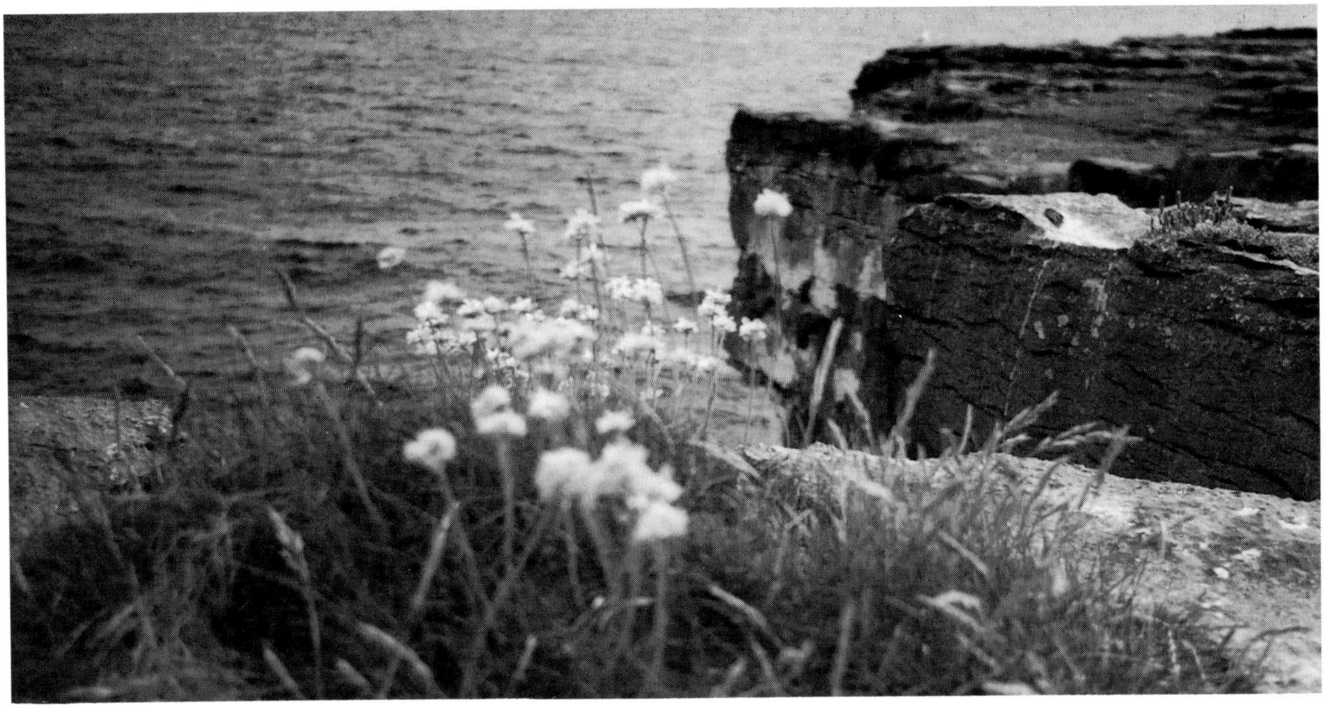

Wildflowers on the cliffhead at Ail an Thoir – Liam O'Flaherty's sacred place on Aran.

Soon after his return from America after the war, O'Flaherty wrote a poem about the wildflowers on the Aran cliffs that endure all that Nature can throw upon them – including the soiling dirt of bird droppings. The poet asked why this was, the flowers replying that they were content, happy listening to the voice of the sea. Those flowers and the cliffs below them to the east of Gort na gCapall had been since his childhood a sacred place to which he brought only his special friends. As Liam O'Flaherty has no grave, this cliffhead at Cill an Ara Thoir, within the sound of the sea's voice, remains the natural memorial to his life and vision.

Na Blátha Craige

Adúirt mé leis na blátha:
'Nach suarach an áit a fuair sibh
Le bheith ag déanamh aeir,
Teannta suas anseo le bruach na haille,
Gan fúibh ach an chloch ghlas
Agus salachar na n-éan,
Áit bhradach, lán le ceo
Agus farraige cháite,
Ní scairteann grian anseo
Ó Luan go Satharn
Le gliondar a chur oraibh'.
Adúirt na blátha craige:
'Is cuma linn, a stór,
Táimid faoi dhraíocht
Ag ceol na farraige.'

Principal Writings of Liam O'Flaherty

(with their dates of first publication)

Thy Neighbour's Wife (novel) – October 1923
The Black Soul (novel) – April 1924
Spring Sowing (stories) – September 1924
The Informer (novel) – September 1925
Civil War (story) – November 1925
The Terrorist (story) – February 1926
Darkness (play) – May 1926
The Tent (stories) – June 1926
Mr Gilhooley (novel) – October 1926
The Child of God (story) – December 1926
The Wilderness (novel) – serialised, January-June 1927 [first published in volume form 1978]
The Life of Tim Healy (biography) – June 1927
The Fairy Goose (stories) – December 1927
The Assassin (novel) – May 1928
Red Barbara and Other Stories – August 1928
The Mountain Tavern (stories) – April 1929
A Tourist's Guide to Ireland (satire) – June 1929
The House of Gold (novel) – September 1929
The Return of the Brute (novel) – October 1929
Joseph Conrad: an appreciation – April 1930
Two Years (autobiography) – July 1930
The Ecstasy of Angus (fantasia) – June 1931
I Went to Russia (political commentary) – June 1931
A Cure for Unemployment (satire) – June 1931
The Puritan (novel) – January 1932
The Wild Swan (stories) – March 1932
Skerrett (novel) – July 1932
The Martyr (novel) – January 1933
Shame the Devil (autobiography) – April 1934
Hollywood Cemetery (novel) [London] – November 1935
Famine (novel) – January 1937
The Short Stories of Liam O'Flaherty [London] – November 1937
Land (novel) – May 1946
Two Lovely Beasts (stories) – July 1948
Insurrection (novel) – October 1950
Dúil (gearrscéalta) – Iúil 1953
The Stories of Liam O'Flaherty [New York] – June 1956
Irish Portraits (stories) – August 1970
The Pedlar's Revenge & Other Stories – August 1976
All Things Come of Age (a tale for children) – February 1977
A Test of Courage (a tale for children) – June 1977

The Letters of Liam O'Flaherty
edited by A.A. Kelly – for publication September 1996

Further Reading
Sources of Extracts

Further Reading

This book is based in part on research by the present author; but he has also drawn extensively upon the important writings of other critics and bibliographers listed below. I am also grateful to those who over the years have shared with me their recollections and thoughts about Liam O'Flaherty, including his daughter Pegeen O'Sullivan, Christine Daly, Michael O'Riordan, Lord Killanin, Seamus Cashman, Fr Dermod McCarthy, O.Z. Whitehead, Proinsias MacAonghusa, Fr Sean Farragher, Pat Langan and many others (including some Aran Islanders). I am also grateful to Kathleen Walsh, for help with the Gaelic; John Wyse Jackson, for help with the English; and Bobby Allen and Damien Maddock, for the photographs. However, the whole intricate story of Liam O'Flaherty's life yet remains to be told.

Jefferson, George. *Liam O'Flaherty: A Descriptive Bibliography of His Works.* Dublin: Wolfhound Press, 1993.

Costello, Peter. *The Heart Grown Brutal – The Irish Revolution in Literature from Parnell to the death of Yeats, 1892 – 1939.* Dublin: Gill and Macmillan, 1972.

O'Flaherty, Liam. 'Autobiographical Note' in John Gawsworth (ed.), *Ten Contemporaries.* London: Joiner and Steele, 1934.

Doyle, Paul A. *Liam O'Flaherty* (Twayne Irish Writers Series). New York: Twayne, 1972.

Kelly, A. A. *Liam O'Flaherty: The Story Teller.* London: Macmillan, 1976.

Kelly, A. A. (ed). *The Letters of Liam O'Flaherty.* Dublin: Wolfhound Press, 1996.

O'Brien, James H. *Liam O'Flaherty.* Lewisburg, Pa.: Bucknell University Press, 1973.

Ó hEithir, Breandán. '*Skerrett* [by] Liam O'Flaherty', in Proinsias O Conluain (ed.), *Islands and Authors.* Cork: The Mercier Press, 1983. pp59-71.

Sheeran, Patrick F. *The Novels of Liam O'Flaherty.* Dublin: Wolfhound Press, 1979.

Zneimer, John. *The Literary Vision of Liam O'Flaherty.* Syracuse, New York: Syracuse University Press, 1970.

Sources of extracts arranged by chapter

Prelims: 'The Wave' from *Spring Sowing* (1924)

Aran: 'The Struggle' from *Spring Sowing* (1924)

Rockwell & Blackrock: extract from 'Benedicamus Domino' from *Spring Sowing* (1924)

The Student: 'The man of genius' from the introduction to *Bitter Water* by Heinrich Hauser (1929)

The Great War: 'And the life of man...' from *The Return of the Brute* (1929)

The Travels of Bill Ganly: 'Rio Bay' from *Two Years* (1930)

The Heat of Revolution: 'The Sniper' from *Spring Sowing* (1924)

The Chrysalis Breaks: 'The Cow's Death' from *Spring Sowing* (1924)

The Land of Tim Healy: 'Wolf Lanigan's Death' from *Spring Sowing* (1924)

The Brutal Part of Life: 'The spirit of revolution' from the introduction to *The Back-to-Backs* by J.C. Grant (1930)

To Russia and Back: 'A gypsy girl in Moscow' from *I Went to Russia* (1931)

The Injured Heart: 'A gratuitous act' from *The Puritan* (1932)

Hollywood: 'Two sides of Hollywood' from *Hollywood Cemetery* (1935)

Wanderings: 'The Blight Comes' from *Famine* (1937)

The Landscape of the Past: (1) 'The way to act' from *Land* (1946); and (2) 'Patriotism' from *Insurrection* (1950)

Return to Aran: 'An tAonach', as *Dúil* (1953)

Spring Sowing: 'Spring Sowing' from *Spring Sowing* (1924)

passage from *Mr Gilhooley* (1926) with the Geneva Window;

passage from 'The Pedlar's Revenge' (1952) with illustration

statement in support of the Spanish Republic, from *Authors Take Sides on the Spanish Civil War* (1937)

'Na Blátha Craige' as *Nuabhearsaiocht 1939-1949,* Seán Ó Tuama a roghnaigh

List of Illustrations

Colour Plates

Section 1

1. Slide File; 2. tp lt and rt Michael Diggin - bt Slide File; 3. tp Michael Diggin - bt Slide File; 4. Both Michael Diggin; 5. Slide File; 6. Tom Kelly; 7. Tom Kelly; 8. Tom Kelly.

Section 2

1. Harry Kernoff, Portrait of Liam O'Flaherty; courtesy of Geraldine O'Sullivan.Reproduced by permission of the Estate of Herry Kernoff. Photo: Robert Allen; 2. Harry Clarke, scene from *Mr Gilhooley*, detail from stained glass panel 6 of The Geneva Window 1929, collection of the Wolfsonian Foundation, Miami Beach, Florida. Reproduced by permission; 3. James Dwyer, Collier's, vol. 131 (16), 18 April 1953, 55. Private collection. Photo: Robert Allen; 3. 4. Tp unidentified, Esquire, vol. 38 (3), Sept. 1952, 39. Private collection - bt John Groch, Esquire, vol. 42 (1), July 1954, 33. Private collection. Photos: Robert Allen; 5. Charles Fennell. Reproduced courtesy of Frank Fennell; 6. Morton Roberts, Collier's, vol. 132 (4), 25 July 1953, 39. Private collection. Photo: Robert Allen; 7. Michael Diggin; 8. Tom Kelly.

Section 3

1. Tom Kelly; 2. all Michael Diggin; 3. tp Tom Kelly - bt Michael Diggin; 4. Michael Diggin; 5. Charles Fennell. Reproduced by courtesy of Frank Fennell Photography; 6. Charles Fennell. Reproduced by permission of Frank Fennell Photography; 7. Slide File; 8. Tom Kelly.

Black & White illustrations

Credits for monochrome pictures - pp. 2/3: Slide File. 6: Charles Fennell, courtesy Frank Fennell Photography. 7: Irish Architectural Archive. 8: Charles Fennel, courtesy of Frank Fennell Photography. 10: Agnes Pataux. 13: courtesy Seamus Cashman. 16: Lawrence Collection, National Library of Ireland. 17: both Lawrence Collection, National Library of Ireland. [19:??Marion Litton.] 20: Lawrence Collection, National Library of Ireland; courtesy Sean Farragher. 22: Peter Costello; courtesy Sean Farragher. 25: Peter Costello. 28: Peter Costello. 30: both Imperial War Museum. 31: both Imperial War Museum. 35: courtesy Peter Costello. 38: Peter Costello. 39: Peter Costello; Central Catholic Library. 41: tp Central Catholic Library; bt Cashman Collection, RTE. 42: Cashman Collection, RTE. 43: Collection, RTE. 48: E.O. Hoppé, Mansell Collection. 52:?? Marion Litton. 52, 53: RKO Radio Pictures 1935, courtesy of the British Film Institute.British International Pictures 1929, courtesy of the British Film Institute. 54: Peter Costello; RKO Radio Pictures 1935, courtesy of the British Film Institute. 57: private collection. 58: private collection 59: drawing Jeanette Dunne from *The Wilderness* (Wolfhound Press 1978). 66: bt Central Catholic Library; tp lt and rt Hilda Roberts 1927, Central Catholic Library. 68: Central Catholic Library. 70, 71: from *The Face and Mind of Bolschevism* by R. Fülop-Miller (1927). 72: from *Two Years* by Liam O'Flaherty (1930); illustration Lucy Kilroy from *The Ecstasy of Angus* (Wolfhound Press, 1978). 74: tp courtesy Pegeen O'Sullivan; bt from *Shame the Devil* (1934). 75: courtesy Pegeen O'Sullivan. 77: tp lt and rt courtesy Antoine Powell, *Oileáin Árann* (Wolfhound Press); bt Irish Architectural Archive. 80: courtesy British Film Institute. 84: Kobal Collection. 86: from *The Devil's Playground*, Columbia Pictures, courtesy British Film Institute.] 87: New York Times Syndication. 89: Hilda O'Malley, private collection. 91: National Library of Ireland. 98: Lawrence Collection, National Library of Ireland. 102: illustration Walter Paget, Pearse Museum, courtesy Pat Cooke. 105, 106 and 108: courtesy Seamus Cashman. 107 and 109: Agnes Pataux. 112: rt drawing Gertrude Degenhardt, by kind permission; lt courtesy Seamus Cashman. 112: courtesy Seamus Cashman. 113: Pat Langan, courtesy *Irish Times*. 114 courtesy Seamus Cashman 119: private collection.

Books by Liam O'Flaherty available from Wolfhound Press

Novels (available in paperback editions)

Famine

Skerrett

The Black Soul

Thy Neighbour's Wife

Insurrection

The Assassin

The Wilderness (also limited edition; hardcover edition illustrated by Jeannette Dunne)

Short Stories

The Pedlar's Revenge & Other Stories (limited edition)

Short Stories (The Pedlar's Revenge)

The Ecstasy of Angus (illustrated by Lucy Kilroy)

Autobiography

Shame the Devil

The Letters of Liam O'Flaherty, ed A. A. Kelly

For Children

All Things Come of Age & The Test of Courage (illustrated by Terence O'Connell)

Forthcoming

A Tourist Guide to Ireland (illustrated by Gertrude Degenhardt), 1997

The Collected Stories of Liam O'Flaherty (two vols), 1997. Edited and introduced by A. A. Kelly.

The Return of the Brute, 1997

The Puritan, 1998

The House of Gold, 1998

For information on these and other forthcoming reissues of Liam O'Flaherty's novels, short stories and prose writings, please write to us at:
Wolfhound Press, 68 Mountjoy Square, Dublin 1.